Assessing Political Representation in Europe

It has long been realised that democratic governance requires a two-way flow of influence. Governments must be able to respond to what people want and people must be able to react to what governments do. These mechanisms of democratic governance have contributed to two research traditions: one, the responsible party approach, views policy change as a consequence of 'electoral turnover'; and the other, the dynamic representation approach, views policy change as occurring in 'rational anticipation' of electoral repercussions.

The aim of this book is to evaluate the state of political representation in contemporary Europe in the light of these two approaches. The chapters present fresh insight into issue congruence between voters and parties and into the extent of dynamic representation. The chapters are logically clustered into three groups: one group of scholars bases their work on the 'responsible party model' and applies it to voters and European parties and party groups; a second group of scholars demonstrates the importance of institutional structures on the degree of issue congruence; and a third group of scholars examines the reciprocal nature of dynamic representation and the effects of institutions on the opinion-policy connection.

This book was previously published as a special issue of *West European Politics.*

Christine Arnold is an Assistant Professor at Maastricht University, Netherlands. Her research interests are in comparative politics, EU politics and European integration, public opinion, political representation, large-scale data analysis and quantitative methods. Her articles have been published in *Political Studies*, *West European Politics*, *International Studies Quarterly*, *European Union Politics* and other journals. Work for this book was partially completed while she was a Marie Curie Fellow at the European University Institute, Florence, Italy.

Mark N. Franklin was the Inaugural Stein Rokkan Professor of Comparative Politics at the European University Institute, Florence, Italy. He is an Emeritus Professor at Trinity College Connecticut, USA, currently visiting the

Massachusetts Institute of Technology, USA. His main research interests lie in British, European and American government and political economy, political methodology, and the attitudes and behaviour of elites and mass publics. Work for this book was completed while he was a Fellow in Residence at the Netherlands Institute for Advanced Studies in the Social Sciences and Humanities.

West European Politics Series

Edited by
***Klaus H. Goetz**, University of Potsdam, Germany*
***Anand Menon**, King's College London, UK*
***Wolfgang C. Müller**, University of Vienna, Austria*

West European Politics has established itself as the foremost journal for the comparative analysis of European political institutions, politics and public policy. Its comprehensive scope, which includes the European Union, makes it essential reading for both academics and political practitioners. The books in this series have originated from special issues published by *West European Politics.*

Immigration Policy in Europe
The politics of control
Edited by Virgine Guiradon and Gallya Lahav

Norway in Transition
Transforming a stable democracy
Edited by Oyvind Osterud

Policy Change and Discourse in Europe
Edited by Claudio M. Radaelli and Vivien Schmidt

Politics and Policy in Greece
The challenge of 'modernisation'
Edited by Kevin Featherstone

France's Political Institutions at 50
Edited by Emiliano Grossman and Nicolas Sauger

Interest Group Politics in Europe
Lessons from EU Studies and Comparative Politics
Edited by Jan Beyers, Rainer Eising and William A. Maloney

Italy – A Contested Polity
Edited by Martin Bull and Martin Rhodes

European Politics
Pasts, presents, futures
Edited by Klaus H. Goetz, Peter Mair and Gordon Smith

The Politics of Belgium
Institutions and policy under bipolar and centrifugal federalism
Edited by Marleen Brans, Lieven De Winter and Wilfried Swenden

Towards a New Executive Order in Europe
Edited by Deirdre Curtin and Morten Egeberg

The Structure of Political Competition in Western Europe
Edited by Zsolt Enyedi and Kevin Deegan-Krause

Accountability and European Governance
Edited by Deirdre Curtin, Peter Mair and Yannis Papadopoulos

Understanding Electoral Reform
Edited by Reuven Y. Hazan and Monique Leyenaar

Dynamics of Change in the European Union
Edited by Daniel Naurin and Anne Rasmussen

Assessing Political Representation in Europe
Edited by Christine Arnold and Mark N. Franklin

Assessing Political Representation in Europe

Edited by
Christine Arnold and Mark N. Franklin

Routledge
Taylor & Francis Group
LONDON AND NEW YORK

First published 2014
by Routledge

2 Park Square, Milton Park, Abingdon, Oxfordshire OX14 4RN
711 Third Avenue, New York, NY 10017

Routledge is an imprint of the Taylor & Francis Group, an informa business

First issued in paperback 2018

British Library Cataloguing in Publication Data
A catalogue record for this book is available from the British Library

ISBN13: 978-0-415-71120-3 (hbk)
ISBN13: 978-1-138-37740-0 (pbk)

Typeset in Times New Roman
by Taylor & Francis Books

Publisher's Note
The publisher accepts responsibility for any inconsistencies that may have arisen during the conversion of this book from journal articles to book chapters, namely the possible inclusion of journal terminology.

Contents

Citation Information

The chapters in this book were originally published in *West European Politics*, volume 35, issue 6 (October 2012). When citing this material, please use the original page numbering for each article, as follows:

Chapter 1
Introduction: Issue Congruence and Political Responsiveness
Christine Arnold and Mark N. Franklin
West European Politics, volume 35, issue 6 (October 2012) pp. 1217-1225

Chapter 2
European Parliament Elections and Political Representation: Policy Congruence between Voters and Parties
Rory Costello, Jacques Thomassen and Martin Rosema
West European Politics, volume 35, issue 6 (October 2012) pp. 1226-1248

Chapter 3
Mechanisms of Issue Congruence: The Democratic Party Mandate
Tom Louwerse
West European Politics, volume 35, issue 6 (October 2012) pp. 1249-1271

Chapter 4
Partisan Sorting and Niche Parties in Europe
James Adams, Lawrence Ezrow and Debra Leiter
West European Politics, volume 35, issue 6 (October 2012) pp. 1272-1294

Chapter 5
Intra-Party Democracy and Party Responsiveness
Ron Lehrer
West European Politics, volume 35, issue 6 (October 2012) pp. 1295-1319

Chapter 6
Institutional Context and Representational Strain in Party–Voter Agreement in Western and Eastern Europe
Robert Rohrschneider and Stephen Whitefield
West European Politics, volume 35, issue 6 (October 2012) pp. 1320-1340

Chapter 7
Parties' Positions on European Integration: Issue Congruence, Ideology or Context?
Christine Arnold, Eliyahu V. Sapir and Catherine de Vries
West European Politics, volume 35, issue 6 (October 2012) pp. 1341-1362

Chapter 8
Strategic Incentives, Issue Proximity and Party Support in Europe
Lorenzo De Sio and Mark N. Franklin
West European Politics, volume 35, issue 6 (October 2012) pp. 1363-1385

Chapter 9
The Causal Flow between Public Opinion and Policy: Government Responsiveness, Leadership, or Counter Movement?
Armen Hakhverdian
West European Politics, volume 35, issue 6 (October 2012) pp. 1386-1406

Chapter 10
Political Institutions and the Opinion–Policy Link
Christopher Wlezien and Stuart N. Soroka
West European Politics, volume 35, issue 6 (October 2012) pp. 1407-1432

Please direct any queries you may have about the citations to
clsuk.permissions@cengage.com

Notes on Contributors

James Adams is Professor and Director of Graduate Studies at the University of California at Davis, USA. He studies voting behaviour, parties' election strategies and political representation in Western Europe and the United States. His work encompasses both spatial models of party competition and empirical analyses of parties' policy programmes.

Christine Arnold is an Assistant Professor at Maastricht University, Netherlands. Her research interests are in comparative politics, EU politics and European integration, public opinion, political representation, large-scale data analysis and quantitative methods. Together with Mark Franklin and Christopher Wlezien she is Co-PI in the project the "Database for Political Responsiveness", funded by the Dutch Organization for Scientific Research (NWO). Her articles have been published in *Political Studies, West European Politics, International Studies Quarterly, European Union Politics* and other journals.

Rory Costello is a Lecturer at the University of Limerick, Ireland. He received his PhD from Trinity College Dublin in 2009. His dissertation examined decision-making under bicameralism in the European Union. He has expertise in EU politics, legislative decision-making, voting behaviour and empirical democratic theory.

Lorenzo De Sio is Assistant Professor at LUISS Guido Carli, Rome, Italy. His research interests are in elections, voting behaviour and party competition models, as well as in quantitative methods in political science.

Catherine de Vries is Professor in European Politics in the Department of Politics and International Relations at the University of Oxford, UK, and University Lecturer in Comparative European Politics and Government at Lincoln College. She is also an affiliated Associate Professor in the Department of Political Science at the University of Amsterdam, the Netherlands. Her research and teaching interests lie in the fields of political behaviour, public opinion, EU politics and European integration and quantitative methods in political science.

Lawrence Ezrow is a Professor of Government at the University of Essex, UK. His research interests are in comparative political representation, party competition, elections, and political parties. He has published *Linking Citizens and Parties*, and his articles have been published in the *American Journal of Political Science, British Journal of Political Science, Journal of Politics, World Politics* and other journals.

Mark N. Franklin was the Inaugural Stein Rokkan Professor of Comparative Politics at the European University Institute, Florence, Italy. He is an Emeritus Professor at Trinity College Connecticut, USA, currently visiting the Massachusetts Institute of Technology, USA. His main research interests lie in British, European and American government and political economy, political methodology, and the attitudes and behaviour of elites and mass publics. His books include *The Decline of Class Voting* (1985), *Electoral Change* (1992, co-authored), *Choosing Europe* (1996, co-authored), *Voter Turnout* (2004) and *The Economy and the Vote* (2007, co-authored).

Armen Hakhverdian is Assistant Professor in the Department of Political Science at the University of Amsterdam, Netherlands. Previously, he was a post-doctoral researcher in the same department and a Max Weber Fellow at the European University Institute in Florence, Italy. His research interests include political representation, public opinion, political institutions and political inequality.

Ron Lehrer is a graduate student at the University of Essex, UK. His research interests are in intra-party politics, party competition, coalition politics and political representation.

Debra Leiter is an Assistant Professor in the Department of Political Science at the University of Missouri-Kansas City. Her research focuses on the intersection of elections, voters, and political parties in Western Europe. Her work has been published in the *British Journal of Political Science* and *Comparative Political Studies.*

Tom Louwerse is Assistant Professor in the Department of Political Science at Trinity College Dublin, Ireland. He received his PhD from Leiden University, the Netherlands. His research interests include political representation, legitimacy, political parties and parliamentary politics.

Robert Rohrschneider is the Sir Robert Worcester Distinguished Professor of Political Science at the University of Kansas, USA. His main research interests include comparative political behaviour and parties, and German and European politics. His books include *Learning Democracy* (1999) and *The Strain of Representation* (2012, with Stephen Whitefield). His articles have appeared in the *American Journal of Political Science, Journal of Politics* and *Comparative Political Studies*, among others.

Martin Rosema is Assistant Professor of Political Science at the University of Twente, Netherlands. His main area of expertise is the psychology of voting. He has published on topics such as partisanship, strategic voting, and electoral turnout. Other themes in his ongoing research are the role of emotions and voting advice applications. He is co-editor of *How Democracy Works: Political Representation and Policy Congruence in Modern Societies. Essays in Honour of Jacques Thomassen* (2011).

Eliyahu V. Sapir is a Lecturer in the Department of Political Science at Maastricht University, Netherlands. He was previously a Postdoctoral Research Fellow at the Methods and Data Institute, University of Nottingham, and the Database on Political Responsiveness, Maastricht University. Sapir specialises in massive data collections, management and analysis, and is developing models of cyber-infrastructure for political and social science research. His research interests are in EU politics, electoral politics, comparative democratisation, political methodology, survey methodology, complex data linking, social statistics, text analysis and data visualisation.

Stuart N. Soroka is Associate Professor and William Dawson Scholar in the Department of Political Science at McGill University in Montreal, Canada. His research focuses on interactions between public opinion, public policy, and mass media. He has published *Degrees of Democracy* and *Agenda-Setting Dynamics in Canada.*

Jacques Thomassen is Emeritus Professor of Political Science in the School of Management and Governance at the University of Twente, Netherlands. He is a member of the Royal Netherlands Academy of Arts and Sciences. His expertise is in democratic theory, political representation, electoral research and legitimacy in the European Union.

Stephen Whitefield is Professor of Politics at the University of Oxford, UK, as well as Rhodes Pelczynski Tutorial Fellow in Politics, Pembroke College. His research interests focus on post-Communist comparative politics and societies and more recently (in his book with Robert Rohrschneider, *The Strain of Representation*) on comparisons of Western and Eastern European party systems and electorates.

Christopher Wlezien is Hogg Professor of Government at the University of Texas at Austin, USA. He has published widely in the areas of elections, public opinion, and public policy, and his books include *Degrees of Democracy*, *Who Gets Represented?*, and *The Timeline of Presidential Elections.* He was founding co-editor of the *Journal of Elections, Public Opinion and Parties* and currently is Associate Editor of *Public Opinion Quarterly* and *Parliamentary Affairs.*

Introduction: Issue Congruence and Political Responsiveness

CHRISTINE ARNOLD and MARK N. FRANKLIN

It has long been realised that democratic governance requires a two-way flow of influence. Governments must be able to respond to what people want and people must be able to react to what governments do. These preconditions for democratic governance have been central to two research traditions on political representation. One of these, the responsible party approach, views policy change as a consequence of 'electoral turnover', while the other, the dynamic representation approach, focuses on policy change that occurs in 'rational anticipation' of electoral repercussions. The aim of this volume is to evaluate the state of political representation in contemporary Europe and to advance our understanding of the topic by presenting fresh insights both on the extent to which there exists issue congruence between voters and parties and the degree to which there is dynamic representation in the policy responses of representatives. This introduction describes in some detail the nature of the two approaches and then briefly summarises the contributions made in the remainder of the volume.

Normative democratic theory tells us that in a representative democracy, as a minimal requirement, there should be some linkage between the interests of citizens and the public policies enacted by their representatives. Many political commentators believe that contemporary democratic institutions in Europe are facing a severe challenge, not least due to the scope of present economic turbulence. With the imperatives of financial markets and the constraints placed on governments by policy commitments made at the supranational level, national decision-makers may well find themselves less able to take policy positions in line with public preferences and to change public policies in response to the demands of their citizens (Streeck and Meertens 2010). At the same time, ever more demanding voters are holding parties and governments accountable and are electorally rewarding or punishing them based on the degree to which they are seen to have governed in line with voters' interests (Mair 2007, 2010, 2011). Given these dynamics, the question of the extent and quality of democratic representation has moved to the forefront of both academic and public debates.

The aim of this volume is to evaluate the state of political representation in contemporary Europe. The articles advance our understanding of the topic by presenting fresh insight both of the extent to which there exists issue congruence between voters and parties and the degree to which there is dynamic representation in the policy responses of representatives.

It has long been realised that democratic governance requires a two-way flow of influence. Governments must be able to respond to what people want and people must be able to react to what governments do (Pitkin 1967). What people want can be expressed most forcefully in election outcomes, and the idea of issue congruence focuses on these. It has its roots in a report published by a committee of the American Political Science Association (Committee on Political Parties 1950; Ranney 1954) and is generally referred to as the 'responsible party model' of political representation. This model assumes that political representation takes place when the policies enacted by governing political parties closely reflect the wishes of those who elected those parties to government office. A problem with this approach is deciding how close 'closely' needs to be in order for us to decide that parties in government are behaving responsibly. Moreover, much government policy-making happens between elections, and the question of whether such policy-making is responsible cannot be addressed by looking only at election outcomes.

The idea of dynamic representation has its roots in work (Page and Shapiro 1983, 1992) that tries to overcome both these problems by using opinion poll data to see whether government policies change in response to changes in public opinion. In this approach, concern for the extent of congruence between public opinion and policy is replaced by concern for the extent to which policy is adjusted to track opinion change. With this approach the possibility of a perfect match between change in opinion and change in policy is not out of the question, and so one can imagine a metric for evaluating responsiveness of policy to opinion in terms of the length of time it would take for a match to occur (in the absence of further adjustments, which of course are always needed) with a quicker match implying better responsiveness. A problem with this approach is that one could in principle find policies that hardly matched public demands still changing in response to changes in those demands.

These two research traditions are each associated in practice with a second distinction, between changes in policy made in 'rational anticipation' of electoral repercussions and changes in policy made as a consequence of 'electoral turnover' (Stimson et al. 1995). The responsible party approach focuses largely on the second of these mechanisms of policy change while the dynamic representation approach customarily focuses on the first of them; though both approaches can and sometimes do address both mechanisms of policy change.

The mechanism of electoral turnover has thus been extensively studied in work on issue congruence, which examines how close a match there is between the wishes of voters and the policy stances of political parties (Golder and Stramski 2010; Powell 2004). Building on the work of Miller and Stokes (1963), in the responsible party model the links in the chain of delegation rest on the assumptions that parties offer coherent choices, citizens have clearly defined preferences on policy dimensions and in turn base their voting choices on these policy preferences (Mair 2008; Thomassen and Schmitt 1997, 1999). Elected parties once in government carry out policies that are in line with the campaign promises they had made and thus the preferences of the majority of the electorate will be reflected in government policy (Dalton 1985; Katz 1997; Ranney 1954; Thomassen 1994). Results of earlier research, both in a comparative perspective and in single country studies, indicate that voters and parties are indeed rather close on the left–right dimension (Mattila and Raunio 2006; Thomassen and Schmitt 1999), while research on EU integration produces mixed findings, some of which show agreement between voters and parties (van der Eijk and Franklin 1991; Rohrschneider and Whitefield 2007), while other work shows clear divergence, especially when it comes to specific policy areas (Hooghe 2003; Thomassen and Schmitt 1997).

Turning to the mechanism of rational anticipation, this has been studied primarily in work on dynamic representation that emphasises, first, whether public demand for policy is responded to by policy-makers who make changes in policy supply (Jacobs and Shapiro 1994; Page and Shapiro 1983, 1992) and, second, the way in which negative feedback in public opinion works as a corrective in case policy demands are met. Christopher Wlezien, in his seminal work on the thermostatic model of public opinion, provided the groundwork for much of the research on dynamic representation (Soroka and Wlezien 2010; Wlezien 1995, 2004; Wlezien and Soroka 2007), detailing precisely how the mechanisms of policy representation and public responsiveness work hand in hand. Building on this work and using a time-series approach, additional research has confirmed that governments indeed regularly react to public opinion not just on election day, but throughout the course of a legislative term (Boelstad 2012; Erikson *et al.* 2002; Hakhverdian 2010; Hobolt and Klemmensen 2008; Jennings and John 2009). Research on the opinion–policy nexus has recently been extended by explicitly examining the conditional influence of political institutions on the causal connection between public opinion and policy-making (Wlezien and Soroka 2011).

The contributions in this volume are logically clustered into three groups. One group of scholars bases its work on the 'responsible party model' and tries to elaborate the findings of earlier work in the same tradition applied to voters and to European parties and party groups; a second group of scholars extends the original model by demonstrating the importance of institutional structures and political information on the degree of issue congruence; a third group examines the reciprocal nature of dynamic representation and the effects of political institutions on the opinion–policy connection.

The first set of contributions in this volume extends our understanding of issue congruence in four important ways: (1) by demonstrating the extent to which there is congruence in the most recent European Parliament elections across distinct policy dimensions; (2) by explicitly testing the degree to which parties, once in office fulfil their electoral mandate by continuing to favour policy positions they put forward during election campaigns; (3) by demonstrating the extent to which, for niche parties, rank-and-file citizens update their policy beliefs in line with the wider informational environment; and (4) by demonstrating the importance of intra-party institutions for understanding whether parties respond to their supporters or to the median voter.

Costello, Thomassen and Rosema (2012) examine how well the system of political representation works on the European level by assessing the degree to which the views of citizens are matched by the policy views of political representatives. The authors extend the responsible party model by distinguishing three unique dimensions of political contestation: a traditional left/right dimension which is strongly associated with economic issues, a cultural dimension that correlates with the GAL-TAN dimension as found by Hooghe et al. (2002) and includes issues such as immigration, and finally a European integration dimension. Given the presence of these separate dimensions, the authors then assess the extent to which there is congruence between voters and parties on each of them. The findings suggest that congruence between parties and their voters is considerably higher on the left/right dimension than on the culture and EU dimensions. Furthermore, these insights are corroborated by an analysis of the coherence of the political groups which demonstrates that, for the left–right dimension, most of the variation in policy positions occurs between rather than within the political groups while, for the culture dimension, the political groups are internally fragmented. For the EU dimension there is a low degree of fragmentation but the variation between the political groups is rather small. In brief, the authors confirm the widely documented existence of a gap between political elites and the electorate on European integration and highlight the existence of a second gap, namely on the cultural dimension. Furthermore, the distance between voters and party groups on the left–right dimension is small enough to provide a modicum of hope for adequate representation relating to issues on this dimension.

Louwerse (2012) extends our understanding of the responsible party model by assessing the extent to which parties fulfil their collective mandate. Specifically, he examines whether there are systematic differences in the linkages between voters and politicians when comparing the United Kingdom (a majoritarian democracy) with the Netherlands (a consensus democracy) and whether these differences vary over time. Louwerse assesses the differences in issue salience and issue positions by comparing the campaign pledges of parties with the speeches delivered in parliament during the following legislative period. The findings suggest that mandate fulfilment in terms of issue salience in absolute terms is higher for British parties while in relative terms it is higher for Dutch parties. Regarding issue congruence, Louwerse finds a reasonable level of congruence and no significant differences between the majoritarian and consensus democracy types – albeit for the British parties the positions taken by government party frontbenchers are slightly closer to the parties' electoral positions.

Adams, Ezrow and Leiter (2012) revisit the question of partisan sorting, which has to do with the extent to which the mass public adjusts its preferred left–right policy position in response to shifts in its preferred parties' policy stances as measured by political experts. Their findings suggest that supporters of niche parties, such as Green, Communist and Radical Right parties, indeed exhibit substantial and statistically significant patterns of partisan sorting while such a pattern cannot be observed for mainstream parties. This result is further corroborated by a significant relationship between lagged expert perceptions of niche party shifts and current shifts in party supporters' left–right positions, thereby minimising the possibility of a reciprocal link in which niche party elites merely respond to the policy preferences of their supporters. In a nutshell, the findings of this paper suggest that, for niche parties, rank-and-file supporters indeed respond to the wider information environment and update their policy beliefs in line with their parties' policy statements in party manifestos, while supporters of other parties do not systematically exhibit such behaviour – at least as regards their left–right policy positions.

Lehrer (2012) extends our understanding of party strategies by emphasising the importance of the 'selectorate'. The findings demonstrate the importance of intra-party institutions by showing that inclusive parties tend to respond to the mean party supporter, while exclusive parties respond to the median voter position in two-party systems.

The second set of contributions in this volume extends our understanding of issue congruence in three important ways: (1) by systematically considering the conditional effect of electoral institutions on congruence; (2) by examining the institutional context in which political parties operate and the effect this has on the policy positions parties are likely to take; and (3) by extending our understanding of issue congruence by focusing on the interaction between party strategy and voting behaviour, sharpening our knowledge about the extent to which parties strategically choose specific issues in order to minimise electoral risk and to reap the benefits of electoral opportunities.

Rohrschneider and Whitefield (2012) demonstrate that the impact of electoral institutions on congruence is conditional on the characteristics of voters – in particular, their degree of partisanship and the associated changing balance between partisans and independents in the electorate. Controlling for the relative numbers of partisan and independent voters, parties' abilities to mitigate the representational strain depends on the characteristics of electoral institutions. These authors show that majoritarian institutions in a highly partisan electorate increase the ideological distance between parties and voters, since parties tend to converge to the centre while voters are spread across the ideological spectrum. This partisan mode of representation predominates when a large majority of voters consist of loyal party supporters. In contrast, majoritarian institutions in a highly dealigned electorate tend to decrease the ideological distance to independent voters, since voters in such a system are to a greater degree concentrated in the ideological centre. In consequence, when a large portion of the electorate is independent, majoritarian systems are found to be significantly better at diminishing the distance between parties and independent voters, while, when the proportion of unaligned voters is small, consensus regimes are more advantageous for issue congruence. This finding has interesting implications for electoral politics in the United States, but that is beyond its remit.

Arnold, Sapir and de Vries (2012) examine the correlates of parties' position on European integration, specifically focusing on the impact of voters' positions, parties' characteristics (such as ideology, incumbency and party size) and party system characteristics (such as the degree of fractionalisation and polarisation). In summary, their findings suggest that parties' positions on EU integration are affected by the preferences of the general electorate, reaffirming that, overall, parties are indeed responsive to voters' preferences in the realm of European integration. Furthermore, extremist position on the left–right scale along with party system characteristics such as fractionalisation and polarisation are strong predictors of parties' position on the EU, albeit the influence of polarisation is indirect. The impact of ideology, incumbency and party size is moderated by the institutional context in which parties operate. Parties' positions on the EU are not just a function of parties' characteristics, but rather a combination of parties' electoral success and the context in which they find themselves.

De Sio and Franklin (2012) add a new facet to our understanding of issue congruence. In this contribution, the issues parties choose to campaign on are seen as a strategic choice to minimise electoral risk (that is, to avoid issues that may be divisive within a party's support base) and to reap the benefits of electoral opportunities (that is, to play up issues that are widely supported outside the party). The issue yield model developed in this contribution has previously been employed to show that parties emphasise those issues on which they expect to benefit the most. In this contribution, voters are shown to make their choices on the basis of those issues that indeed serve the strategic interests of the parties they voted for. The paper confirms the relevance of issue yield especially for small party strategies: if small parties stress an issue that promises high yield they can narrow the gap in effects of issues that normally separate them from large parties, thus making themselves considerably more attractive to voters.

The third set of contribution focuses on dynamic representation and extends our understanding of political representation in two important ways: (1) by examining the causal relationship between public opinion and policy and (2) by considering the conditional effect of political institutions on the causal relationship between public opinion and policy-making.

Armen Hakhverdian (2012) provides an assessment of the causal relationship between public opinion and policy. The paper starts from the premise that, for democratic representation to occur, public opinion must play a key role in policy-making. The paper sets out to examine whether a reciprocal link exists between public opinion and policy and, if so, whether the feedback from policy to the public is positive (indicating leadership) or negative (thermostatic – which this author terms corrective). The paper enhances our understanding of dynamic representation by confirming the existence of a strong influence of public opinion on decision-makers. The effect is particularly strong on vulnerable incumbents, indicating that a threat to a government's re-election prospects enhances the strong relationship between public opinion and policy. This demonstrates that the electoral context matters for political responsiveness. While the paper finds only limited evidence of policy influencing public opinion, a notable contribution is to demonstrate that, for popular governments, there is a positive relationship between prior policy change and subsequent opinion change whereas for unpopular governments this relationship is negative. This again extends our understanding of dynamic representation by highlighting the conditional nature of the policy–opinion nexus.

The concluding contribution by Wlezien and Soroka (2012) provides a valuable comparison of dynamic representation across 17 countries through time, accounting for differences both in government institutions and electoral institutions. The key findings are that publics do perceive policy changes and that governments do respond to changing public preferences. This confirms the insights gained from earlier research on dynamic representation and shows them to be robust to variations in institutional context. Furthermore, this contribution refines our understanding of representation by demonstrating that there is a conditional effect of political institutions, whereby governments in proportional systems are less responsive to changes in public opinion. These findings challenge the conventional academic wisdom about the impact of electoral systems on democratic representation (Lijphart 1999; Powell 2000) and underline again the need to take the institutional context into consideration when examining the degree of policy representation and public responsiveness.

Taken together, these articles provide a window into the evolving research traditions that study political representation in all its facets, together with a rich addition to the burgeoning literature on representation processes.

References

Adams, James, Lawrence Ezrow, and Debra Leiter (2012). 'Partisan Sorting and Niche Parties in Europe', *West European Politics*, 35:6, 1272–94.

Arnold, Christine, Eliyahu V. Sapir, and Catherine de Vries (2012). 'Parties' Positions on European Integration: Issue Congruence, Ideology or Context?', *West European Politics*, 35:6, 1341–62.

Boelstad, Joergen (2012). 'Thermostatic Voting: Presidential Elections in Light of New Policy Data', *PS Political Science and Politics*, 45:1, 44–50.

Committee on Political Parties (1950). 'Toward a More Responsible Two-Party System', *American Political Science Review* 44 (supplement).

Costello, Rory, Jacques Thomassen, and Martin Rosema (2012). 'European Parliament Elections and Political Representation: Policy Congruence between Voters and Parties', *West European Politics*, 35:6, 1226–48.

Dalton, Russell J. (1985). 'Political Parties and Political Representation. Party Supporters and Party Elites in Nine Nations', *Comparative Political Studies*, 18:3, 267–99.

De Sio, Lorenzo, and Mark N. Franklin (2012). 'Strategic Incentives, Issue Proximity and Party Support', *West European Politics*, 35:6, 1363–85.

Erikson, Robert S., Michael B. Mackuen, and James A. Stimson (2002). *The Macro Polity*. Cambridge: Cambridge University Press.

Golder, Matt, and Jacek Stramski (2010). 'Ideological Congruence and Electoral Institutions', *American Journal of Political Science*, 54:1, 90–106.

Hakhverdian, Armen (2010). 'Political Representation and Its Mechanisms: A Dynamic Left–Right Approach for the United Kingdom', *British Journal of Political Science*, 40:4, 835–56.

Hakhverdian, Armen (2012). 'The Causal Flow between Public Opinion and Policy: Government Responsiveness, Leadership, or Counter Movement? Evidence from the United Kingdom', *West European Politics*, 35:6, 1386–1406.

Hobolt, Sara, and Robert Klemmensen (2008). 'Government Responsiveness and Political Competition in Comparative Perspective', *Comparative Political Studies*, 41:3, 309–37.

Hooghe, Liesbet (2003). 'Europe Divided? Elite vs. Public Opinion on European Integration', *European Union Politics*, 4:3, 281–305.

Hooghe, Liesbet, Gary Marks, and Carol Wilson (2002). 'Does Left/Right Structure Party Positions on European Integration?', *Comparative Political Studies*, 35:8, 965–89.

Jacobs, Lawrence, and Robert Shapiro (1994). 'Public Opinion, Institutions, and Policy Making: Studying Substantive Democracy', *PS: Political Science and Politics*, 27, 9–17.

Jennings, Will, and Peter John (2009). 'The Dynamics of Political Attention: Public Opinion and the Queen's Speeches in the United Kingdom', *American Journal of Political Science*, 53:4, 838–54.

Katz, Richard S. (1997). *Democracy and Elections*. New York: Oxford University Press.

Lehrer, Ron (2012). 'Intra-Party Democracy and Party Responsiveness', *West European Politics*, 35:6, 1295–1319.

Lijphart, Arnd (1999). *Patterns of Democracy*. New Haven, CT: Yale University Press.

Louwerse, Tom (2012). 'The Mechanisms of Issue Congruence: The Democratic Mandate', *West European Politics*, 35:6, 1249–71.

Mair, Peter (2007). 'Political Parties and Party Systems', in Paolo Grazioano and Maarten Vink (eds.), *Europeanization: New Research Agenda*. Basingstoke: Palgrave Macmillan, 154–66.

Mair, Peter (2008). 'The Challenge to Party Government', *West European Politics*, 31:1–2, 211–34.

Mair, Peter (2010). 'Political Representation and Government in the European Union', *Journal of European Public Policy*, 17, 20–35.

Mair, Peter (2011). 'Is Governing Becoming More Contentious?', in Martin Rosema, Bas Denkers, and Kees Aarts (eds.), *How Democracy Works: Political Representation and Policy Congruence in Modern Societies*. Amsterdam: Amsterdam University Press, 77–86.

Mattila, Mikko, and Tapio Raunio (2006). 'Cautious Voters – Supportive Parties: Opinion Congruence between Voters and Parties on the EU Dimension', *European Union Politics*, 7:4, 427–49.

Miller, Warren E., and Donald E. Stokes (1963). 'Constituency Influence in Congress', *American Political Science Review*, 57:1, 45–56.

Page, Benjamin, and Robert Shapiro (1983). 'The Effects of Public Opinion on Policy', *American Political Science Review*, 77:1, 175–90.

Page, Benjamin, and Robert Shapiro (1992). *The Rational Public: Fifty Years of Trends in Americans' Public Preferences*. Chicago: University of Chicago Press.

Pitkin, Hanna (1967). *The Concept of Representation*. Berkeley: University of California Press.

Powell, Bingham G. (2000). *Elections as Instruments of Democracy*. New Haven, CT: Yale University Press.

Powell, Bingham G. (2004). 'Political Representation in Comparative Perspective', *Annual Review of Political Science*, 7, 273–96.

Ranney, A. (1954). *The Doctrine of Responsible Party Government*. Urbana, IL: University of Illinois Press.

Rohrschneider, Robert, and Stephen Whitefield (2007). 'Political Parties, Public Opinion and European Integration in Post-Communist Countries', *European Union Politics*, 7:1, 141–60.

Rohrschneider, Robert, and Stephen Whitefield (2012). 'Institutional Context and Representational Strain in Party–Voter Agreement in Western and Eastern Europe', *West European Politics*, 35:6, 1320–40.

Soroka, Stuart N., and Christopher Wlezien (2010). *Degrees of Democracy: Politics, Public Opinion and Policy*. New York: Cambridge University Press.

Stimson, James A., Michael B. Mackuen, and Robert S. Erikson (1995). 'Dynamic Representation', *American Political Science Review*, 89:3, 543–65.

Streeck, Wolfgang, and Daniel Mertens (2010). *An Index of Fiscal Democracy*. MPIfG 10/3. Cologne: Max Planck Institute for the Study of Society.

Thomassen, Jacques (1994). 'Empirical Research into Political Representation: Failing Democracy or Failing Models?', in M. Kent Jennings and Thomas E. Mann (eds.), *Elections at Home and Abroad: Essays in Honor of Warren Miller*. Ann Arbor, MI: University of Michigan Press, 237–65.

Thomassen, Jacques, and Hermann Schmitt (1997). 'Policy Representation', *European Journal of Political Research*, 32, 165–84.

Thomassen, Jacques, and Hermann Schmitt (1999). 'Issue Congruence', in Hermann Schmitt and Jacques Thomassen (eds.), *Political Representation and Legitimacy in the European Union*. Oxford: Oxford University Press, 186–208.

Van der Eijk, Cees, and Mark N. Franklin (1991). 'The European Elections of 1989', *The European Journal of Political Research*, 19:1, 31–54.

Wlezien, Christopher (1995). 'The Public as Thermostat: Dynamics of Preferences for Spending', *American Journal of Political Science*, 39, 981–1000.

Wlezien, Christopher (2004). 'Patterns of Representation: Dynamics of Public Preferences and Policy', *Journal of Politics*, 66:1, 1–24.

Wlezien, Christopher, and Stuart Soroka (2007). 'The Relationship between Public Opinion and Policy', in Russell Dalton and Hans-Dieter Klingemann (eds.), *Oxford Handbook of Political Behavior*. Oxford: Oxford University Press.

Wlezien, Christopher, and Stuart Soroka (2011). 'Federalism and Public Responsiveness to Policy', *Publius: The Journal of Federalism*, 41, 31–52.

Wlezien, Christopher, and Stuart N. Soroka (2012). 'Political Institutions and the Opinion–Policy Link', *West European Politics*, 35:6, 1407–32.

European Parliament Elections and Political Representation: Policy Congruence between Voters and Parties

RORY COSTELLO, JACQUES THOMASSEN and MARTIN ROSEMA

It is often said that European Parliament elections fail as an instrument to express the will of the European people. However, while the elections are not contested at the European level and are often dominated by national issues, this does not necessarily imply that they fail to connect policy views of voters and representatives. This article examines policy congruence between voters and candidates, utilising the candidate and voter surveys of the European Election Study 2009. First, it demonstrates that policy preferences of candidates and voters are constrained by three separate policy dimensions. Second, it shows that the quality of representation is high in terms of left/right, the main dimension of conflict in European politics, but lower on the cultural and European integration dimensions. Finally, it establishes that in some cases the aggregation of national parties in political groups in the European Parliament poses problems for effective political representation.

The referendums on the Constitutional Treaty in 2005 in the Netherlands and France and the referendum on the Lisbon Treaty in 2008 in Ireland revealed a major lack of congruence between the policy views of the political elites and the electorate. The most extreme case was the Netherlands where a clear majority (62 per cent) of the electorate voted 'nee' in the referendum, against the will of the major political parties in parliament, together occupying 85 per cent of the seats. Obviously, the great majority of voters were far more Eurosceptic than their political leaders. A similar phenomenon is the sudden rise of populist parties across Western Europe. To a large extent their success is built on their crusade against non-western immigrants, in particular from Muslim countries, and the 'Islamisation' of Western societies. Just like the issue of Europeanisation this development suggests a failure of the traditional mainstream parties to represent the policy views of the electorate. Our main contention in this paper is that this is due to the fact that policy positions on such issues are not constrained by the main dimension of contestation in European politics, the left/right dimension.

We develop our argument as follows. In the next section we discuss the main conditions for an effective process of representation. One of these conditions is that both at the level of political parties and the electorate issue positions are constrained by the same ideological dimension. We argue that in the European context this can only be the left/right dimension. The section that follows describes the policy dimensions that form the basis for electoral competition in European Parliament elections. We argue that policy preferences at the level of candidates as well as voters are structured in terms of three distinct dimensions: the left/right dimension, a cultural dimension, and a European integration dimension. We hypothesise that political representation in the European Parliament will only be effective on issues constrained by the main dimension of political contestation in European politics, that is, the left/right dimension.

We test this hypothesis on the basis of data on the 2009 European Parliament elections. We first examine the dimensionality of the issue space in each country using confirmatory factor analysis. The goal is to identify whether policy issues are constrained by the left/right dimension or form several separate policy dimensions. Our second research goal is to examine the level of congruence between voters and candidates across different policy dimensions at the national level. As the left/right dimension is the primary dimension of contestation in domestic European politics, we expect that there will be a relatively high level of congruence between voters and representatives on this dimension. To the extent that issues are not related to this left/right dimension, we expect that the level of congruence will be lower. In the last part of the analysis we examine to what extent the national parties are compatible policy-wise and hence whether the process of political representation is still effective when we aggregate it to the level of the political groups in the European Parliament. Finally, we reflect on the implications of our findings for the quality of representation in the European Union and its member states.

The Requirements for Effective Political Representation

What constitutes an effective process of political representation depends on one's view on the function of this process. In modern (theories of) representative democracy there is hardly any dispute about the main function of this process: it should connect, either directly or indirectly, the policy preferences of the citizenry to public policy. The key actors in this process, in addition to the voters, are political parties. They directly or indirectly translate their electoral mandate into public policy. Directly in majoritarian democracies where a single party gets an electoral mandate to implement its policy programme, indirectly in consensus democracies where after the elections parties in parliament have to form a coalition government based on a compromise between their policy programmes (Powell 2000). In both systems the first important step in connecting the policy preferences of the voters to public policy is that elections connect these preferences to the policy views of political parties and their representatives in parliament. In this paper we focus on this first step by examining to what degree the policy views of political representatives match the views of the citizens in the context of the European Parliament and hence how well the system of political representation works on the European level.

For elections to function as instruments to link citizens' policy preferences with the policy positions of representatives, two main requirements must be met. First, the parties must offer a choice to the electorate in terms of their policy proposals. Second, voters must vote according to their policy preferences. These conditions are familiar elements of the Responsible Party Model of representation (see e.g. American Political Science Association 1950; Katz 1997; Thomassen 1994). The common assumption is that if both conditions are met, the electoral process will lead to policy congruence between a particular parliamentary party and the voters who voted for it.

However, as argued elsewhere (Thomassen 1994, 1999), these two requirements do not guarantee policy congruence between voters and representatives. Even when parties offer distinct policy programmes and all voters vote according to their issue positions, the election outcome does not necessarily convey an unequivocal electoral mandate to political parties on any given policy issue. Political parties offer a package deal to the voter. By voting for a particular party, voters are forced to vote for the whole package, even though they might favour another party on some issues. Consequently, it is possible that a party represents the view of a minority of its voters on individual issues.

The problem is only avoided when the voters voting for a particular party because of their position on a particular issue(-dimension) agree with the other policy positions of that party as well. Logically, this will only occur when these issue positions, both at the level of political parties and at the level of the electorate, are highly correlated – i.e. when both political parties, in the composition of their programmes, their representatives in parliament, in their legislative behaviour, and voters, when they decide which party they will vote for, are constrained by the same ideology. If that is the case then voters, by using this ideology or belief system as a shortcut, can vote for the party that represents their policy preferences best without even knowing the position of political parties on each and every issue (Downs 1957). Only when this condition is met will elections connect the policy preferences of the voters for a particular party across a range of issues to the policy position of the party of their choice.

Examining the effectiveness of political representation at the level of the European Parliament is even more complicated than at the national level.

A familiar criticism of the system of political representation at the European level is that there is no such system. European political parties as such do not compete for the votes of a European electorate. European elections are fought by national political parties and mainly on national issues, voters make their choice on the basis of their opinions on national issues and their perception of national political parties on these issues, and, as a consequence, European elections fail as an instrument of democracy at the European level, that is, they fail to link the policy preferences of the European people to the decision-making process in the European Parliament.

However, even though it is true that there is no European system of political representation as such, this does not necessarily mean European elections fail as an instrument of linkage. If the requirements spelled out above are met within each member state this will lead to policy congruence between voters and their national MEPs. Furthermore, if the various national systems are compatible – in terms of having similar sets of parties putting forward similar policy programmes, based on the same ideological dimension – then they can be successfully aggregated at the European level if like-minded national political parties jointly form political groups in the European Parliament. This in turn would lead to congruence between the policy positions of these transnational political groups and the people who (indirectly) voted for them. Taking this into account is relevant, because the general pattern is that MEPs vote in accordance with the majority of their political group in the European Parliament (Hix *et al.* 2007: 137). Therefore, the compatibility of the national political parties jointly forming political groups in the European Parliament is an additional requirement to be met for an effective process of political representation at the European level.

Policy Dimensions in European Parliament Elections

It has often been argued that party competition in European democracies can be largely reduced to a single dimension of left/right (e.g. Sani and Sartori 1983). Empirical research seems to confirm that left/right is the main dimension of contestation. Voters in general have no problem locating themselves on the left/right dimension; they have a clear perception of where the main political parties stand; and they vote in large numbers for parties near their own position on this dimension (van der Brug and van der Eijk 1999; van der Brug *et al.* 2009; van der Eijk *et al.* 2005). Therefore, the language of 'left' and 'right' seems to create a unidimensional discourse providing the common yardstick for masses and elites that is required in a model of political representation (Huber and Powell 1994). Research also shows that vote choice in European elections is strongly related to left/right positions (van der Eijk *et al.* 1996: 359).

In terms of content, the left/right dimension is most closely associated with economic questions, such as the redistribution of wealth and the role of the state in the economy. As Hooghe *et al.* (2004: 164) put it, the left/right dimension 'constrains the positions that parties take on competing versions of capitalism in Europe'. Support for the economic interpretation of the left/right dimension is also provided by the cross-national study of Benoit and Laver (2006). They find that in all EU countries, except for Malta and Austria, party positions on the issue of 'taxes and spending' were significantly correlated with positions on the general left/right dimension. Due to the dominance of the left/right dimension in shaping party competition across countries, the national systems of political representation in EU member states are largely compatible. This is the case even after the 2004 enlargement of the European Union with 10 new member states, mainly from Central and Eastern Europe. As a consequence these national systems of political representation can be aggregated to the European level without losing much of their effectiveness. Even though there is not much of a truly European system of political representation, European party groups are remarkably distinct (competitive) and internally cohesive with regard to the left/right dimension, while voters across member states mainly vote according to their position on the left/right dimension (Rosema and de Vries 2011; Schmitt and Thomassen 2009; van der Brug *et al.* 2009).

All these studies suggest that the process of political representation is likely to be effective on the left/right dimension and therefore on issues constrained by this dimension. However, they do not really prove that this process is effective on each and every issue. This will only be the case when all policy issues are encompassed or constrained by this single dimension. This requirement is unlikely to be met. On the contrary, a growing body of research suggests that attitudes and policy positions on issues like law and order, European unification, immigration and the place of ethnic minorities in society are *not* constrained by the left/right dimension (Hooghe *et al.* 2004; Kriesi *et al.* 2006). If this is the case, whereas at the same time the behaviour of both political parties and voters at election time is still dominated by the left/right dimension, elections are doomed to fail as an instrument of linkage with regard to such issues.

The idea that the space of political conflict in most modern Western societies can be reduced to a single ideological dimension was never undisputed. In Western Europe the religious cleavage used to be a second dimension of conflict in addition to the left/right dimension, basically understood as a class cleavage. Although it might be true that this dimension is no longer a *dimension of conflict* but 'only' a *dimension of identification* (Sani and Sartori 1983), people might still use it as a compass guiding them on moral issues. A second more or less classic dimension is the libertarian-authoritarian dimension (Kitschelt 1994; Lipset 1966). Lipset (1966) was the first to argue that the traditional parties on the left were not representative of their voters on this dimension. Whereas these parties tend to combine a left position on the (socio-economic) left/right dimension with a libertarian position, their voters, in particular as far as they are less well educated, tend to combine a position on the left with a traditional or authoritarian position on non-material issues.

Recently this discussion has been brought back to life, mainly because of the rise of populist parties. It is difficult to understand their success in the simple left/right framework. For example, Kriesi *et al.* (2006, 2008) argue that the antagonism between winners and losers of the contemporary process of globalisation leads to a conflict between *integration* and *demarcation*. They expect that this new conflict dimension will increasingly take on an ethnic or nationalist character. Also, they expect that new issues like European integration and immigration will be absorbed into this cultural dimension. The cultural dimension has been gaining in importance as it has become the primary basis on which new parties or transformed established parties seek to mobilise their electorate and therefore has developed into a second dimension of conflict (Kriesi *et al.* 2006, 2008). The cultural dimension is conceptually strongly related to the classic libertarian-authoritarian dimension. The same applies to the GAL-TAN dimension (green/alternative/libertarian vs. traditional/authoritarian/nationalist) introduced by Hooghe *et al.* (2004).

While the cultural dimension is distinct from the left/right dimension, most studies find that it is not entirely separate. In terms of the positions of European political parties in Western Europe, Marks *et al.* (2006) find a moderately strong correlation between the two dimensions, with parties on the left typically associated with libertarian (or GAL) positions, and parties on the right associated with more authoritarian (or TAN) positions. In contrast, the relationship was found to be in the opposite direction for parties in former communist countries of Central and Eastern Europe: parties on the right (with free market economic policies) tend to be more liberal on cultural matters and more in favour of European integration than parties on the left. This suggests that on this dimension the major political groups in the European Parliament will have difficulty meeting the requirement of the compatibility of national party delegations (cf. van der Brug *et al.* 2009; Voeten 2009).

In both Kriesi's and Hooghe's conceptual framework the issue of European integration is part of the cultural or GAL-TAN dimension respectively. However, in analyses of the issue positions of both members of the European Parliament and members of the national parliaments of the member states, European integration clearly came out as a separate dimension, distinct from both the left/right and libertarian-authoritarian dimensions (McElroy and Benoit 2007; Thomassen and Schmitt 1999). European integration appears not completely independent from left/right, though, in particular at the elite level, because parties opposing European integration are typically found relatively close to the extremes of the left/right dimension, whereas centrist parties are characterised by more favourable attitudes towards European integration (Hooghe *et al.* 2004; Rosema and de Vries 2011; Schmitt and Thomassen 2009). These findings lead us to expect that policy preferences can be understood best in terms of three distinct, but moderately correlated, dimensions of political contestation: the traditional left/right dimension, which is strongly associated with economic issues, a cultural dimension, which strongly overlaps with GAL-TAN and incorporates issues like immigration, and a dimension related to the issue of European integration.

The Dimensionality of the Policy Space

To test our hypotheses we use data from the Candidate Study and Voter Study of the European Election Study 2009 (EES 2009) (Giebler *et al.* 2010; van Egmond *et al.* 2010). The Candidate Study surveyed a total of 1,576 candidates from all 27 member states. The sample focused on parties that received over half the national electoral threshold and excluded candidates very low on the party list. On average, there were 58 respondents per member state. However, this varied widely, from seven respondents in Bulgaria to 258 respondents in the UK. The Voter Study surveyed 27,069 individuals from all 27 member states, with a minimum of 1,000 respondents per country. Data files and documentation are available from the project website: http://www.piredeu.eu.

The present study employs 11 attitudinal items contained in both the candidate and voter surveys, listed in Table 1. These items were selected as they measure different aspects of the three policy dimensions discussed in the previous section, namely the economic left/right dimension, the cultural dimension, and the EU dimension. It was also important to have a balance in terms of the orientation of the items – in other words, to include both positively worded and negatively worded items with respect to the

TABLE 1
DESCRIPTION OF SURVEY ITEMS IN EUROPEAN ELECTION STUDY 2009

Item	Description
Redistribution	Income and wealth should be redistributed towards ordinary people
State	Public services and industries should be in state ownership
Enterprise	Private enterprise is the best way to solve (country's) economic problems
Immigration	Immigration to (country) should be decreased significantly
Sentences	People who break the law should get much harsher sentences than now
Marriage	Same-sex marriage should be prohibited by law
Abortion	Women should be free to decide on matters of abortion
Trust	You trust the institutions of the European Union
Parliament	The European Parliament takes into consideration the concerns of European citizens
Referendum	EU treaty changes should be decided by referendum
Democracy	How satisfied are you with the way democracy works in the EU? (4-point scale)

Note: All items were measured using a 5-point Likert scale with values ranging between 1 (strongly agree) and 5 (strongly disagree), except the 'democracy' item, which was measured using a four-point scale with values ranging between 1 (very satisfied) and 4 (not at all satisfied).

dimension being measured – in order to be able to identify an acquiescence bias in the data. Ten of the selected items elicited a response to a statement on a 5-point Likert scale, while one item used a 4-point scale.

The first set of analyses examines the structure of policy views among voters and candidates. Confirmatory factor analysis was conducted using STATA version 12.0 to test our expectations regarding the policy space in each country. Maximum Likelihood (ML) estimation was used for the analysis, with missing data handled by listwise deletion.[1] The candidate data and voter data are examined together, in order to produce comparable estimates of their respective positions on the underlying dimensions, enabling us to determine the degree of policy congruence. We also looked at voters and candidates separately (results not presented). A comparable structure was found for both levels, the main differences being that for candidates, positions are more tightly constrained by the underlying dimensions (indicated by higher factor loadings for the candidate data than the voter data) and the dimensions are somewhat more strongly correlated with each other.

The model we test is shown in Figure 1. It assumes a three-dimensional policy space: an economic left/right dimension, on which the three economic variables load; a cultural dimension, on which four items load; and an EU dimension, on which four items load. Correlations between these latent factors are also expected (indicated by the double-headed arrows).

FIGURE 1
PATH DIAGRAM FOR THE STRUCTURE OF POLICY PREFERENCES

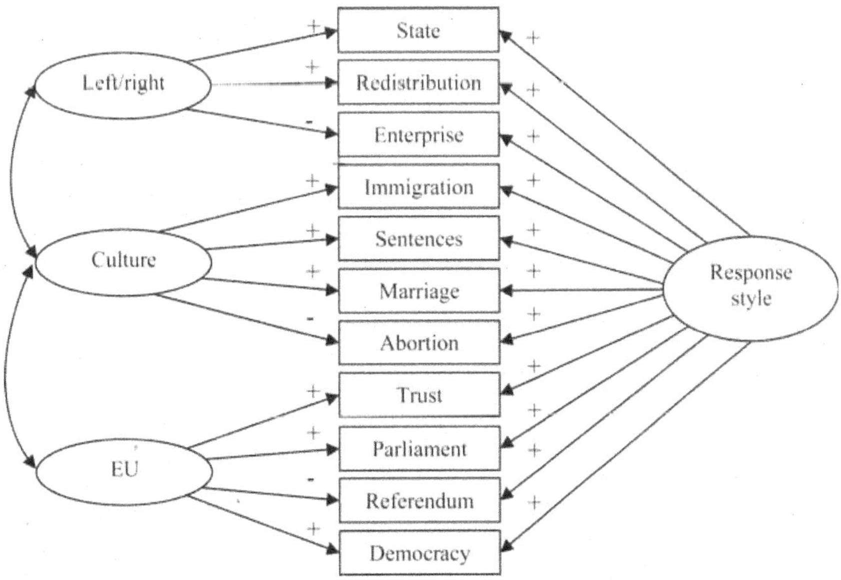

Note: Error paths not included.

In addition to the factors corresponding to the three policy dimensions a 'response style' factor is included in the model. We include this factor to address a measurement problem in the data. As is common in Likert items, there is evidence of acquiescence bias, that is, a tendency among some respondents to agree with statements regardless of their content (McClendon 1991). This tendency is picked up by the inclusion of the response style factor, which follows the recommendations of Billiet and McClendon (2000) and Welkenhuysen-Gybles *et al.* (2003). There is no reason to believe that different items will be affected differently by acquiescence (Welkenhuysen-Gybles *et al.* 2003: 707), so the style factor is constrained to have an identical loading on all of the Likert items in the model (but loads freely on the non-Likert item 'democracy'). The style factor is further constrained to be uncorrelated with each of the three 'content' factors (Billiet and McClendon 2000: 612).[2] An additional test confirmed that the response style factor does indeed measure acquiescence.[3]

For member states in Western Europe the standardised factor loadings are presented in Table 2. In each of these countries the four-factor model (three policy dimensions plus the response style factor) provided a good fit with the data, as discussed in more detail below. In general, the factor loadings (which have a possible range of −1 to +1) are reasonably strong and in the anticipated direction. Only the item about abortion has consistently low loadings, which suggests that in most countries this issue is not incorporated in the cultural dimension. We kept the item, though, in order to maintain a mix of pro-trait and contra-trait items for each dimension.

In Central and Eastern Europe our model was not always supported by the data, as shown in Table 3. In five countries (Czech Republic, Estonia, Poland, Slovakia and Slovenia) the model that included three policy dimensions plus the response style factor provided a good fit with the data. In Bulgaria, Romania and Hungary, however, a simpler model containing just two policy factors performed better than the full model: a broad left/right factor on which the economic and cultural items load, and a separate EU factor. For four countries no acceptable model was found: Greece, Malta, Lithuania and Latvia.[4] For reasons of comparability, these four countries are not included in the analyses below of policy congruence between voters and parties.

Model fit indices and the inter-factor correlations for each country are listed in Table 4. The adequacy of the fit is evaluated using a number of recommended statistics (Brown 2006: 87). The standardised root mean square residual (SRMR) measures the extent to which the correlations from the input matrix are adequately predicted by the model; good-fitting models have values below 0.08. The root mean square error of approximation (RMSEA) expresses the degree of model misspecification; values below 0.08 can indicate an acceptable model fit, while values below 0.06 indicate a good fit. The Comparative Fit Index (CFI) evaluates the fit of the model in comparison to a baseline model on a scale of 0 to 1; values above 0.90 can be

TABLE 2
RESULTS OF CONFIRMATORY FACTOR ANALYSIS OF POLICY PREFERENCES: FACTOR LOADINGS BY COUNTRY FOR WESTERN EUROPE

	Item	AT	BE	CY	DK	FI	FR	DE	IE	IT	LU	NL	PT	ES	SE	UK
Left/right	State	0.47	0.23	0.16	0.40	0.43	0.50	0.61	0.26	0.10	0.58	0.48	0.29	0.32	0.58	0.48
	Redistribution	0.43	0.67	0.25	0.18	0.56	0.41	0.55	0.61	0.17	0.16	0.36	0.44	0.34	0.61	0.42
	Enterprise	−0.72	−0.29	−0.28	−0.73	−0.21	−0.60	−0.63	−0.22	−0.34	−0.26	−0.35	−0.27	−0.61	−0.61	−0.80
Culture	Immigration	0.79	0.57	0.15	0.77	0.67	0.76	0.77	0.60	0.77	0.58	0.61	0.66	0.45	0.78	0.73
	Sentences	0.62	0.41	0.19	0.67	0.57	0.57	0.54	0.41	0.48	0.53	0.53	0.36	0.44	0.54	0.64
	Marriage	0.40	0.25	0.53	0.30	0.45	0.52	0.41	0.24	0.44	0.28	0.39	0.29	0.54	0.46	0.52
	Abortion	−0.15	−0.11	−0.25	−0.13	−0.12	−0.42	−0.08	−0.06	−0.07	−0.10	−0.24	0.04	−0.49	−0.30	−0.22
EU	Trust	0.75	0.63	0.68	0.75	0.71	0.83	0.67	0.81	0.88	0.66	0.73	0.72	0.77	0.77	0.82
	Parliament	0.75	0.62	0.49	0.58	0.59	0.70	0.68	0.62	0.56	0.64	0.66	0.66	0.62	0.64	0.73
	Referendum	−0.54	−0.36	−0.15	−0.36	−0.49	−0.39	−0.39	−0.26	−0.06	−0.39	−0.49	−0.28	−0.20	−0.49	−0.55
	Democracy	0.48	0.41	0.35	0.54	0.48	0.56	0.45	0.47	0.22	0.51	0.46	0.45	0.37	0.65	0.60
Style	(Mean loading across items)	0.21	0.28	0.37	0.10	0.21	0.20	0.22	0.20	0.23	0.22	0.18	0.24	0.22	0.13	0.20

Note: Countries are abbreviated as follows. AT: Austria; BE: Belgium; CY: Cyprus; DK: Denmark; FI: Finland; FR: France; DE: Germany; IE: Ireland; IT: Italy; LU: Luxembourg; NL: The Netherlands; PT: Portugal; ES: Spain; SE: Sweden; UK: The United Kingdom.

TABLE 3

RESULTS OF CONFIRMATORY FACTOR ANALYSIS OF POLICY PREFERENCES: FACTOR LOADINGS BY COUNTRY FOR CENTRAL AND EASTERN EUROPE

		Four-factor solution					Three-factor solution			
	Item	**CZ**	**EE**	**PL**	**SK**	**SI**		**BU**	**HU**	**RO**
Left/right	State	0.46	0.51	0.47	0.70	0.29	**Left/right**	0.55	0.58	0.51
	Redistribution	0.51	0.28	0.33	0.38	0.23		0.54	0.37	0.34
	Enterprise	−0.27	−0.33	−0.57	−0.45	−0.30		−0.44	−0.15	−0.52
Culture	Immigration	0.65	0.39	0.38	0.41	0.42		0.34	0.62	0.27
	Sentences	0.33	0.41	0.53	0.18	0.16		−0.05	0.29	0.32
	Marriage	0.37	0.43	0.51	0.41	0.72		0.38	0.50	0.27
	Abortion	−0.04	−0.02	−0.28	0.02	−0.39		−0.12	−0.15	−0.07
EU	Trust	0.71	0.75	0.75	0.74	0.65	**EU**	0.82	0.78	0.66
	Parliament	0.73	0.67	0.54	0.5	−0.26		0.67	0.62	0.64
	Referendum	−0.31	−0.14	−0.38	−0.17	−0.26		−0.15	−0.38	−0.29
	Democracy	0.50	0.47	0.46	0.48	0.43		0.33	0.49	0.36
Style	(Mean loadings across items)	0.22	0.26	0.23	0.27	0.24	**Style**	0.26	0.31	0.28

Note: Countries are abbreviated as follows. CZ: Czech Republic; EE: Estonia; PL: Poland; SK: Slovakia; SI: Slovenia; BU: Bulgaria; HU: Hungary; RO: Romania.

TABLE 4
RESULTS OF CONFIRMATORY FACTOR ANALYSIS OF POLICY PREFERENCES: MODEL FIT AND INTER-FACTOR CORRELATIONS BY COUNTRY

	Model fit			Inter-factor correlations			
	RMSEA	CFI	SRMR	Left/right culture	Left/right EU	Culture EU	*N*
Western Europe							
Austria	0.067	0.917	0.067	−0.42	−0.04	−0.57	667
Belgium*	0.066	0.834	0.054	−0.22	−0.14	−0.45	674
Cyprus	0.042	0.900	0.042	−0.40	−0.69	−0.05	671
Denmark*	0.060	0.910	0.048	−0.63	−0.11	−0.15	715
Finland	0.078	0.835	0.061	0.01	−0.48	−0.53	600
France	0.054	0.947	0.041	−0.70	−0.39	−0.22	600
Germany	0.079	0.851	0.062	−0.17	−0.25	−0.29	788
Ireland	0.050	0.900	0.043	0.27	−0.18	−0.42	721
Italy	0.049	0.917	0.047	−0.64	0.07	−0.36	657
Luxembourg	0.066	0.833	0.056	−0.03	−0.20	−0.33	721
Netherlands	0.099	0.745	0.072	−0.29	−0.26	−0.46	652
Portugal	0.055	0.889	0.048	0.43	−0.41	−0.57	503
Spain	0.057	0.891	0.046	−0.73	−0.13	−0.10	588
Sweden	0.060	0.929	0.044	−0.07	−0.57	−0.28	782
UK	0.077	0.914	0.052	−0.54	0.33	−0.64	732
Mean				*−0.28*	*−0.23*	*−0.36*	
Central/Eastern Europe (3 factors)							
Czech Republic	0.082	0.812	0.060	0.57	−0.34	−0.48	411
Estonia	0.067	0.862	0.053	0.67	−0.53	−0.49	419
Poland	0.064	0.865	0.053	0.33	−0.34	−0.58	334
Slovakia	0.080	0.822	0.063	0.67	−0.33	−0.62	350
Slovenia	0.065	0.835	0.062	−0.10	−0.58	−0.12	530
Mean				*0.43*	*−0.43*	*−0.46*	
Central/Eastern Europe (2 factors)							
Bulgaria	0.056	0.906	0.051	–	−0.42	–	339
Hungary	0.053	0.943	0.050	–	−0.85	–	378
Romania	0.059	0.875	0.056	–	−0.59	–	324
Mean					*−0.62*		

Note: RMSEA: Root Mean Square Error of Approximation. CFI: Comparative Fit Index. SRMR: Standardised Root Mean Square Residual.
*Minor modifications to the basic model were made for these countries. See note 2.

taken as an acceptable fit, and values above 0.95 indicate a good fit (Brown 2006: 87).

For most countries the four-factor model was superior to a model with fewer factors (i.e. a model without the style factor, or models with fewer policy factors). Ten countries score well on all three fit indices. Most of the other countries (both east and west) have acceptable SRMR and RMSEA scores but are below the 0.90 threshold for CFI. Only the Netherlands and the Czech Republic perform poorly on two of the three measures of model fit. Overall, taking into account the fact that any model will perform better in some countries than in others, the model that includes three policy dimensions plus a response style factor can be taken to be a reasonably good fit for the data.

The direction and the strength of the correlations between the content factors are also of interest (see Table 4). The first thing to note is that the correlations are generally modest (there is only one instance of an inter-factor correlation above 0.80, which is sometimes taken as a cut-off point for discriminant validity; see Brown 2006: 32), supporting the conclusion that the three policy dimensions are indeed distinct. In terms of the direction of the relationships, there are notable differences between west and east. For nearly all Western European countries, there is a negative correlation between the left/right and culture factors. Given the way the factors are oriented, this means those on the left on economic issues tend to be liberal on cultural issues, as expected. In contrast, there is a moderately strong positive correlation between these two factors for nearly all countries in Central and Eastern Europe (CEE). In line with the findings of Marks *et al.* (2006), this implies that economically leftist voters and candidates from CEE countries are culturally conservative.

These differences between east and west are not found for the other correlations. For all countries, there is a negative correlation between the culture and EU factors, implying that culturally conservative respondents tend to be more Eurosceptic. There is also a negative correlation between the left/right and EU factors for most countries, indicating that left-wing respondents tend to be more opposed to EU integration. However, this relationship is quite weak in several Western European countries. This does not necessarily mean that the factors are not related, because the analysis focuses on linear relationships and previous research identified a non-linear relationship (Hooghe *et al.* 2004; Schmitt and Thomassen 2009). However, those findings concerned the EU as a whole and focused on the elite level. At the mass level and when focusing on individual countries, those patterns are much weaker (Rosema and de Vries 2011: 209).

To summarise, the confirmatory factor analysis shows that the attitudes of voters and candidates are not constrained by a single dimension. Rather, three separate policy dimensions were found to best capture the observed variation: an economic left/right dimension, a cultural dimension and an EU dimension. In only three countries (Hungary, Bulgaria and Romania) two policy dimensions produced the best fit. Thus, the assumption implicit in the Responsible Party Model of representation – that the opinions of voters and representatives on all relevant issues are constrained by a single dimension – does not hold. This raises the possibility that the congruence between voters and representatives will be weak for certain types of issues.

Analysis of Policy Congruence between Voters and Representatives

We have argued that the level of agreement between voters and representatives will vary across policy domains: issues that are related to the left/right dimension are expected to be associated with higher levels of congruence than issues that are independent of this dimension. To test these expectations, we compare the positions of voters and candidates from each national party on the three dimensions identified in the previous section. Factor scores (predicted values for each latent factor) are produced for each dimension on the basis of the confirmatory factor analysis reported in the previous section. The advantage of using factor scores instead of additive indices is that they enable us to control for acquiescence bias, as done in the above analysis. The factor scores are standardised variables with a mean of zero.

Policy congruence is analysed by determining how close each national party is to its voters on each dimension.[5] National party positions are measured as the mean position of their candidates. The proximity of parties to their voters is measured as the mean absolute difference between the position of each voter and the position of the party he or she voted for. To increase the reliability of the estimates, only parties that have at least five candidates and 40 voters with valid responses to all 11 items are included in the analysis. So in countries where the response rate of the candidate survey was low, several parties had to be excluded. This also applies to several small parties, which did not meet the criterion of the voter survey. In addition, the four countries for which an acceptable factor solution was not found (Greece, Malta, Lithuania and Latvia) are excluded. In total, 39 national parties meet all selection criteria and these are now focused on.

The policy congruence between voters and parties is presented in Figure 2. Each bar represents the mean absolute difference between a national party and its voters on a particular dimension. The results are organised by party groups and by country. The first panel gives the results for 12 parties affiliated with the centre-right European People's Party (EPP). The difference between parties and voters is smallest on the left/right dimension in nearly all countries. The only exception is Slovakia, where the party is closest to its voters on the culture dimension.

The second panel in Figure 2 shows the results for eight parties affiliated with the Progressive Alliance of Socialists and Democrats (S&D). Again, parties and their voters are found to match best on the left/right dimension, the only exceptions being Belgium and Germany, where parties are slightly closer to their voters on the culture dimension. The pattern is repeated for parties affiliated with the Alliance of Liberals and Democrats for Europe (ALDE) and the Group of the Greens/European Free Alliance (Greens). In both cases, parties perform best on the left/right dimension in all but one of the countries analysed.

For the smaller party groups (the European Conservatives and Reformists Group (ECR), the Confederal Group of the European United Left–Nordic Green Left (EUL-NGL) and Europe of Freedom and Democracy Group (EFD)), there are very few national parties that meet our selection criteria. For four out of the five national parties included, the parties are closer to their voters on the left/right dimension than on the other two dimensions. This is somewhat surprising, given the emphasis these parties typically place on issues related to the other two dimensions. Because of the low number of

FIGURE 2
DIFFERENCES BETWEEN VOTERS AND PARTIES ON THREE POLICY DIMENSIONS

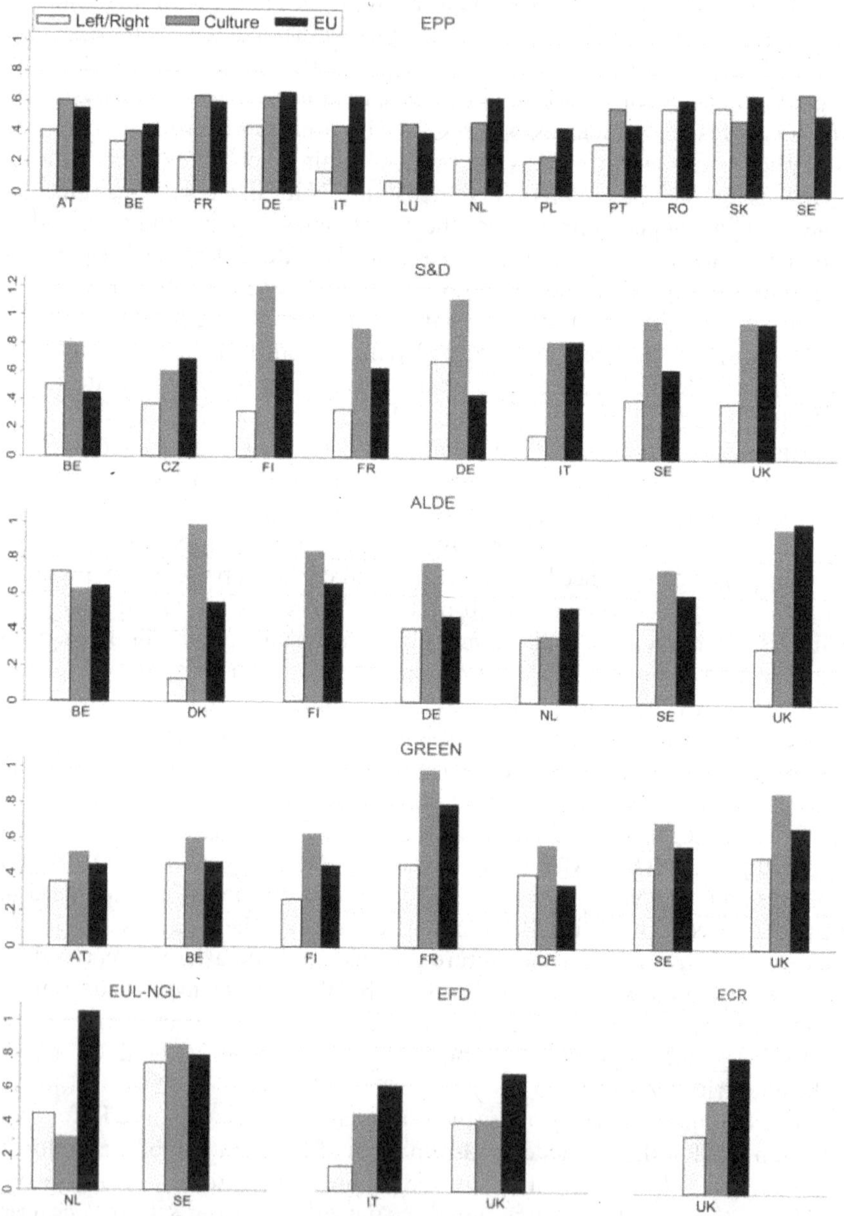

Note: Entries are the mean absolute difference between the voter positions and the party position. Countries are abbreviated as follows. AT: Austria; BE: Belgium; CY: Cyprus; CZ: The Czech Republic; DK: Denmark; EE: Estonia; FI: Finland: FR: France; DE: Germany; IE: Ireland; IT: Italy; LU: Luxembourg; NL: The Netherlands; PL: Poland; PT: Portugal; RO: Romania SI: Slovenia; SK: Slovakia; ES: Spain; SE: Sweden; UK: The United Kingdom.

national parties, however, we cannot reach strong conclusions about these party groups.

The differences between positions of parties and their voters are illustrated in Figure 3, which plots the mean position of voters against the mean position of candidates for each party on the three dimensions. When the mean positions of candidates and voters for a particular party are the same, the party will be placed on the 45 degree reference line. For the left/right dimension, the mean positions of candidates and voters are relatively close together, with most parties placed on or close to the reference line. The differences that exist follow a pattern, in that parties on the right (i.e. where the mean candidate has a high score on this dimension) tend to be slightly to the right of their average voter, while parties on the left tend to be slightly to the left of their average voter. For the culture dimension, the mean position of candidates for most parties is higher than the mean position of their voters. Given the way this dimension is orientated, this indicates that candidates for most parties are more liberal than their voters on cultural issues.

For the EU dimension, the mean position of candidates is lower than that of voters for most parties. This implies that candidates are typically more in favour of EU integration than their voters. The three outliers at the top right corner of the graph are parties associated with EUL-NGL and EFD, where the mean candidate position is strongly anti-EU. The average size of the gap between mean candidate and mean voter positions is 0.26 on the left/right dimension, 0.52 on the culture dimension and 0.41 on the EU dimension.

The Compatibility of National Parties within Political Groups

So far, we have established that an important requirement for an effective process of political representation is not met. Instead of a single left/right dimension three separate policy dimensions can be identified in most EU member states, with different relationships between these dimensions for CEE and Western European countries. As expected, the congruence between parties and their voters is consistently higher on the economic left/right dimension than on the culture and EU dimensions. In this section, we investigate whether the process of political representation is still effective when transferred to the EU level. As argued above, this will only be the case when an additional requirement is met, i.e. when the policy positions of the national parties from each political group are compatible. If national parties represent their voters well on the left/right dimension and have similar positions on this dimension to the other parties in their political group, then we can infer that the groups represent their voters well, albeit indirectly. In a similar way, how well voters are represented on the culture and EU dimensions depends in part on how well national parties from the same political group in the European Parliament match in those terms.

To estimate policy positions for national parties that are comparable across countries, the confirmatory factor analysis model was applied to the

FIGURE 3
COMPARISON OF MEAN POSITIONS OF CANDIDATES AND VOTERS FOR NATIONAL PARTIES

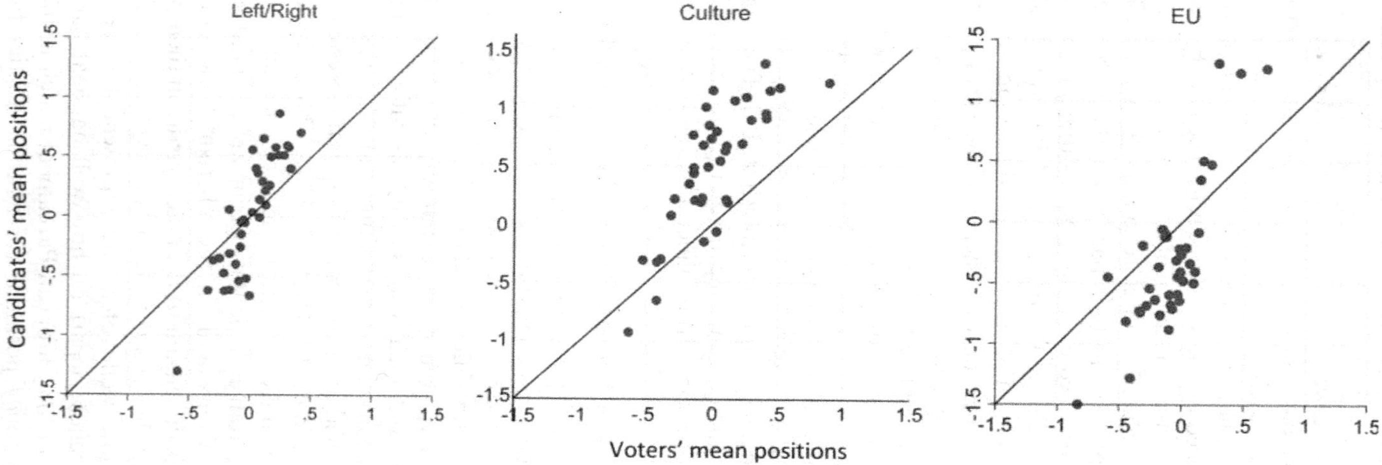

candidate data with all 27 countries included together. As before, national parties with fewer than five candidates with valid responses to all 11 items are excluded from the analysis. A total of 61 national parties are included as a result (the breakdown by political group is as follows: 15 EPP, 10 S&D, 10 ALDE, 12 Green, 4 ECR, 6 GUE-NGL and 4 EFD). The model has an acceptable fit on most indicators (SRMR = 0.06; CFI = 0.93; RMSEA 0.09), and the three policy dimensions having strong loadings (>0.5) on all items. Factor scores were produced for each of the three policy dimensions on the basis of this analysis. The position of each national party on the three dimensions was calculated as the mean position of its candidates.

Figure 4 shows the position of the national parties from each political group on the three policy dimensions. For the left/right dimension, clear differences are apparent between groups on the left (GUE-NGL, Green and S&D) and groups on the right (ALDE, EPP, ECR, EFD). The national parties for each group are generally clustered closely together, although some differences are apparent, particularly in the Green and ALDE groups. No significant differences are apparent between Western European countries (represented by the white circles) and CEE countries (represented by black circles). Overall, political group membership explains 77 per cent of the variation in all national party positions on this dimension, and 67 per cent of the variation in the positions of national parties associated with the three largest groups (EPP, S&D and ALDE).[6] Such high figures can only be reached if the political groups are to a considerable extent both cohesive and distinctive.

Turning to the culture dimension, more significant internal divisions are apparent in several political groups, and these divisions appear to follow geographic lines. For the Greens, S&D and ALDE, parties from CEE countries are noticeably more conservative than their Western European counterparts. The internal differences are smallest for the relatively extreme GUE-NGL group and for ECR. Political group membership explains less variation in party positions on this dimension compared to the left/right dimension: the figure for all parties is 69 per cent, and for parties from the three largest groups it is 55 per cent.

Finally, a noticeably different picture emerges for the EU dimension. The smaller fringe parties (GUE-NGL, Greens, ECR and EFD) appear quite divided on this dimension, although tending towards the anti-EU end of the spectrum. The larger centre parties (EPP, S&D and ALDE) are more cohesive, but there are no significant differences between them, as they all take similar pro-EU positions. The percentage of variation in party positions explained by group membership is relatively high when all parties are analysed (74 per cent), but the figure is just 14 per cent for the three largest parties. This low figure results from the lack of distinctiveness of the major parties on the EU dimension.

The graphs in Figure 4 also reveal something else, namely how positions of the political parties on the three dimensions are related (keeping in mind

FIGURE 4
POSITIONS OF NATIONAL PARTIES ON THREE POLICY DIMENSIONS, ORGANISED BY POLITICAL GROUP IN THE EUROPEAN PARLIAMENT

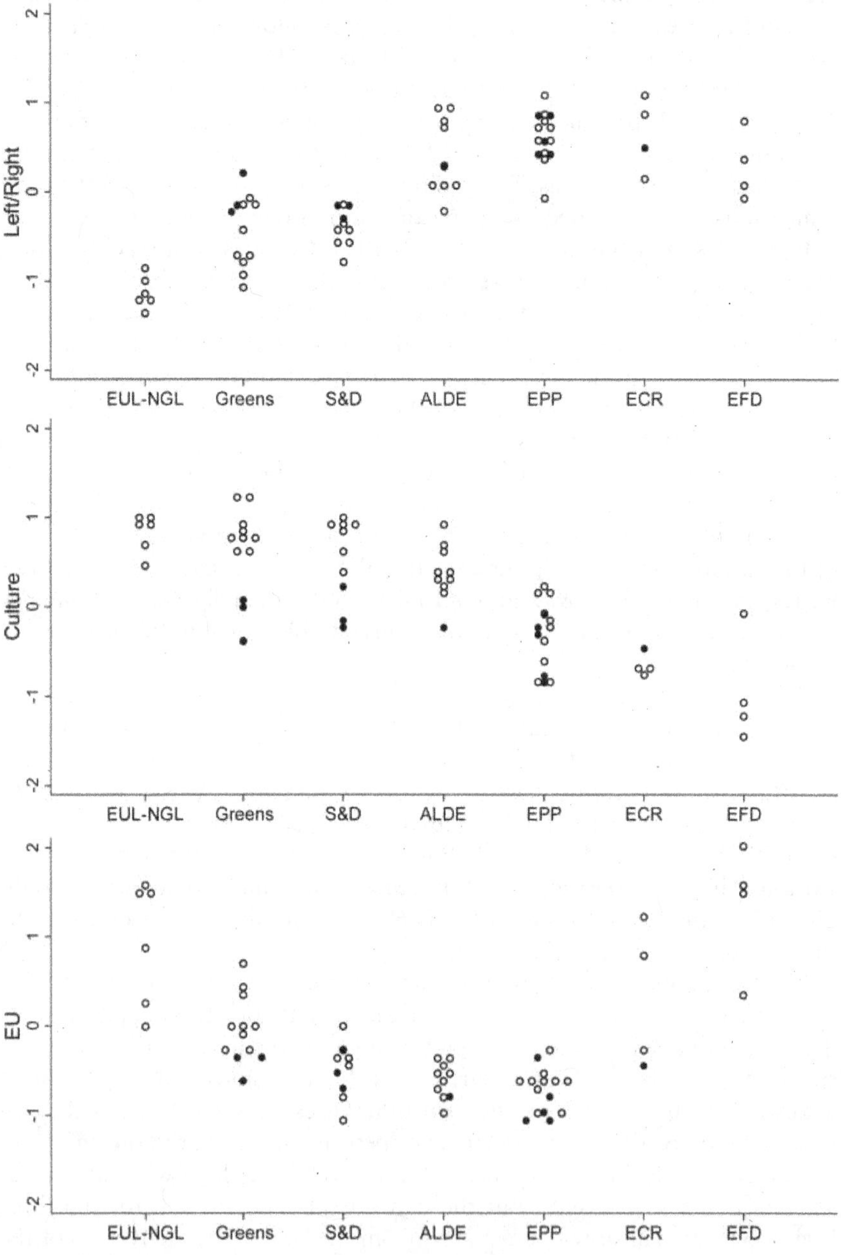

Note: The position of each national party is the mean position of its candidates. Parties from Western European countries are represented by white circles; parties from Central and Eastern European countries are represented by black circles.

that the positions of the groups are not always very clear due to internal differences). Comparing the first and second graphs, there is a general tendency for political groups with parties that take leftist positions on the left/right dimension to take liberal positions on the cultural dimension. A comparison of the first and third graph reveals that at the elite level the left/right and EU dimensions are also related, though in a different way. The relationship is not linear but follows the familiar pattern: party groups close to the centre of the left/right dimension favour European integration more strongly, whereas party groups further to the left and further to the right take a more Eurosceptic position.

In conclusion, the coherence and compatibility of political groups is highest on the left/right dimension, with most of the variation in positions occurring between rather than within political groups. The groups are generally more internally fragmented on the culture dimension, while for the EU dimension the largest groups are relatively cohesive, but not distinctive.

Conclusion

The system of political representation may be viewed as a means to establish the democratic ideal of policy congruence between citizens and representatives, and ultimately congruence between citizens' preferences and government policy (Powell 2000). In this paper we have examined how well the system of democratic representation works at the level of the European Union. We have not only analysed policy congruence between voters and their representatives in the European Parliament, but also highlighted one of the conditions necessary to enable policy congruence between voters and representatives: namely, that the attitudes of voters and positions of parties on the key issues are constrained by one ideological dimension. The implications of this were analysed in the context of the 2009 European Parliament elections on the basis of voter and candidate data from the European Election Study.

Confirmatory factor analysis of voters' and candidates' political opinions revealed that in fact this crucial condition is not met in the context of elections to the European Parliament. In line with research on previous European Parliament elections (Thomassen and Schmitt 1999), it was found that three dimensions were necessary to describe the policy attitudes of voters and candidates: an economic left/right dimension, a cultural dimension capturing attitudes towards a broad range of social issues, and a dimension capturing attitudes towards the EU. The correlations between these dimensions are generally modest, particularly when voters alone are considered.

These findings have two important implications. First, the fact that policy preferences are not structured in terms of a single dimension implies that if voters would fully base their choice on their policy preferences, this still does not guarantee that parties in parliament will reflect the policy preferences of their voters. Second, the fact that the dimensions are not highly correlated at the mass level makes it difficult for political parties to organise in such a way that citizens will find options that reflect their preferences on all three dimensions.

An analysis of the level of agreement between voters and parties on the three policy dimensions confirms this. Congruence was found to be higher on the left/right dimension than on the culture and EU dimensions for nearly all of the national parties analysed. On the culture dimension, most parties were found to have more liberal positions than their voters; while on the EU dimension, most parties were found to have more pro-EU positions than their voters.

It has long been noted that a gap exists between political elites and the electorate on issues of European integration. The findings here suggest that a substantial gap also exists on the cultural dimension. This may explain the success of populist parties across Europe in mobilising voters on issues related to this dimension. The sad news is that with policy preferences that are weakly structured at the level of citizens, adequate representation on different types of issues becomes difficult. However, representation can work well on particular sets of issues. We found this to be the case on issues related to the economic left/right dimension. As long as the majority of the European Parliament's legislative workload relates to economic issues such as the regulation of the single market, European elections do fulfil an important function in linking citizens' and representatives' policy preferences.

Notes

1. While ML assumes the data are continuous, it is generally found to work well on ordinal data on at least 5-point scales (Harrington 2008). As a robustness check, an alternative Weighted Least Squares estimation was also conducted. There is disagreement in the literature as to which approach performs better in the presence of ordinal variables (Brown 2006: 388). However, the results from the two procedures were similar and the ML estimates are reported here.
2. The exact same model was applied to each country, with two minor exceptions. For Belgium, it was necessary to allow the 'response style' factor to load freely on the 'parliament' item in order to achieve convergence. This might be explained by the fact that this question appeared in a different part of the survey from most of the other items. For Denmark, it was necessary to allow the covariation in the error terms for the 'marriage' and 'abortion' items to reach a good model fit.
3. The items in the factor analysis are a mix of positively and negatively worded items, but a perfectly balanced set was not available. To test if the response style factor does indeed measure acquiescence, and not attitudes, we compare it with a balanced set of 18 items using 5-point scales in the candidate survey. We follow a procedure suggested by Billiet and McClendon (2000: 622–3) and apply it to candidates from the UK (the country with the highest number of candidates in the data, at 258). Acquiescence is measured using an additive scale that identifies the number of items that respondents agreed with. When this variable is included as an additional indicator for the response style factor in the confirmatory factor analysis, the loading was very high (standardised loading = −0.93). This supports the conclusion that the response style factor does indeed measure acquiescence.

4. The full model (with three policy factors plus the response style factor) did not achieve convergence for these countries. Lack of convergence is a common problem with confirmatory factor analysis, particularly with complex models (Brown 2006: 74). A simpler model with two policy factors was not an acceptable fit, having several insignificant factor loadings.
5. In a small number of cases, there are two or more parties from the same country affiliated with a particular political group in the European Parliament. These parties are treated as one single party in the present analysis.
6. This is based on the R^2 of an analysis of variance of party positions, with party group membership as the independent variable (cf. Schmitt and Thomassen 2009: 37).

References

American Political Science Association (1950). *Toward a More Responsible Two-Party System.* New York: Rinehart & Company, Inc.

Benoit, K., and M. Laver (2006). *Party Policy in Modern Democracies.* Abingdon: Routledge.

Billiet, J.B., and J.M. McClendon (2000). 'Modeling Acquiescence in Measurement Models for Two Balanced Sets of Items', *Structural Equation Modeling*, 7:4, 608–28.

Brown, T.A. (2006). *Confirmatory Factor Analysis for Applied Research.* New York: The Guilford Press.

Downs, A. (1957). *An Economic Theory of Democracy.* New York: Harper.

Giebler, H., E. Haus, and B. Weßels (2010). *2009 European Election Candidate Study – Codebook, Advance Release.* Berlin: WZB.

Harrington, D. (2008). *Confirmatory Factor Analysis.* Oxford: Oxford University Press.

Hix, S., A.G. Noury, and G. Roland (2007). *Democratic Politics in the European Parliament.* Cambridge: Cambridge University Press.

Hooghe, L., G. Marks, and C. Wilson (2004). 'Does Left/Right Structure Party Positions on European Integration?', in G. Marks and M. Steenbergen (eds.), *European Integration and Political Conflict.* Cambridge: Cambridge University Press, 120–40.

Huber, J., and G.B. Powell (1994). 'Congruence between Citizens and Policymakers in Two Versions of Liberal Democracy', *World Politics*, 46:3, 291–326.

Katz, R.S. (1997). *Democracy and Elections.* New York: Oxford University Press.

Kitschelt, H. (1994). *The Transformation of European Social Democracy.* Cambridge: Cambridge University Press.

Kriesi, H., H. Grande, R. Lachat, M. Dolezal, S. Bornschier, and T. Frey (2006). 'Globalization and the Transformation of the National Political Space: Six European Countries Compared', *European Journal of Political Research*, 45:6, 921–56.

Kriesi, H., E. Grande, R. Lachat, M. Dolezal, S. Bornschier, and T. Frey (2008). *West European Politics in the Age of Globalization.* Cambridge: Cambridge University Press.

Lipset, S.M. (1966). *Political Man.* London: Mercury Books.

Marks, G., L. Hooghe, M. Nelson, and E. Edwards (2006). 'Party Competition and European Integration in the East and West: Different Structure, Same Causality', *Comparative Political Studies*, 39:4, 155–75.

McClendon, M.K. (1991). 'Acquiescence and Recency Response-Order Effects in Interview Surveys', *Sociological Methods and Research*, 20:1, 60–103.

McElroy, G., and K. Benoit (2007). 'Party Groups and Policy Positions in the European Parliament', *Party Politics*, 13:1, 5–28.

Powell, G.B. (2000). *Elections as Instruments of Democracy. Majoritarian and Proportional Visions.* New Haven, CT: Yale University Press.

Rosema, M., and C.E. de Vries (2011). 'Assessing the Quality of European Democracy: Are Voters Voting Correctly?', in M. Rosema, B. Denters and K. Aarts (eds.), *How Democracy Works: Political Representation and Policy Congruence in Modern Societies (Essays in Honour of Jacques Thomassen).* Amsterdam: Amsterdam University Press/Pallas Publications, 199–219.

Sani, G., and G. Sartori (1983). 'Polarisation, Fragmentation and Competition in Western Democracies', in H. Daalder and P. Mair (eds.), *Western European Party Systems: Continuity and Change*. Beverly Hills and London: Sage, 307–40.

Schmitt, H., and J. Thomassen (2009). 'The European Party System after Enlargement', in J. Thomassen (ed.), *The Legitimacy of the European Union after Enlargement*. Oxford: Oxford University Press, 23–43.

Thomassen, J.J.A. (1994). 'Empirical Research into Political Representation: Failing Democracy or Failing Models', in M.K. Jennings and T.E. Mann (eds.), *Elections at Home and Abroad: Essays in Honor of Warren Miller*. Ann Arbor: University of Michigan Press, 237–64.

Thomassen, J.J.A. (1999). 'Political Communication between Political Elites and Mass Publics: The Role of Belief Systems', in W. Miller, R. Pierce, J. Thomassen, R. Herrera, S. Holmberg, P. Esaiasson and B. Wessels (eds.), *Policy Representation in Western Democracies*. Oxford: Oxford University Press, 33–58.

Thomassen, J.J.A., and H. Schmitt (1999). 'Partisan Structures in the European Parliament', in R.M. Katz and B. Wessels (eds.), *The European Parliament, the National Parliaments, and European Integration*. Oxford: Oxford University Press, 129–48.

Van der Brug, W., and C. van der Eijk (1999). 'The Cognitive Basis of Voting', in H. Schmitt and J.J.A. Thomassen (eds.), *Political Representation and Legitimacy in the European Union*. Oxford: Oxford University Press, 129–60.

Van der Brug, W., M. Franklin, M. Popescu, and G. Tóka (2009). 'Towards a European Electorate: One Electorate or Many?', in J.J.A. Thomassen (ed.), *The Legitimacy of the European Union after Enlargement*. Oxford: Oxford University Press, 65–88.

Van der Eijk, C., M. Franklin, and E. Oppenhuis (1996). 'The Strategic Context: Party Choice', in C. Van der Eijk and M.N. Franklin (eds.), *Choosing Europe? The European Electorate and National Politics in the Face of the Union*. Ann Arbor: University of Michigan Press, 332–65.

Van der Eijk, C., H. Schmitt, and T. Binder (2005). 'Left–Right Orientations and Party Choice', in J. Thomassen (ed.), *The European Voter*. Oxford: Oxford University Press, 167–91.

Van Egmond, M.H., E.V. Sapir, W. van der Brug, S.B. Hobolt, and M.N. Franklin (2010). *EES 2009 Voter Study Advance Release Notes*. Amsterdam: University of Amsterdam.

Voeten, E. (2009). 'Enlargement and the "Normal" European Parliament', in J.J.A. Thomassen (ed.), *The Legitimacy of the European Union after Enlargement*. Oxford: Oxford University Press, 93–114.

Welkenhuysen-Gybels, J., J. Billiet, and B. Cambré (2003). 'Adjustment for Acquiescence in the Assessment of the Construct Equivalence of Likert-type Score Items', *Journal of Cross-Cultural Psychology*, 34:6, 702–22.

Mechanisms of Issue Congruence: The Democratic Party Mandate

TOM LOUWERSE

Issue congruence between voters and parties can be achieved if voters and parties follow the party mandate model. A central requirement of this model is that parties fulfil their electoral mandate. This article studies collective party mandate fulfilment by comparing parties' election manifestos with the parliamentary speeches of their politicians in two countries: a typical consensus democracy, the Netherlands, and a typical majoritarian democracy, the United Kingdom. The central question is whether a difference in collective mandate fulfilment exists between these two types of democracy. Contrary to previous findings, this study finds that such a difference does not exist, at least not with regard to the two countries analysed. This can be explained by the way in which the party mandate is conceptualised. The article also analyses the development of party mandate fulfilment over time and finds no evidence for the idea that collective mandate fulfilment is declining.

The policy link between voters and party politicians has received considerable attention (Blais and Bodet 2006; Golder and Stramski 2010; Powell 2000, 2009). Not only is congruence between the opinions of politicians and voters desirable from the perspective of democratic theory, policy differences are also increasingly important to understand how people vote (van der Eijk and Franklin 2009). The party mandate model provides a mechanism for establishing issue congruence: voters authorise parties to pursue a set of policies on their behalf (Thomassen 1994). An important requirement for this model to work is that parties observe their mandates.

Most work on the question of mandate fulfilment compares parties' election manifestos with government policies (Klingemann *et al.* 1994; Mansergh and Thomson 2007; Royed 1996). While this is a good way to measure to what extent government parties manage to put their pledges into action, it ignores the representative dimension of authorisation, most importantly the role of parliament. This article takes a different approach: it compares the electoral party competition with the *parliamentary* party competition. An important advantage of this approach is that it allows the study of mandate fulfilment by both government and opposition parties.

It remains an open question which type of institutional setting creates the most suitable circumstances for a properly functioning party mandate system (Klingemann *et al.* 1994; Mansergh and Thomson 2007; Powell 2009). In particular, there is debate on the merits of consensus and majoritarian democracy (Lijphart 1999). The findings of existing studies of issue congruence and the party mandate are mixed. Related to this is the question how the functioning of the party mandate model changes over time. The literature on electoral behaviour and party position change suggests that both voters and parties have changed significantly over the last 50 years. How have these changes affected party policy representation? This results in two related research questions. First, does a difference exist between majoritarian and consensus democracies in terms of parties' (collective) mandate fulfilment? Second, how has mandate fulfilment developed over the last 60 years?

The article studies these questions with regard to two cases: one typical majoritarian democracy, Great Britain, and a typical consensus democracy, the Netherlands. It compares parties' election manifestos with their MPs' speeches in parliament, which are analysed using the novel *Wordfish* text analysis algorithm. The novel approach and data used here present a picture of mandate fulfilment that runs counter to the prevailing wisdom.

The Party Mandate Model

If it is desirable to have a link between the preferences of voters and those of their representatives, one should be interested in how this is achieved. More specifically, what kind of (institutional) mechanism can bring about such linkage between voters and politicians? A particularly influential answer to this question has been presented by proponents of the party mandate model (APSA 1950; Ranney 1954; Thomassen 1994). They argue that a choice between competing parties with different electoral programmes can bring about issue congruence.

The traditional way in which the party mandate model is conceived is that it provides the winning party a mandate for government (Ranney 1954). In the ideal type situation there are only two parties, one of which will receive the support of a majority of voters and will go into government. This party is then said to be mandated to carry out its electoral commitments. If it does so indeed, there is a link between the will of (the majority of the people) and the policies of the government.

An alternative way to look at the party mandate is by treating it as a parliamentary mandate. This view considers whether parties fulfil their representative role in a good way: do political parties take similar policy stances before and after elections? This is important, first, because parliament usually is the principal (public) political arena. From the perspective of representative democracy this makes the way in which parliament operates a highly relevant question. Democracy, it can be argued, does not only require that the decisions that are made reflect the will of the people, but also that the opinions and interests of the people are taken into account in the actions that representatives take. Second, parliament presents a vital link in the 'chain of representation' (Müller 2000). Whereas existing studies have often compared the start of the chain, the preferences of the electorate, with (almost) the end, government decisions, this study focuses on a smaller section of the representative chain, namely the link between voters and their party representatives in parliament. This sheds more light on what happens between the act of voting and the decisions that are eventually made. Furthermore, it is important to know for voters if parties' electoral positions are a good predictor of their parliamentary behaviour to avoid adverse selection problems (Müller 2000).

Approach

Previous research into mandate fulfilment has been conducted in either of two fashions: the pledge approach or the saliency approach (Klingemann *et al.* 1994; Mansergh and Thomson 2007; Royed 1996). Both approaches are concerned with the extent to which the electoral mandate is translated into government policy output, either in the form of governmental decisions (the pledge approach) or government spending (the saliency approach). Thus, both approaches take a government mandate perspective, comparing parties' promises to what the government does. From this perspective the mandate of opposition parties is not very important, because the opposition party lost the election and has in fact no mandate to govern.

From the perspective of political representation, however, opposition parties' mandates are as important as government parties' mandates. The fact that opposition parties are not in government, either because they lost the election or because they were left out in the government formation process, does not alter the fact that their voters should be able to expect representation along the lines of the opposition party's mandate. Opposition parties might want to adjust some of their policy positions in order to be able to defeat the government at the next election (especially in majoritarian systems), but their voters should be able to expect a degree of congruence between what opposition parties say before and after elections. While the losing party in an election may have failed to win a mandate to government, it still managed to gain a mandate to represent in parliament.

By shifting the focus from the government mandate to the parliamentary mandate one can present a more inclusive picture of mandate fulfilment, incorporating both government and opposition parties. Rather than comparing parties' pledges to government policy outcomes, I compare how parties behave during the election to their behaviour in parliament, or more specifically what they *say* before and after elections. Of course, requiring parties simply to act in parliament according to their electoral mandate is in a way less demanding than actually having to implement the pledges. This is why one should expect that levels of mandate fulfilment are relatively high. Whereas the actual implementation can be frustrated by many external factors, such as economic growth, civil society opposition or legal procedures (Mansergh and Thomson 2007), how parties behave in parliament is very much their own choice – the fact that some policies are difficult to implement is no excuse for not pursuing them. However, this does not imply that parliamentary 'talk is cheap': parliamentary debates are not a philosophical debate devoid of any real-world implications. In some ways parliamentary debates may be conceived as very long motivations of parliamentary voting behaviour (Proksch and Slapin 2009). Parties and MPs have incentives to vote in line with their speeches if only to avoid criticisms of other parties and negative media attention. Thus, while it may be easier to talk about things in parliament than to actually get them done, making a speech does bear certain costs.

The existing approaches differ with respect to what they study: the pledge approach looks at specific electoral pledges in election manifestos, while the saliency approach measures party issue saliency. The pledge approach only looks at part of the picture: it cannot deal very well with a changing policy agenda and is one-sided in that it only looks at the question whether pledges are enacted – not whether what is enacted is pledged (Louwerse 2011). The saliency approach offers a more comprehensive test of party mandate fulfilment, although it is limited to a particular understanding of the nature of party competition (Klingemann *et al.* 2006). As it tests whether parties' electoral issue priorities are related to government spending patterns, it is well suited to measure changes in the political agenda (Klingemann *et al.* 1994). However, it ignores parties' position differences to a large degree: talking a lot about a particular subject does not necessarily imply that a party also wants to spend more on it or what specific policies it wishes to pursue (Royed 1996: 52–4). In addition, issues that do not directly relate to government spending at all, such as regulation and medical-ethical issues, cannot be taken into account in the analysis.

The application of spatial theory to the party mandate mitigates these problems and allows researchers to shift from studying the government mandate to the parliamentary mandate. It does so by offering a party system approach to the question of the party mandate. Rather than looking at the fulfilment of pledges by individual parties, it looks at the congruence of the electoral party competition and the parliamentary party competition. Instead of looking whether specific pledges have been fulfilled, I study whether the structure of the party competition (that is parties' positions relative to each other) is similar before and after elections. To put it simply, if the social democrats are to the 'left' of the Christian democrats during the election, we also expect them to be in that position in the parliamentary competition. By comparing the structure of the party competition, one can compare the electoral and parliamentary competition even when the parliamentary agenda changes.

This shift.from a party-level to a party system-level analysis is similar to the one that Golder and Stramski (2010) have proposed in the context of issue congruence. They argue that the existing one-to-one congruence measures (congruence between a single voter and a single party) and many-to-one congruence measures (congruence between all voters and the median legislator or the government) should be appended by a measure of many-to-many congruence: whether the distribution of voter preferences is similar to the distribution of legislators' preferences. Similarly, I argue that the analysis of the party mandate should be extended by analysing the congruence between parties' pre-election positions and their parliamentary positions. A voting decision is, after all, a choice *between* parties: if the configuration of parties is very different between the electoral and parliamentary arena, a voters' decision may not have been optimal. The electoral competition should be a good predictor of where parties stand in parliament in relation to each other. Thus, this study shifts the analysis from individual mandate fulfilment to what may be called collective mandate fulfilment.

The mandate itself is conceptualised here with respect to two dimensions. First, there is the question of what parties talk about, or issue saliency. It can be argued that the issues that matter most to parties during elections should also be the most important issues in parliament. The second aspect is what parties actually say on these issues, or issue positions. Parties' relative issue positions on issue dimensions should be similar before and after the election if their mandate is to be deemed fulfilled.

Explaining Differences in Mandate Fulfilment

The first research question is how the institutional setup of a country is related to *collective* mandate fulfilment. Is there a difference between majoritarian (or countries with majoritarian or plurality electoral systems) and consensus democracies (countries with proportional electoral systems) (Lijphart 1999)? This difference between two types of institutional settings has been central in the literature on issue congruence (Blais and Bodet 2006; Golder and Stramski 2010; Powell 2000) and mandate fulfilment (Klingemann *et al.* 1994; Thomson 2001). In terms of issue congruence majoritarian and consensus democracies seem to be similar, although some authors argue that consensus democracies outperform majoritarian countries (Powell 2000). Pledge fulfilment studies, on the other hand, have found that majoritarian democracies perform better in terms of pledge fulfilment (Mansergh and Thomson 2007). How then, do institutions relate to *collective* mandate fulfilment?

The traditional argument is that majoritarian democracies show higher levels of mandate fulfilment, because their characteristic single-party governments are in a better position to enact their electoral pledges than the coalition governments usually found in consensus democracies (Thomson 2001: 174). Majoritarian democracy provides a short 'chain of representation' from voters to a single-party government that can do exactly what it promised, whereas coalition governments in consensus democracies have to compromise and therefore cannot enact the whole of their election manifesto. This argument is, however, primarily directed at the government mandate, not the parliamentary mandate. In parliament, parties in a coalition government are relatively free to outline their own policy position, as long as this does not threaten the stability of the government. In fact, this is one of the major roles of the parliamentary party group: to voice the viewpoints of the party, rather than the coalition. However, in the case of single-party government in majoritarian democracies there is usually no distinction between the position of the government and that of the parliamentary party: the government is also the frontbench of the parliamentary party group. This restricts their parliamentary behaviour, because as the government they are directly responsible for the resulting policies and accountable for the whole of government (in the broad sense of the word). Government party backbenchers do have some liberty to voice authentic party policy stances, so we would expect them to be closer to the electoral position of the party than the frontbench. All in all, I expect that there is no difference in the extent to which government parties in majoritarian democracies are able to fulfil their parliamentary mandates compared to government parties in consensus democracies.

Collective mandate fulfilment by opposition parties is expected to be relatively low in majoritarian democracies. Opposition parties in majoritarian parliaments generally have few powers (Döring 1995). The other major party is in government and there is usually little that the opposition can do about it. Majoritarian opposition normally involves opposing what the government wants, even when it had originally been in the opposition party manifesto. Consensus democracies are characterised by relatively powerful parliaments, for example in terms of setting their own agenda and powerful committee systems (Döring 1995; Sieberer 2011). Furthermore, the opposition is usually not united, but consists of several parties that do not necessarily agree on an alternative for the current government. As a result, these parties do not have a dominant strategy to oppose every government proposal: as much as they want to pose as an alternative for the government parties, they also need to distinguish themselves from the other opposition parties. It seems much more attractive to stay true to their electoral mandate and try and use parliamentary prerogatives to influence policy – often not without success: Mansergh and Thomson (2007) found that opposition parties in countries with proportional representation are able to implement more of their pledges than those in non-proportional countries.[1]

Taking these arguments together, I argue that there is reason to expect that collective mandate fulfilment is higher in consensus democracies than in majoritarian democracies:

> *Hypothesis 1:* Collective mandate fulfilment is higher in a consensus democracy than in a majoritarian democracy.

The second question of this article is whether collective mandate fulfilment has changed over time. The literature on party change suggests that the process of dealignment has made electoral politics more volatile (Daalder and Mair 1983; Dalton 1984; Katz and Mair 2009). Parties no longer cater to a specific socio-demographic constituency, but try to catch all voters or rather occupy a specific niche in a cartelised party system. One can distinguish two arguments about the influence these changes have had on the representative relationship between parties and voters. Some authors argue that parties are no longer agents of the people, but rather agents of the state (Katz and Mair 1995). Parties are merely a public utility that is supplied by the state to offer citizens a way of influencing politics (van Biezen 2004). In addition, the end of the Cold War has fostered a process of globalisation and European integration; politicians have put major areas of policy-making outside the realm of the traditional (national) political institutions. This has severely limited the stakes of the electoral competition (Katz and Mair 2009: 754). Just as democratic elections are, according to Katz and Mair (1995: 22) 'dignified parts of the constitution', one could argue that election manifestos are merely a part of this electoral ritual and have little substantive impact. The room for political influence by voters is limited, because of the party cartel: parties may pretend to cater to specific voter groups, but in fact offer little choice to citizens. This leads to a decline of the representative link and also to the extent that parties fulfil their mandates (Mair 1997). After all, in a cartel party system, parties have little incentive to adhere to their promises as ex post electoral control mechanisms no longer function properly, because the difference between winning and losing in politics has diminished (Katz and Mair 1995). This leads to the expectation that collective mandate fulfilment has declined over time:

> *Hypothesis 2:* Collective mandate fulfilment has declined over the last 60 years.

Kitschelt (2000) argues that the opposite is true: because the links between parties and particular constituencies have declined, the electoral market is now more competitive than before. Parties have much to win and lose in elections and will therefore listen better to voters than in the past. Kitschelt argues that the political cartel cannot successfully limit electoral competition: there is always a possibility that new parties enter the political arena. Indeed, the relative success of radical right-wing populist parties seems to suggest that if there was a cartel, it could not prevent the entrance of significant challengers (de Lange 2008). All in all, this seems to suggest that in order to keep citizens satisfied, parties should be better motivated to implement their manifesto than in the past. In essence, the above hypothesis is also a test of Kitschelt's counter-argument: if no evidence of a decline is found, but rather of an increase in mandate fulfilment, this would lend support to his argument.

Data and Methods

This article uses original data collected from 12 elections and the subsequent parliamentary periods in the Netherlands and Great Britain. While ideally a large number of cases would be used to test the two hypotheses, this would be very resource intensive – even with computer-assisted techniques. The selection of two typical cases, one majoritarian democracy (Great Britain) and one consensus democracy (the Netherlands), provides a research design that allows inferences to be drawn from a limited number of cases. The two selected countries are placed on opposite ends of Lijphart's (1999) executive-parties dimension, which captures differences in electoral and party systems, the type of government and corporatism/pluralism, while they are relatively similar in terms of GDP per capita, democratic history and EU membership. To compare mandate fulfilment over time, I have selected one election per decade between 1950 and 2010 – the selected cases are not consecutive so as to limit the direct influence from one selected election to another.

Parties' issue saliency and positions are estimated by means of computer-assisted analysis of election manifestos and parliamentary debates. The choice to analyse text is motivated by the need to collect data for quite some time in the past and the need to compare parties' policy preferences on a rather short time-scale (before and after elections) for which other sources, such as (expert) surveys are not suitable. Party manifestos, while certainly not the only message that parties present to voters during elections, are regarded as the most authoritative statement of a parties' policy views (Klingemann *et al.* 2006; Pellikaan *et al.* 2007). Parliamentary speeches compare most directly to manifestos as they are both political texts. I opted to analyse speech rather than voting behaviour because the latter captures only a small subset of parliamentary behaviour and is often strategically motivated (Proksch and Slapin 2009: 589–90).

The estimates of issue saliency for each party are derived from a dictionary-based content analysis technique. For each of the 20-odd major issue categories in the Comparative Agenda Project's (Breeman *et al.* 2009; UK Policy Agendas Project 2010) coding scheme, a list of keywords has been drawn up (the dictionaries). Each paragraph of text was classified into the category of which the keywords appeared most frequently (corrected for the length of the keyword list). The same dictionaries were used for each set of election manifestos and the parliamentary speeches from the subsequent period. The paragraphs that remained unclassified by this method, e.g. if no keywords could be found or there was a tie between issue categories, were estimated by means of a Support Vector Machine (Fan *et al.* 2008). The classified categories were used here as a training set. This procedure yields reasonably reliable classifications: machine–human coder reliability for a subset of the data yields a Krippendorff's alpha between 0.6 and 0.7.

The issue position estimates were acquired by applying Wordfish, a novel approach that distils parties' issue positions from word counts in political texts (Proksch and Slapin 2008; Slapin and Proksch 2008). The underlying assumption of the Wordfish algorithm is that parties that use similar words have a similar policy position or, to put it more formally, that word counts are a function of parties' issue positions. The advantage of this method over other methods of automated content analysis, such as Wordscores, is the fact that no reference texts are needed, e.g. one does not have to 'instruct' the computer what is 'left' and what is 'right', but policy positions are derived directly from the data (Laver *et al.* 2003). The method has shown to produce valid and reliable estimates for the analysis of manifestos and parliamentary speech, although it has not yet been used to compare those two sources (Proksch and Slapin 2009). It is exactly this comparison that provides a challenge for applying the Wordfish algorithm, because word usage in election manifestos is in most cases quite different from word usage in parliamentary speech. Manifestos are carefully crafted written documents, usually composed by multiple authors, while parliamentary speeches are usually single-authored or made up on the spot. These differences make it difficult to directly compare manifestos with parliamentary speech using a word count-based algorithm. However, this is not strictly necessary for the research question at hand. The idea of collective mandate fulfilment is that there is congruence between the electoral and parliamentary competition, i.e. that parties' *relative* positions are similar. Thus, it is sufficient to analyse parliamentary speeches and manifestos separately and compare the resulting estimates of parties' relative issue positions on issue dimensions.

Wordfish produces one-dimensional estimates of party positions. While a single dimension might be adequate to capture the competition in some countries, such as Great Britain, the party competition in other countries, such as the Netherlands, is usually regarded as multidimensional (Pellikaan *et al.* 2007). To distinguish between parties' positions on different issues, Wordfish can be applied to separate pieces of text. For example, to capture parties' positions on the issue of foreign affairs, one can select the parts of the manifestos or parliamentary debates that deal with that issue and run a Wordfish analysis on only those texts. In this way, I was able to distinguish between parties' positions on four to eight issue dimensions, depending on the case at hand. The selection of relevant text was based on the text classification procedure described above. However, a number of the 20 issue categories in that analysis contained too little text to arrive at robust Wordfish estimates. Therefore, I combined the 19 or 20 (Netherlands) issue categories to a smaller number: five categories in Britain and four (1952–1977) and eight (1982–2006) for the Netherlands. The combinations were based on a substantive understanding of the issues, and are largely comparable to the dimensions that other party position estimation techniques use (Laver 2006; Lowe *et al.* 2011). This resulted in party positions on between four and eight issue dimensions. The subsequent analysis compares parties' positions on these dimensions before the election with those in parliament.[2] One observation in the subsequent analysis is thus a party's saliency of or position on an issue dimension in a particular time period (election and subsequent parliament).

Results: Types of Democracy

Issue Saliency

The first aspect of collective mandate fulfilment is that parties talk about similar things before and after elections: issue saliency congruence. Issue saliency was expressed as the percentage of text that was devoted to a particular issue. I first estimated an OLS regression model that explains parliamentary issue saliency by electoral issue saliency. How well does a party's attention for an issue during the election predict its attention for that issue in parliament? To establish whether there was a difference between parties from the Netherlands and the United Kingdom, the model also includes a country dummy variable and the interaction effect between manifesto issue saliency and the country dummy. The results are presented as model 1 in Table 1. The coefficient for issue saliency manifesto shows that one percentage point more issue saliency in parliament leads to a predicted 0.477 percentage point increase in parliamentary issue saliency, in the Netherlands. To estimate the effect for the British parties, we have to add to

TABLE 1
EXPLAINING PARTIES' ISSUE SALIENCY IN PARLIAMENT

	Model 1	Model 2
(Intercept)	0.026*	−0.001
	(0.001)	(0.001)
Issue saliency manifesto	0.477*	0.121*
	(0.018)	(0.014)
UK	−0.005	0.000
	(0.003)	(0.002)
Issue saliency manifesto * UK	0.125*	−0.110*
	(0.038)	(0.033)
Mean issue saliency parliament		0.890*
		(0.020)
UK * Mean issue saliency parliament		0.101*
		(0.042)
N	1502	1502
R^2	0.410	0.785
adj. R^2	0.409	0.784
Resid. sd	0.031	0.019

Note: Ordinary Least Squares regression estimates. Standard errors in parentheses.
*Indicates significance at $p < 0.05$.

this the coefficient of the interaction effect (Issue saliency manifesto * UK). The net effect for Britain is 0.572, which is significantly higher.

The data thus suggest that mandate fulfilment in terms of issue saliency is higher in the United Kingdom than in the Netherlands. However, this seems to be the result of the fact that British parties are more alike in terms of issue saliency. For instance, all parties talk much more about macro-economy than about foreign trade, both in their manifestos and in parliament, which makes issue saliency levels higher than in the Netherlands. The most important aspect about issue saliency in terms of the collective mandate is, however, that parties that talk much more about an issue in their manifesto compared to other parties, also talk more about it than other parties in parliament. This is relative issue saliency congruence, which was studied by including the mean issue saliency in parliament (for a specific issue in a specific case) in the model. When parties 'just' follow average attention for an issue very closely, this coefficient will be high at the cost of the predictive power of the issue saliency of that issue in their own manifesto. The model also includes the interaction between this variable and the country dummy variable, to estimate the difference between the Netherlands and the United Kingdom.

The very high coefficients for the mean issue saliency in parliament in model 2 show that the between-issue variation of issue saliency is much larger than the between-parties issue saliency. Once mean parliamentary issue saliency is added to the model, the predictive value of a party's manifesto issue saliency drops significantly. For the Dutch observations, it is only 0.121 and for the British parties it is even as low as 0.02 (not significant). The difference between the two countries is significant. The conclusion is that while in absolute terms the British parties show higher levels of issue saliency congruence, in relative terms the Dutch parties score higher.

Issue Positions

The second aspect of collective mandate fulfilment, issue position congruence, was analysed in two ways. First, I calculated a simple difference score between a party's (relative) electoral position and its (relative) parliamentary position. For the UK, I differentiated between the frontbench and the backbenchers (except for the Liberals who were all treated as the party's frontbench, because of their small size), because of the different roles they play in parliament.[3] Figure 1 displays the mean of those scores, weighted by the saliency of each issue. The grey dots display the score for each party, while the black line indicates an over-time trend based on the six elections selected for this study. There are notable differences between parties, in some cases ranging from (almost) no difference between electoral and parliamentary positions to a difference of 1.5, which is quite large, bearing in mind that we are dealing with parties' positions on standardised dimensions, which effectively run between −2 and +2. In addition, there is a substantial

FIGURE 1
DISTANCES BETWEEN ELECTORAL AND PARLIAMENTARY POSITIONS

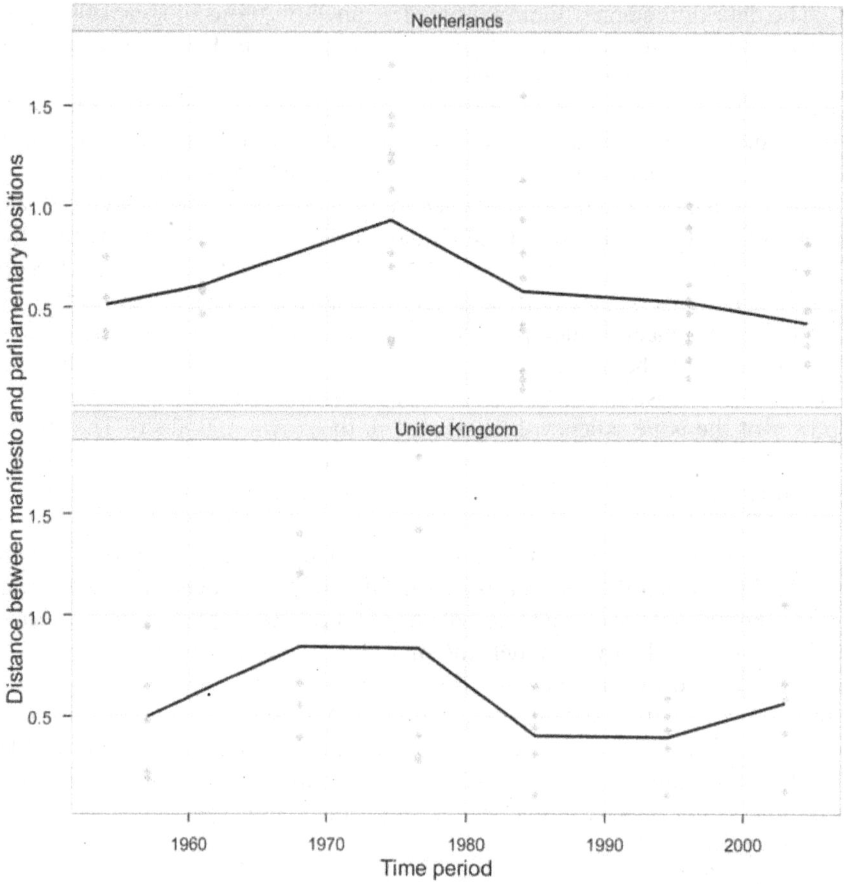

Note: The figure displays the mean distance between a party's electoral and its parliamentary positions on each of the issue dimension, weighted by the saliency of those dimensions (grey dots). The black line indicates the average of those values per country per period. The Figure only includes the selected cases for this study, plotted at the midpoint of the parliamentary period.

difference between time periods: in the 1970s (and to a lesser extent the 1960s), differences between electoral and parliamentary positions are larger than in other years. This can be understood in light of the transformation of politics from the post-war welfare state compromise to the neo-liberal synthesis. Given these between-parties and over-time differences, the difference between the United Kingdom and the Netherlands is only very small.

To test whether the observed difference between the Netherlands and the United Kingdom is significant, I estimated a regression model, much like the one used above.[4] The dependent variable is a party's relative issue position in parliament. The independent variables are its relative issue position in the manifesto, a country dummy variable and the interaction of these two variables (see Table 2). The coefficient of manifesto position indicates how much the parliamentary position changes when the manifesto position changes by one point. This is 0.614 points for the Netherlands; for Britain one has to add 0.077 for the interaction effect, which results in a net effect of 0.691. Thus, parties do not, on average, follow their manifesto position perfectly, but the level of congruence is quite reasonable. The difference between the Netherlands and Britain is, however, not significant.

The regression analysis was based on data that differentiated between frontbench and backbenchers in the British cases. There is, however, an argument to be made that the 'party line' of any party is represented by the frontbench rather than the backbenchers. After all, while statements of the frontbench are considered to represent what the parliamentary party thinks and wants, speeches by backbenchers are not necessarily considered to present the party line – and usually present multiple positions reflecting the respective 'wings' within a party. Model 2 fits this interpretation by including only the frontbench observations. Here, the coefficient for the Dutch parties remains virtually the same as in the previous analysis, 0.625, while the coefficient for the British parties drops significantly to 0.337. Apparently, mandate fulfilment for British frontbenchers is substantially lower than for its backbenchers. Closer inspection of the data shows that this is related to two features. First, the position of the government party frontbench is consistently more moderate than that of its backbenchers. Taking into account that scores have been standardised, this implies that the positions of the backbenchers are closer to the party's electoral positions. Second, the position of the Liberals/Liberal Democrats changes quite substantially between elections and parliament: during elections they usually oppose the incumbent government, while they take more of a middle ground in parliament. This lowers their levels

TABLE 2
EXPLAINING PARTIES' ISSUE POSITIONS IN PARLIAMENT

	Model 1	**Model 2 (frontbench)**
(Intercept)	0.030	−0.003
	(0.042)	(0.042)
Manifesto position	0.614*	0.625*
	(0.041)	(0.044)
Country: UK	−0.042	0.063
	(0.064)	(0.086)
Manifesto position * Country: UK	0.077	−0.288*
	(0.065)	(0.092)
N	440	382
R^2	0.489	0.365
adj. R^2	0.486	0.360
Resid. sd	21.103	0.712

Note: Ordinary Least Squares regression estimates. Standard errors in parentheses.
*Indicates significance at $p < 0.05$.

of mandate fulfilment, which has a negative effect on the levels of mandate fulfilment of the three frontbenches combined.

Although there is some evidence that the Dutch parties score better than their British counterparts, other analyses are inconclusive. Therefore, I have to conclude that hypothesis 1 which stated that a consensus democracy performs better than a majoritarian democracy in terms of collective mandate fulfilment is not supported by the data.

Results: Changes Over Time

Issue Saliency

Whether collective mandate fulfilment has changed over time is analysed by calculating a measure of issue saliency congruence, which measures the percentage of party attention before and after an election that has not shifted (cf. Pedersen 1979). If a party's issue saliency for each issue is exactly the same in the electoral and parliamentary competition, thus when it devotes exactly as much attention to each issue in both arenas, their congruence score equals 100. The score is 0 when a party only talks about issues in parliament which it did not discuss at all in the manifesto. The congruence formula is:

$$\text{congruence}_p = 100 - \frac{1}{2}\sum_{i=1}^{n} \left|\text{saliency} \cdot \text{manifesto}_{ip} - \text{saliency} \cdot \text{parliament}_{ip}\right|$$

Where p is a party and i_1, i_2 ... i_n are the issues.

The mean congruence scores for Britain and the Netherlands are displayed in Figure 2. Over the whole research period, there was an increase of issue saliency congruence in both countries. For Britain, the increase took place between the 1950s and 1980s, while congruence in the Netherlands followed a more erratic, but gradually upward, pattern.

A similar pattern is found when adapting the regression model presented above to analyse change over time. In order to do this, I included dummy variables for each time period (instead of the country dummy variables), with the first as the reference category. In addition, I included the interaction effect between each of the time period dummy variables and the manifesto issue saliency. Thus, the model explains parliamentary issue saliency by means of manifesto issue saliency, time period and their interaction. As the standard regression table with interaction effects is rather difficult to interpret, I present a graphical representation (Figure 3) of the total effect of manifesto issue saliency on parliamentary issue saliency in each time period (the regression table is available from the author) (Brambor *et al.* 2006). This shows that in the 1950s (which includes one election and subsequent parliament from each country) one percentage point more saliency in manifesto leads, on average, to 0.4 more percentage points of issue saliency in parliament. Over time, the coefficient becomes

FIGURE 2
MEAN ISSUE SALIENCY CONGRUENCE SCORE

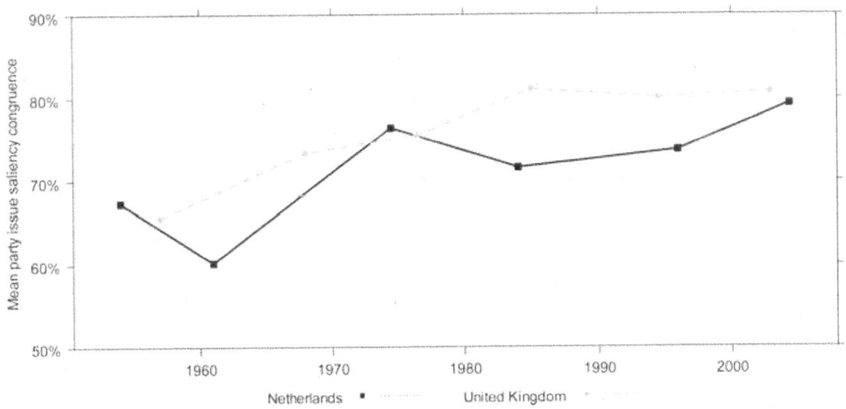

Note: The figure only includes the selected cases for this study, plotted at the midpoint of the parliamentary period.

significantly larger: in the 2000s cases, the marginal effect of manifesto saliency on parliamentary saliency is about 0.7. These findings are statistically significant: the error bars for the earlier periods do not overlap with those of the later periods. The lower panels present the analysis for each country separately. From it, one may deduce that the overall increase of manifesto saliency is mainly the result of an increase in the Dutch cases. While there is also a slight increase in the British cases, this fails to achieve statistical significance. This reflects a larger degree of stability in the issue agenda in the United Kingdom, which was also observed above.

The increase in issue saliency congruence in the Dutch case can be explained by two factors. Firstly, the length and nature of election manifestos has changed. While manifestos in the 1950s were short pamphlets in which only the most important policy issues were discussed, modern manifestos read almost like an encyclopaedia in which the reader may find a party's position on a broad range of issues. Debate in parliament has always focused on a relatively broad range of issues. Thus, by making their manifestos more encompassing parties have increased the congruence between manifesto and parliamentary issue saliency. Second, political competition has changed substantially in the Netherlands. Until the end of the 1960s, elections were almost like a census: voting behaviour could be explained very well by religion and class (Andeweg and Irwin 2009). Elections were very much about mobilisation, and, in order to do this, parties needed to stress issues that mattered to their voters. In parliament, however, they could focus on a broader range of issues in the interest of the state. As this structure of 'pillarisation' declined, parties were less certain about their electoral basis. Talking about similar issues in parliament and in the manifesto became more important.

FIGURE 3
THE EFFECT OF MANIFESTO ISSUE SALIENCY ON PARLIAMENTARY ISSUE SALIENCY IN DIFFERENT TIME PERIODS

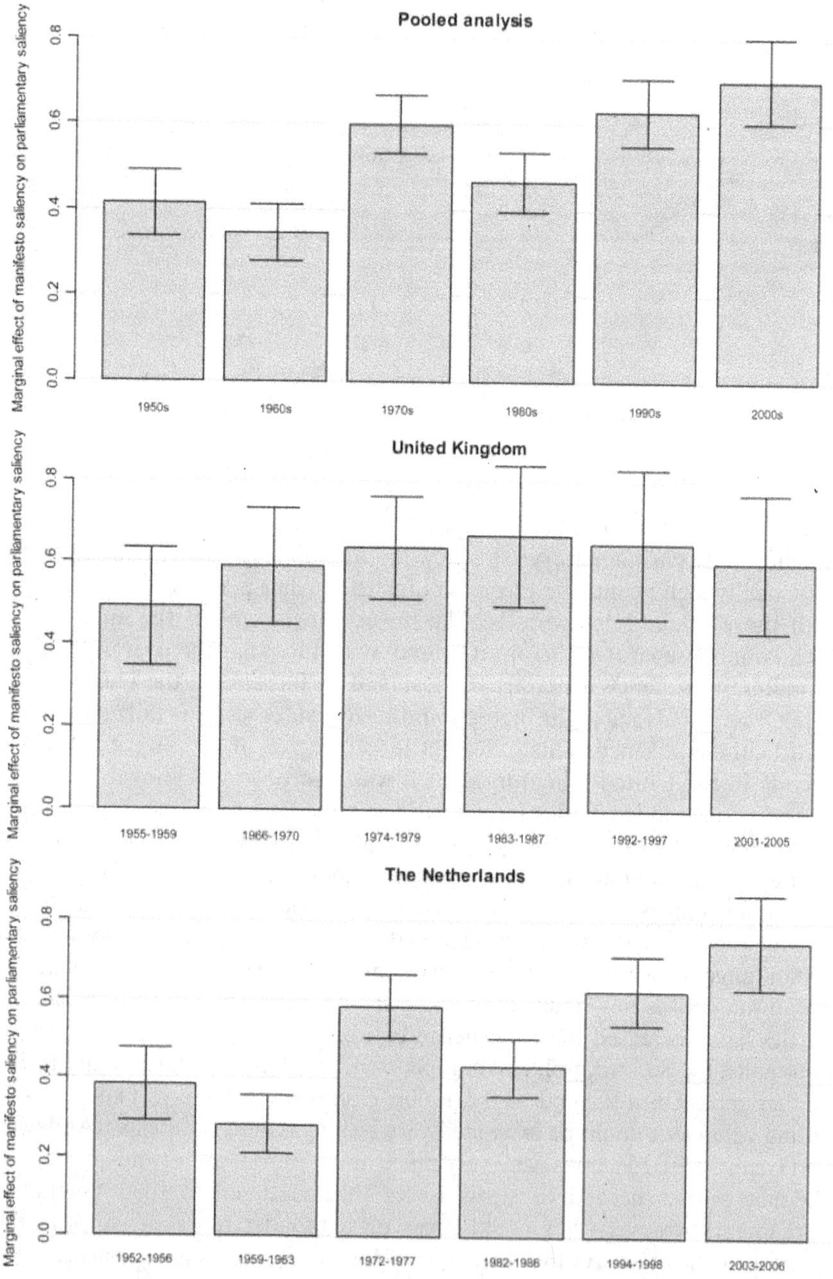

Note: Error bars indicate 95 per cent confidence intervals.

FIGURE 4
THE EFFECT OF MANIFESTO ISSUE POSITIONS ON PARLIAMENTARY ISSUE POSITIONS IN DIFFERENT TIME PERIODS

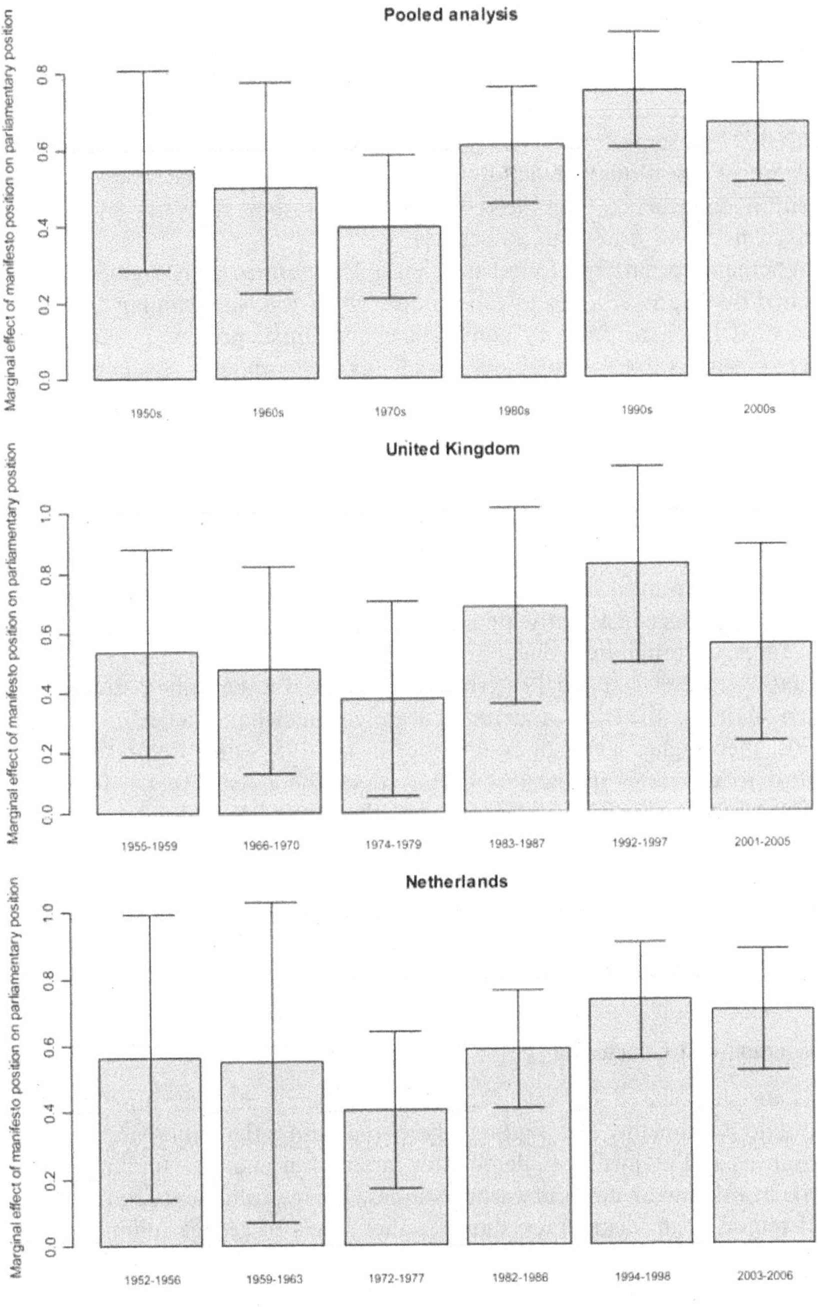

Note: Error bars indicate 95 per cent confidence intervals.

Issue Positions

In the discussion of Figure 1 above I made some preliminary remarks on changes over time in party position congruence. The distances between parties' relative electoral and parliamentary positions indicate that the 1970s score particularly poorly in these terms. Overall, there seems a slight decline of the distances in the Netherlands, with the 2003–2006 case showing the lowest distance scores of the six Dutch cases. In Britain, the 1983–1987 and 1992–1997 cases showed the lowest distances between manifesto and parliament positions. Generally, over-time changes over time in party position congruence seem to be small, but rather show an increase of congruence over time than a decrease.

Whether the patterns found in Figure 1 are statistically significant was studied by means of a regression model, which was very similar to the one presented for issue saliency congruence over time: parties' parliamentary issue positions were explained by means of manifesto issue positions, dummy variables for each time period (first time period as reference category) and the interaction between these dummy variables and manifesto issue positions capturing change over time. Figure 4 presents the marginal effects for each time period (the regression table is available from the author). Note that the confidence intervals are much larger than in the previous analysis, because the number of observations for parties' positions is lower. The pooled analysis of Dutch and British observation shows that congruence was consistently higher in the last three time periods than in the first three, although only one difference (between the 1990s and 1970s cases) actually achieves statistical significance. Essentially the same pattern holds when analysing the two countries separately: somewhat of a decline until the 1970s, then higher levels of congruence in the 1980s and 1990s. Only with regard to the cases in the last decade does there seem to be more of a difference between the Netherlands and the United Kingdom. In the UK, issue position congruence has declined (not significant), while it remained more or less stable in the Netherlands. The overall picture is that there is certainly no decline of issue position congruence – where there are over-time differences, these show an increase of issue position congruence over time. Therefore, the second hypothesis is rejected.

Discussion and Conclusion

This article focused on one aspect of the party mandate model: party mandate fulfilment. The findings here regarding the difference between consensus and majoritarian democracy in terms of mandate fulfilment seem to be at odds with those of earlier studies. Pledge fulfilment studies found that majoritarian democracy shows higher levels of pledge fulfilment than consensus democracy (Mansergh and Thomson 2007). Klingemann *et al.* (1994) found that the linkage between manifesto issue saliency and government spending priorities is clearer in majoritarian countries –

although Great Britain did not do particularly well in their analysis, it clearly outperformed the Netherlands. My analysis shows that differences between the two countries are small, but if there are any they suggest that the consensus system of the Netherlands shows higher rather than lower levels of mandate fulfilment than the majoritarian British case. How can these differences be explained? First, this article has compared parties' manifestos to their parliamentary behaviour, rather than government policy output. In this fashion, the (parliamentary) mandate of opposition parties is taken more fully into account. As I argued above, there is reason to expect that opposition parties are in a relatively better position to enact their parliamentary mandate in consensus democracies. Whereas one-party governments are in a better position to enact specific manifesto policies than coalition governments, in terms of parliamentary policy representation, majoritarian and consensus democracy are on equal footing.

Second, I have studied the 'collective' mandate of parties: rather than looking at specific pledges of individual parties, I compared party competition before and after elections. This allows for a more inclusive comparison, as it does not just look at whether parties pursue in parliament what they promised, but also how their parliamentary behaviour relates to their electoral mandate. Exactly because one-party governments are in a good position to implement pledges, pledge-making has become very much a strategic game in majoritarian democracies, with parties and media keeping tallies on the implementation of pledges. As a result, parties might try to avoid making certain pledges. These strategic elements have less influence on a spatial analysis of party position: if a party decides to avoid making certain pledges (and thus has a centrist electoral position), but implements these policies (meaning a more outspoken parliamentary position), the spatial analysis will pick up on a change in a party's position.

The above result has consequences for the debate on institutional reform. Discussions on institutional reform in Britain and the Netherlands regularly refer to the relative advantages of both political systems (e.g. Power Inquiry 2006: 180–217). Many of these arguments relate to the degree of linkage between voters and politicians. For example, one of the proponents of introducing majoritarian elements into the Dutch democracy has argued that this would lead to higher levels of issue congruence, because of higher levels of mandate fulfilment (van Thijn 1967). This is what I called the 'chain-of-representation' argument: majoritarian democracy offers a clear chain of representation (one party wins a majority and forms a government), which would ensure that parties are better able to implement their mandates (Ranney 1954). Indeed, if the criterion is that government parties fulfil their election pledges in government, majoritarian democracy seems to be the system of choice (Royed 1996; Thomson 2001). My findings, and indeed those of students of issue congruence (Blais and Bodet 2006; Golder and Stramski 2010; Powell 2000), suggest that in terms of collective policy representation (in parliament) there either is not much of a difference between institutional arrangements or that proportional (consensus) democracies fare better. While there might be other reasons to choose for one institutional arrangement or the other, participants in the institutional reform debate should use the 'chain-of-representation' argument more cautiously.

More caution is also warranted with regard to the often-heard claim that party representation is in decline. My analysis did not find evidence of a decline of collective mandate fulfilment. On the contrary, issue saliency congruence has increased in the Netherlands. These findings seem to support, at least to a degree, the arguments put forward by Kitschelt (2000) on how party (system) change would affect political representation. Because parties' traditional links with specific groups in society (based on class or religion) have diminished, they need to be more sensitive to what voters want and to take better notice of their manifesto rather than less. Voting behaviour is by no means unstructured, but voters are more inclined to change between ideologically proximate parties than in the past (van der Meer *et al.* 2012). The reason that I do not find an increase of all aspects of mandate fulfilment might be that the mechanisms described by Kitschelt will first and foremost lead to an increase of policy responsiveness: parties responding to changes in public opinion. While this might be the case, the current article shows that changes in electoral behaviour do not bring British and Dutch parties to abandon their electoral mandates.

Because this article is limited to an analysis of two countries, inferences about the population of democracies should be made with caution. Nevertheless, it shows that the spatial approach to the party mandate offers an addition to the existing approaches, because it allows us to look at party mandate fulfilment at the party system level. Computer-assisted content analysis techniques enable the analysis of a lot of political text, which would have been unfeasible by hand. While these techniques should be applied with care, doing so yields new insights into how parties operate. Further research can focus on the further improvement of the current techniques, but also on a better understanding of collective party mandate, taking into account more countries and focusing more explicitly on the differences between government and opposition parties' mandate fulfilment. In 2010, exceptional governments were elected both in Britain (a full-fledged coalition) and the Netherlands (a minority government with majority support in parliament). Therefore, these cases arguably provide new evidence concerning the relationship between institutions and party mandate fulfilment.

Acknowledgements

An earlier version of this paper was presented at the Joints Sessions of Workshops of the European Consortium for Political Research, St. Gallen, Switzerland, 12–17 April 2011. I am grateful for comments and suggestions of the participants of this workshop, in particular Christine Arnold, Simon

Bornschier, and Mark Franklin, as well as Rudy Andeweg, Jannine van de Maat, Huib Pellikaan and Cynthia van Vonno.

Notes

1. While studying the difference between opposition and government parties' mandate fulfilment in majoritarian and consensus democracies is beyond the scope of the current article. The argument here is merely that taking opposition parties into account in the study of the mandate will lead to a different expectation concerning overall mandate fulfilment in different democratic system.
2. Details regarding technical issues involved in the application of Wordfish to parliamentary speech and manifestos are available from the author's website: http://english.tomlouwerse.nl/.
3. The findings in this article would not be significantly altered if this distinction is not made.
4. I weighted the cases by the manifesto word count, to take the uncertainty of the Wordfish estimates into account.

References

Andeweg, R.B., and G.A. Irwin (2009). *Governance and Politics of the Netherlands*, 3rd rev. ed. Basingstoke: Palgrave Macmillan.

APSA (1950). 'Toward a More Responsible Two-Party System: A Report of the Committee on Political Parties', *American Political Science Review*, 44:3, Part 2: Supplement.

Blais, A., and M.A. Bodet (2006). 'Does Proportional Representation Foster Closer Congruence Between Citizens and Policy Makers?', *Comparative Political Studies*, 39:10, 1243–62.

Brambor, T., W.R. Clark, and M. Golder (2006). 'Understanding Interaction Models: Improving Empirical Analyses', *Political Analysis*, 14:1, 63–82.

Breeman, G., D. Lowery, C. Poppelaars, S.L. Resodihardjo, A. Timmermans, and J. de Vries (2009). 'Political Attention in a Coalition System: Analysing Queen's Speeches in the Netherlands 1945–2007', *Acta Politica*, 44:1, 1–27.

Daalder, H., and P. Mair, eds. (1983). *Western European Party Systems: Continuity and Change*. Beverly Hills, CA: Sage Publications.

Dalton, R.J. (1984). 'Cognitive Mobilization and Partisan Dealignment in Advanced Industrial Democracies', *The Journal of Politics*, 46:1, 264–84.

De Lange, S.L. (2008). *From Pariah to Power: Explanations for the Government Participation of Radical Right-Wing Populist Parties in West European Parliamentary Democracies*. PhD thesis, Universiteit Antwerpen.

Döring, H. (1995). 'Time as a Scarce Resource: Government Control of the Agenda', in *Parliaments and Majority Rule in Western Europe*. Frankfurt: Campus Verlag, 223–46.

Fan, R.-E., K.-W. Chang, C.-J. Hsieh, X.-R. Wang, and C.-J. Lin (2008). 'LIBLINEAR: A Library for Large Linear Classification', *Journal of Machine Learning Research*, 9, 1871–4.

Golder, M., and J. Stramski (2010). 'Ideological Congruence and Electoral Institutions', *American Journal of Political Science*, 54:1, 90–106.

Katz, R.S., and P. Mair (1995). 'Changing Models of Party Organization and Party Democracy: The Emergence of the Cartel Party', *Party Politics*, 1:1, 5–28.

Katz, R.S., and P. Mair (2009). 'The Cartel Party Thesis: A Restatement', *Perspectives on Politics*, 7:4, 753–66.

Kitschelt, H. (2000). 'Citizens, Politicians, and Party Cartellization: Political Representation and State Failure in Post-industrial Democracies', *European Journal of Political Research*, 37:2, 149–79.

Klingemann, H.-D., R.I. Hofferbert, and I. Budge (1994). *Parties, Policies, and Democracy. Theoretical Lenses on Public Policy*. Boulder, CO: Westview Press.

Klingemann, H.-D., A. Volkens, J. Bara, I. Budge, and M. McDonald (2006). *Mapping Policy Preferences II: Estimates for Parties, Electors, and Governments in Central and Eastern Europe, European Union and OECD 1990–2003*. Oxford: Oxford University Press.

Laver, M.J. (2006). 'Legislatures and Parliaments in Comparative Context', in B. Weingast and D. Wittman (eds.), *Oxford Handbook of Political Economy*. Oxford: Oxford University Press, 1–16.

Laver, M.J., K. Benoit, and J. Garry (2003). 'Extracting Policy Positions from Political Texts Using Words as Data', *American Political Science Review*, 97:2, 311–31.

Lijphart, A. (1999). *Patterns of Democracy: Government Forms and Performance in 36 Countries*. New Haven, CT: Yale University Press.

Louwerse, T. (2011). 'The Spatial Approach to the Party Mandate', *Parliamentary Affairs*, 64:3, 425–47.

Lowe, W., K. Benoit, S. Mikhaylov, and M. Laver (2011). 'Scaling Policy Positions From Coded Units of Political Texts', *Legislative Studies Quarterly*, 36:1, 123–55.

Mair, P. (1997). *Party System Change: Approaches and Interpretations*. Oxford and New York: Clarendon Press and Oxford University Press.

Mansergh, L., and R. Thomson (2007). 'Election Pledges, Party Competition, and Policy-making', *Comparative Politics*, 39:3, 311–29.

Müller, W.C. (2000). 'Political Parties in Parliamentary Democracies: Making Delegation and Accountability Work', *European Journal of Political Research*, 37:3, 309–33.

Pedersen, M.N. (1979). 'The Dynamics of European Party Systems: Changing Patterns of Electoral Volatility', *European Journal of Political Research*, 7:1, 1–26.

Pellikaan, H., S.L. de Lange, and T. van der Meer (2007). 'Fortuyn's Legacy: Party System Change in the Netherlands', *Comparative European Politics*, 5:3, 282–302.

Powell, G.B. (2000). *Elections as Instruments of Democracy*. New Haven, CT: Yale University Press.

Powell, G.B. (2009). 'The Ideological Congruence Controversy: The Impact of Alternative Measures, Data, and Time Periods on the Effects of Election Rules', *Comparative Political Studies*, 42:12, 1475–97.

Power Inquiry (2006). 'Power to the People: An Independent Inquiry into Britain's Democracy', available at http://www.powerinquiry.org/report/documents/PowertothePeople_002.pdf (accessed 15 July 2011).

Proksch, S.-O., and J.B. Slapin (2008). *WORDFISH: Scaling Software for Estimating Political Positions from Texts*, available at http://www.wordfish.org/ (accessed 15 July 2011).

Proksch, S.-O. and J.B. Slapin (2009). 'Position Taking in European Parliament Speeches', *British Journal of Political Science*, 40:3, 587–611.

Ranney, A. (1954). *The Doctrine of Responsible Party Government*. Urbana, IL: University of Illinois Press.

Royed, T.J. (1996). 'Testing the Mandate Model in Britain and the United States: Evidence from the Reagan and Thatcher Eras', *British Journal of Political Science*, 26:1, 45–80.

Sieberer, U. (2011). 'The Institutional Power of Western European Parliaments: A Multi-dimensional Analysis', *West European Politics*, 34:4, 731–54.

Slapin, J.B., and S.-O. Proksch (2008). 'A Scaling Model for Estimating Time-Series Party Positions from Texts', *American Journal of Political Science*, 52:3, 705–22.

Thomassen, J.J.A. (1994). 'Empirical Research into Political Representation: Failing Democracy or Failing Models?', in M.K. Jennings and T.E. Mann (eds.), *Elections at Home and Abroad*. Ann Arbor: University of Michigan Press, 237–65.

Thomson, R. (2001). 'The Programme to Policy Linkage: The Fulfilment of Election Pledges on Socio-economic Policy in the Netherlands, 1986–1998', *European Journal of Political Research*, 40:2, 171–97.

UK Policy Agendas Project (2010). 'UK Topics Codebook', available at http://www.policyagendas.org.uk/codebooks/documents/UK_Topics_Codebook_Subtopics&Media_100219.pdf (accessed 29 July 2011).

Van Biezen, I. (2004). 'Political Parties as Public Utilities', *Party Politics*, 10:6, 701–22.
Van der Eijk, C., and M.N. Franklin (2009). *Elections and Voters*. Basingstoke: Palgrave Macmillan.
Van der Meer, T., E. van Elsas, R. Lubbe, and W. van der Brug (2012). *Kieskeurige Kiezers: Een onderzoek naar de veranderlijkheid van Nederlandse kiezers, 2006–2010*. Amsterdam: Universiteit van Amsterdam.
Van Thijn, E. (1967). 'Van partijen naar stembusaccoorden', in E. Jurgens *et al.* (eds.), *Partijvernieuwing?* Amsterdam: Arbeiderspers, 54–73.

Partisan Sorting and Niche Parties in Europe

JAMES ADAMS, LAWRENCE EZROW and DEBRA LEITER

Earlier research has concluded that European citizens do not update their Left–Right policy preferences or their party attachments in response to the content of parties' election manifestos – i.e. partisan sorting is not observed in the mass public in response to shifts in the Left–Right tone of these manifestos. Here we extend this research to analyse whether we observe partisan sorting patterns that correspond with political experts' perceptions of parties' Left–Right policy shifts. Given that these experts plausibly consider all pertinent information when estimating parties' Left–Right orientations – including party elites' speeches, elite interviews, coalition behaviour, and legislative voting patterns – such a finding would imply that citizens do weigh the wider informational environment when updating their Left–Right orientations and their party support, even if they do not attach great weight to the parties' policy manifestos. Our analyses provide support for this hypothesis with respect to niche parties, i.e. green, communist, and radical right parties, but not for mainstream parties.

According to the responsible party model, the link between parties' policy positions and their supporters' policy beliefs is crucial for representative democracy (Sartori 1968). The mass–elite linkages emphasised by the responsible party model have been examined empirically by prominent scholars of political representation (e.g. Dalton 1985; Iversen 1994), who identify close matches between the Left–Right positions of party elites and the positions of their supporters (Dalton 1985).

In a dynamic setting, where parties and voters shift their policy positions over time, the policy correspondence between party elites and their supporters can be maintained through some combination of elites responding to their supporters and these supporters responding to political elites. Specifically, party elites may adjust their policy positions in response to shifts in their supporters' beliefs (which we label party elite responsiveness), or conversely, party supporters may dynamically adjust their preferred policy positions in response to shifts in their preferred party's policy stances (party persuasion). Party supporters may also switch their partisan loyalties in response to parties' policy shifts (partisan switching). The latter two processes, party persuasion and partisan switching, are collectively referred to as partisan sorting (see e.g. Carmines and Stimson 1989; Erikson *et al.* 2002).

In previous research Adams *et al.* (2011) presented empirical evidence that European citizens do not update their perceptions of parties' Left–Right positions in response to the statements the parties publish in their election manifestos, and, furthermore, that European citizens adjust neither their own Left–Right policy orientations nor their party support in response to shifts in the Left–Right tone of these manifestos. However, in related research Fortunato and Stevenson (forthcoming) report remarkable findings that European citizens update their estimates of Left–Right party positions in response to an important facet of parties' observed behaviour, namely the compositions of governing coalitions.[1] Here we extend the research dialogue between Fortunato and Stevenson and Adams *et al.* in two new directions. First, we ask whether we observe partisan sorting in European electorates (Carmines and Stimson 1989), i.e. shifts in citizens' Left–Right policy orientations and/or their party support, in response to the wider informational environment that encompasses all relevant information pertaining to parties' Left–Right positions, not simply the content of parties' manifestos. We evaluate this issue by analysing whether the partisan sorting that we observe in European electorates tracks experts' perceptions of parties' Left–Right position shifts. Because these experts, namely the political scientists and journalists who have responded to the Chapel Hill expert surveys (see e.g. Hooghe *et al.* 2010), are free to weigh all relevant information when estimating parties' Left–Right positions – including the content of party elites' speeches, interviews, and policy manifestos, along with elites' coalition bargaining behaviour and their actual roll-call votes – these experts' perceptions plausibly provide reliable measures of the parties' positions based on all relevant evidence. Second, we evaluate whether we observe greater degrees of partisan sorting in the electorate with respect to niche parties than with respect to mainstream parties, where niche parties are defined as communist, green, and radical right parties – that is, parties that either stake out extreme positions on the Left–Right dimension (communist and radical right parties) or parties that cater to a tightly focused, ideological clientele (green parties).[2] Our focus on niche parties is motivated by previous research which documents that citizens are disproportionately responsive to niche parties' Left–Right shifts, and which argues that this pattern arises because niche parties' supporters are more politically engaged and expressive than are mainstream parties' supporters (Adams *et al.* 2006; Ezrow *et al.* 2011; Hobolt and Spoon 2010).

Our empirical study of mass–elite policy linkages in 14 Western European democracies over the period 1984–2002 supports the hypothesis that the partisan sorting patterns in European electorates track political experts' perceptions of parties' Left–Right policy shifts, but that this pattern is substantively (and statistically) significant for niche parties but not for mainstream parties – a pattern we label the niche party dynamic. Specifically, we find that when the political experts who were interviewed in the Chapel Hill expert surveys perceived that a focal niche party had shifted its ideological position to the left (right), then the mean Left–Right preferences of the niche party's supporters displayed strong tendencies to shift in a direction consistent with these experts' perceptions, a pattern that is consistent with a partisan sorting process whereby rank-and-file citizens update their own Left–Right orientations and/or their party support in response to niche parties' Left–Right shifts. Specifically, we observe a lagged relationship whereby experts' perceptions of niche party shifts were associated with lagged shifts in party supporters' Left–Right positions, a pattern that supports the partisan sorting hypothesis for niche parties and which cannot be explained by a reciprocal process whereby niche party elites respond to their supporters' policy preferences. We label this finding the lagged effects dynamic. By contrast, we uncover no statistically (or substantively) significant evidence of partisan sorting with respect to mainstream parties – i.e. parties that are members of social democratic, liberal, conservative, or Christian democratic party families. We also present evidence that niche party supporters are indeed significantly more politically engaged than are the supporters of mainstream parties (or political independents), a pattern that supports our finding of stronger partisan sorting patterns with respect to niche parties (although we do not claim to definitively parse out the causal mechanisms that underpin our results). Finally, consistent with the results reported in Adams *et al.* (2011), we find no evidence of partisan sorting – from either niche party or mainstream party supporters – in response to shifts in the Left–Right tone of parties' election manifestos.

Our finding, that mass–elite policy linkages differ for niche parties compared to mainstream parties, is consistent with earlier research on this issue. Thus Adams *et al.* (2006) conclude that niche parties suffer sharp electoral reverses when they moderate their Left–Right positions, while mainstream parties' vote shares are (on average) unresponsive to their policy shifts. Ezrow *et al.* (2011) conclude that niche party elites respond disproportionately to their supporters' Left–Right attitudes, in contrast to mainstream party elites who weigh the policy preferences of the entire electorate; as we show below, niche party elites' responsiveness to their supporters makes sense given that these supporters are significantly more politically engaged than are mainstream parties' supporters. Furthermore, our finding that citizens exhibit lagged responses to niche parties' policy shifts meshes with the findings of Adams and Somer-Topcu (2009), who conclude that time lags intervene before citizens update their party evaluations in response to changes in party elites' Left–Right positions.

In toto, our findings imply that while members of the mass public do not systematically update their policy beliefs or their party support in response to the policy statements in party manifestos (as demonstrated by Adams *et al.* 2011), rank-and-file citizens do respond to the wider informational environment – an environment that encompasses party elites' speeches and interviews, their coalition behaviour, and their legislative voting patterns – with respect to niche parties. This is because the mean Left–Right positions of niche parties' supporters track experts' (lagged) perceptions of these parties' Left–Right positions, and these experts, namely the political scientists and journalists who have responded to the Chapel Hill expert surveys, plausibly weigh this wider informational environment when estimating parties' Left–Right positions. However our finding, that mainstream party supporters' Left–Right position shifts do not track shifts in political experts' perceptions of these parties' positions, extends the earlier results reported by Adams *et al.* (2011) that mainstream party supporters' Left–Right shifts also fail to track shifts in the Left–Right tone of these parties' manifestos.

The Link between Parties' Left–Right Images as Perceived by Political Experts and Partisan Sorting in the Electorate: Hypotheses and Empirical Specifications

Hypotheses on Partisan Sorting

Our first hypothesis on partisan sorting in European electorates is motivated in part by the empirical work of Kitschelt (1994), D'Alimonte (1999), Tarrow (1989), and Adams *et al.* (2006), who have analysed the policy attitudes and the personal characteristics of the political elites belonging to green, communist, and radical right political parties, along with the characteristics of these parties' political supporters:

> *H1 (the Niche Party Hypothesis): Partisan sorting processes in the mass public will be stronger with respect to niche parties than with respect to mainstream parties.*

The studies cited above report several findings that imply the Niche Party Hypothesis. First, these studies suggest that niche parties' elites, along with niche parties' activists and rank-and-file supporters, place greater emphasis on policy debates than do the elites and supporters from mainstream parties, who frequently emphasise their party elites' leadership abilities and superior competence to govern the country. In particular, Kitschelt (1994) and D'Alimonte (1999) report findings that niche parties' core supporters are strongly policy-oriented and are highly resistant to ideological 'compromises' by their party's elites – i.e. that these niche party supporters are prepared to abandon the party if they disapprove of its policy direction. To the extent that this is true, we should expect to observe stronger partisan sorting processes with respect to niche parties. Second, and related, niche party supporters are more likely to perceive and react to their preferred party's policy shifts than are mainstream partisans. In this regard, Adams *et al.* (2006) present aggregate-level analyses that document that niche parties' vote shares decline precipitously when they moderate their Left–Right positions – but that there is no systematic relationship between mainstream parties' policy shifts and changes in their support – a finding consistent with the hypothesis that niche party supporters' disproportionately monitor and react to their preferred party's policy positions.

Our second hypothesis relates to the timing of partisan sorting effects in the mass public, specifically to the likelihood that significant time lags may intervene between when party elites shift their policy positions, and when members of the mass public react to these elite-level shifts by changing their party support and/or their policy positions:

> *H2 (the Lagged Effects Hypothesis): Significant time lags may intervene before the mass public reacts to party elites' policy shifts.*

The research on issue evolution and macro-partisanship in the United States motivates the Lagged Effects Hypothesis (Carmines and Stimson 1989; Erikson *et al.* 2002). When party elites' policy behaviour changes, these studies report significant temporal lags with respect to when rank-and-file voters perceive and react to these shifts. For instance, in the case of the issue of racial desegregation, Carmines and Stimson (1989: chapter 7) identify four-year lags between the time when partisan elites' voting patterns change in the US Senate, and when the mass public perceives this change in voting. In addition, Erikson *et al.* (2002: chapter 7) estimate significant lags in the effects of party positions on presidential vote share. These authors argue that when citizens estimate parties' current policy images, they account for the parties' current and past policy positions, and this observation motivates our own perspective on this process:

> where the parties stand in the eyes of the electorate will incorporate both the present platform and past platforms. In the end, while the parties are able to use the platforms as a vehicle for altering the image of where they stand, they can alter that image only slowly over time. (Erikson *et al.* 2002: 258)

Similarly, Pelizzo (2007) documents that Italian voters' perceptions of parties' positions are not highly responsive to parties' current policy manifesto shifts, or to party MPs' current parliamentary voting behaviour, because voters' perceptions are anchored by the parties' *previous* policy behaviour, a strong inertial component which reflects voters' 'historical knowledge' of party positions (Pelizzo 2007: 8).

Finally, Adams and Somer-Topcu (2009) present evidence from 15 Western European democracies which documents that time lags intervene between when political parties shift their Left–Right positions and when their vote shares change, a pattern that supports the Lagged Effects Hypothesis on partisan sorting.

Model Specifications

We analyse the dynamics of citizens' responses to shifts in European parties' Left–Right positions, as these positions are perceived by political experts who might be expected to weigh all information that is pertinent to estimating parties' positions, including party elites' policy statements (in speeches, interviews, and election manifestos) along with their observed behaviour (including coalition behaviour and legislative voting patterns). We ask: when these political experts perceive that a focal party has shifted its Left–Right orientations, do we observe partisan sorting in the electorate that is consistent with these expert perceptions – i.e. do we observe patterns which suggest that citizens are shifting their own Left–Right positions in the same direction as the focal party (a party persuasion process) and/or that citizens are updating their partisan loyalties in response to parties' policy shifts (partisan switching)? Furthermore, do we observe that partisan sorting processes are stronger with respect to niche parties than mainstream parties (the Niche Party Hypothesis), and that time lags intervene before partisan sorting in the electorate occurs in response to party elites' policy shifts (the Lagged Effects Hypothesis)?

In analyses based on panel data we might parse out the extent to which partisan sorting in the electorate reflects partisan switching as opposed to party persuasion (see e.g. Carsey and Layman 2006; Goren 2005; Highton and Kam 2011; Milazzo *et al.* 2012). However, because the data we analyse is time-series cross-sectional, we instead assay the simpler task of estimating the extent to which *either* of these processes is taking place – i.e. we will search for any evidence of voters' partisan sorting that is consistent with political experts' perceptions of parties' Left–Right policy shifts. Our logic is simple: to the extent that parties' Left–Right shifts – as perceived by experts – prompt reactions in the electorate that reflect either partisan switching and/or party persuasion, we should observe that when a party shifts its Left–Right position the mean position of the party's supporters shifts in the same direction. This is because either causal process – party persuasion or partisan switching – generates an aggregate-level pattern whereby the mean Left–Right position of a focal party's supporters tracks the mean position of the party's elites. This test is very simple, and it is also incomplete in that even if we find evidence that party shifts as perceived by political experts correlate with shifts in the mean Left–Right positions of party supporters, we cannot conclude that these associations reflect a causal process of voters reacting to parties, rather than vice versa. However in keeping with the Lagged Effects Hypothesis we will address this causal inference issue via analyses of lagged relationships between parties' policy shifts and shifts in their supporters' positions. On this basis we proceed.

We require longitudinal, cross-national measures of parties' Left–Right positions as perceived by experts, along with measures of the mean Left–Right positions of these parties' supporters, in order to carry out our analyses. Our measure of experts' perceptions of the parties' Left–Right positions is derived from the Chapel Hill expert surveys (CHES) (Hooghe *et al.* 2010). In these surveys, respondents who were considered as experts on the politics of a focal country were asked to place each party in the country's party system on a scale running from 0 ('extreme left') to 10 ('extreme right'), expert placements that we rescaled between 0 and 1. We used these survey responses to compute experts' perceptions of the parties' positions, for each party at each date the Chapel Hill survey was administered (1984, 1996, 1999, and 2002, which were dates oriented towards elections to the European Parliament).[3] For the observations prior to 1999, we note that the CHES study compiles data from previous surveys of experts by Castles and Mair (1984), Huber and Inglehart (1995), and Hix and Lord (1997).

Our longitudinal measure of voters' Left–Right positions and their partisan loyalties is derived from Eurobarometer studies, which have been administered in the following Western European democracies beginning in the early 1970s: Austria, Belgium, Britain, Denmark, Finland, France, Germany, Greece, Ireland, Italy, the Netherlands, Portugal, Spain, and Sweden.[4] These surveys contain the same item in each year in each country, asking approximately 1,000 respondents per country to place themselves on a scale running from 1 (extreme left) to 10 (extreme right), and also to indicate the party (if any) that they supported.[5] We have rescaled the Eurobarometer Left–Right scale to run between 0 and 1 so that it is consistent with the CHES Left–Right scale. Our measure of the Left–Right position of each party's partisan constituency in the focal year is the mean Left–Right self-placement of all Eurobarometer respondents from that year that reported support for the party. We note that the Eurobarometer surveys discontinued the party support question after 2002, so that our analysis of partisan sorting patterns runs from 1984 (the first year of the Chapel Hill expert surveys) until 2002 (the last year the Eurobarometer surveys included the party support question).

We specify a multivariate regression model to search for evidence of partisan sorting in European electorates in response to parties' Left–Right shifts, as perceived by the Chapel Hill experts. As we are interested in how the mean positions of party supporters shift in response to experts' perceptions of parties' Left–Right shifts, we specify a model in which the dependent variable is the change in the party supporters' mean Left–Right position in the year t of the current CHES, compared to party supporters' positions in the year (t − 1) of the previous CHES, as measured by Eurobarometer respondents' Left–Right self-placements and reported party support. We label this variable [*Party j supporters' Left–Right shift* (*t*)]. Our key independent variables are [*Expert perceptions of j's Left–Right shift* (*t*)], which denotes the shift in party *j*'s Left–Right position between the year of the current and the previous Chapel Hill expert surveys, based on the experts' Left–Right party placements, and a lagged version of this variable, [*Expert perceptions of j's Left–Right shift* (*t* – 1)], which denotes the shift in party *j*'s perceived Left–Right position between the previous Chapel Hill expert survey and the survey before that. We include this lagged variable in order to evaluate the Lagged Effects Hypothesis, which specifies that time lags intervene before partisan sorting in the electorate occurs in response to party elites' policy shifts. We also include a lagged version of the dependent variable to control for autocorrelation issues that are otherwise present in the data.[6] Thus our basic specification is:

$$\begin{aligned}[\textit{Party j supporters' Left–Right shift}(t)] &= b_0 + b_1[\textit{Expert perceptions of j's Left–Right shift}(t)] \\ &+ b_2[\textit{Expert perceptions of j's Left–Right shift}(t-1)] \\ &+ b_3[\textit{Party j supporters' Left–Right shift}(t-1)] \qquad (1)\end{aligned}$$

where

Party j supporters' Left–Right shift (*t*) = the change in the mean Left–Right position of party *j*'s supporters in the year *t* of the current Chapel Hill expert survey, compared to the mean supporter position at the year *t* – 1 of the previous Chapel Hill expert survey, based on Eurobarometer respondents' Left–Right self-placements and their party support. The variable [*Party j supporters' Left–Right shift* (*t* – 1)] is similarly defined.

[*Expert perceptions of j's Left–Right shift* (*t*)] – the change in party *j*'s Left–Right position in the year *t* of the current Chapel Hill expert survey compared to party *j*'s position in the year *t* – 1 of the previous Chapel Hill expert survey, based on the mean party placements by the experts interviewed in these surveys. The variable [*Expert perceptions of j's Left–Right shift* (*t* – 1) is similarly defined.

Results

Our analysis encompassed 162 Left–Right shifts by parties and their supporters in 14 European party systems: Austria, Belgium, Britain, Denmark, Finland, France, Germany, Greece, Ireland, Italy, the Netherlands, Portugal, Spain, and Sweden. In order to attenuate error in our measures of the mean Left–Right positions of party supporters, we confined our analyses to policy shifts by political parties that obtained the support of at least 50 Eurobarometer respondents per survey, over the time period for which we measured the change in the mean Left–Right position of the focal party's supporters.[7] (Below we report supplementary analyses that apply to all partisan constituencies that featured at least 10 supporters per Eurobarometer survey). The complete set of parties and elections included in the analyses are reported in Appendix A. Table 1 reports the means and standard deviations of the observed values of the variables in our data set.

Our analyses encompassed 65 parties, each observed over an average of 3.5 elections, and should thus be regarded as time-series cross-sectional data. Estimating a simple regression on the pooled data can lead to erroneous conclusions if there are unobserved differences between partisan constituencies (Hsiao 2003); we address these concerns through the use of robust standard errors clustered by party (Rogers 1993). The lagged dependent variable included in our specifications helps to address the concern of serially correlated errors (Beck and Katz 1995), and a Lagrange multiplier test fails to reject the null hypothesis of no serial correlation.

The parameter estimates for the alternative models that we investigated are reported in Table 2, where the dependent variable [*Party j supporters' Left–Right shift* (*t*)] represents the change in the mean Left–Right self-placements of all Eurobarometer respondents who reported support for the focal party *j* in surveys conducted in the year of the current Chapel Hill expert survey, compared to the mean Left–Right placements of all Eurobarometer respondents who reported support for the focal party *j* in the year of the previous Chapel Hill expert survey.

Column 1 in Table 2 reports the parameter estimates when the model is estimated over all niche parties in our data set, where, following Adams *et al.* (2006), niche parties are defined as parties that are members of the communist, green, and radical right party families, based on the party family codings published by the Comparative Manifesto Project (see Klingemann *et al.* 2006). (Below we report supplementary analyses for alternative definitions of what constitutes a niche party.) To the extent that citizens update either their own Left–Right positions or their party support in response to niche parties' Left–Right shifts – as these shifts are perceived by the Chapel Hill experts – we expect positive and statistically significant

TABLE 1
DESCRIPTIVE STATISTICS: DEPENDENT AND INDEPENDENT VARIABLES

	Mean value	Standard deviation
Party j's supporters' Left–Right shift (t)	−0.020	0.290
Party j's Left–Right shift (t) – experts	0.014	0.496

Note: All of the variables are calibrated along a 0–1 scale, for which higher numbers denote a more right-wing position. The measures of party supporters' Left–Right shifts are drawn from Eurobarometer survey data from Austria, Belgium, Britain, Denmark, Finland, France, Germany, Greece, Ireland, Italy, the Netherlands, Portugal, Spain, and Sweden. The measures of parties' Left–Right positions as perceived by experts are drawn from the Chapel Hill expert surveys. The definitions of these variables are given in the text.

TABLE 2
THE RELATIONSHIP BETWEEN SHIFTS IN PARTY SUPPORTERS' LEFT–RIGHT POSITIONS, AND PARTIES' LEFT–RIGHT SHIFTS AS PERCEIVED BY EXPERTS

	Niche parties (1)		**Mainstream parties (2)**		**Interaction model (3)**	
Experts' perception of party j's Left–Right shift (t)	0.05	(0.05)	0.08	(0.05)	0.08	(0.06)
Experts' perception of party j's Left–Right shift (t – 1)	0.39**	(0.12)	0.02	(0.06)	0.02	(0.07)
[Experts' perception of party j's Left–Right shift (t)] × Niche Party					–0.03	(0.04)
[Experts' perception of party j's Left–Right shift (t – 1)] × Niche Party					0.37**	(0.14)
Niche Party					0.01	(0.01)
Party j supporters' Left–Right shift (t – 1)	–0.26*	(0.13)	–0.33**	(0.09)	–0.33**	(0.10)
[Experts' perception of party j's Left–Right shift (t)] × [Experts' perception of party j's Left–Right shift (t – 1)]					0.04	(10.05)
Intercept	0.01	(0.01)	0.00	(0.00)	0.00	(0.00)
N	42		120		162	
R^2	0.23		0.13		0.17	

***$p \leq 0.01$; *$p \leq 0.05$; two-tailed tests.

Note: Standard errors are in parentheses. For these analyses the dependent variable was the change in the mean self-placement of the focal party's supporters on the Left–Right scale between the year of the current Chapel Hill expert survey and the year of the previous Chapel Hill expert survey, based on Eurobarometer respondents' self-placements. For the analyses reported in column 1, niche parties are defined as members of the communist, green, and nationalist party families, according to the party family codings of the Comparative Manifesto Project (CMP), and the analyses encompass all parties which had at least 50 supporters in the Eurobarometer surveys. For the analyses in column 2, mainstream parties are defined as members of the Social Democratic, Socialist, Liberal, Conservative, and Christian Democratic party families, according to the CMP party family codings. The independent variables are defined in the text.

coefficient estimates on either the [*Party j's perceived Left–Right shift* (*t*) – experts] variable, a result that would be consistent with contemporaneous partisan sorting in the mass public in response to niche parties' Left–Right shifts (although as we discuss below this pattern would also be consistent with a reciprocal relationship whereby party elites respond to their supporters' policy preferences), or a positive and significant coefficient estimate on the lagged version of this variable, which would support the Lagged Effects Hypothesis, that time lags intervene before the mass public reacts to party elites' policy shifts. The coefficient estimates in column 1 in Table 2 reveal that there is no significant contemporaneous statistical association between shifts in niche party supporters' mean Left–Right positions and niche party shifts at the elite level as perceived by experts – i.e. the coefficient estimate on the [*Expert perceptions of j's Left–Right shift* (*t*)] variable is near zero and is statistically significant. However we estimate a statistically significant coefficient ($p < 0.01$) on the lagged version of this variable, [*Expert perceptions of j's Left–Right shift* (*t* – 1)], indicating that –

consistent with the Lagged Effects Hypothesis – time lags intervene between when political experts perceive niche parties' Left–Right shifts and when rank-and-file voters perceive and react to these shifts. Note, furthermore, that the magnitude of the coefficient estimate on the [*Expert perceptions of j's Left–Right shift* (t – 1)] variable, +0.39, is also substantively significant: it implies that a one-unit shift in a niche party's Left–Right position in the previous time period, as perceived by political experts, is associated with a shift of nearly 0.4 units in the mean Left–Right position of the party's supporters during the current time period, where both parties' and the party supporters' shifts are calibrated along identical 0–1 scales.

Our finding, of a lagged relationship between experts' perceptions of niche parties' Left–Right shifts and shifts in the mean positions of niche party supporters is in fact more revealing than a finding of a contemporaneous relationship would be, because it is far easier to sort out the causal processes that underlie this lagged relationship. For a contemporaneous relationship, a tight fit between niche parties' Left–Right shifts and their supporters' Left–Right shifts would be consistent with a causal process whereby rank-and-file voters respond to niche party elites or a process whereby niche party elites respond to their supporters' shifting policy viewpoints. By contrast, our finding that shifts in niche party elites' Left–Right positions (as perceived by experts) are associated with lagged shifts in their supporters' Left–Right positions cannot be due to niche party elites responding to their supporters. Hence we interpret our parameter estimates as evidence of partisan sorting in the mass public with respect to niche parties – i.e. that citizens adjust their own Left–Right policy orientations and/or their party support in response to niche parties' Left–Right shifts (as these shifts are perceived by political experts).

Column 2 in Table 2 reports the parameter estimates when our model is estimated over the set of all mainstream parties in our data set, where mainstream parties are defined as parties that are members of the socialist, social democratic, liberal, conservative, and Christian democratic party families, based on the party family codings published by the Comparative Manifesto Project. Here the parameter estimates on the current and lagged versions of our key independent variable are both near zero and statistically insignificant – i.e. we do not identify any tendency for the (current and legged) shifts in the mean Left–Right positions of mainstream parties' supporters to match up with shifts in these parties' Left–Right positions, as perceived by political experts. These estimates on mainstream parties, in conjunction with the earlier estimates on niche parties reported in column 1, support the Niche Parties Hypothesis, that partisan sorting processes in the mass public are stronger with respect to niche parties than with respect to mainstream parties. And column 3 in Table 2 reports coefficient estimates for a model where we interact the [*Expert perceptions of j's Left–Right shift* (t)] variable (and the lagged version of this variable) with a dummy variable for niche parties. The coefficient estimate on the lagged interactive variable,

[*Expert perceptions of j's Left–Right shift* (t – 1) × *Niche Party*], +0.37, is statistically significant ($p < 0.01$), which again supports the Niche Parties Hypothesis.

Sensitivity Analyses

We performed several tests in order to evaluate whether our central findings, that there is strong evidence of partisan sorting with respect to niche parties and that these effects are lagged, were robust to the inclusion of small parties in our analyses; to an alternative definition of niche parties; and, to the possibility of error in the measurements of our key independent variables, namely parties' current and lagged policy shifts.[8] In order to evaluate the effects of including small parties in our analyses, we re-estimated the parameters of equation 1 on the set of all niche parties in our data set that featured at least 10 supporters in each relevant wave of the Eurobarometer surveys (recall that the analyses reported above were conducted on the set of niche parties that featured at least 50 Eurobarometer supporters per survey). This expanded definition increased the number of relevant niche party supporters' Left–Right shifts in our data set from 42 to 90. Column 2 in Table 3 reports the parameter estimates with these small niche parties included, while for comparison purposes column 1 presents the parameter estimates with small niche parties excluded (column 1 in Table 3 is therefore identical to column 1 in Table 2). This comparison shows that our conclusions are robust to the inclusion of small niche parties: the parameter estimate on the [*Expert perceptions of j's Left–Right shift* (t)] variable is again near zero and is statistically insignificant, indicating that there is no evidence of contemporaneous partisan sorting with respect to niche parties, while the coefficient estimate on the lagged version of this variable, [*Expert perceptions of j's Left–Right shift* (t – 1)], is again positive and statistically significant ($p < 0.05$), which provides evidence of lagged partisan sorting with respect to niche parties. Furthermore the coefficient estimate on the [*Expert perceptions of j's Left–Right shift* (t – 1)] variable when estimated on the set of all niche parties regardless of size, +0.36, is nearly identical to this coefficient when estimated on the set of larger niche parties only (+0.39).

Column 3 in Table 3 reports coefficient estimates using an alternative definition of niche parties, one that includes green and radical right parties but excludes communist parties, a definition that matches the perspective on niche parties advanced by Meguid (2008) and Spoon (2011).[9] With communist parties excluded from the niche party category, the number of niche party supporters' Left–Right shifts in our data set drops from 42 to 25. However, our conclusions are robust to this alternative definition of niche parties: the parameter estimate on the [*Expert perceptions of j's Left–Right shift* (t)] variable is again near zero and is statistically insignificant, while the coefficient estimate on the lagged version of this variable, [*Expert perceptions of j's Left–Right shift* (t – 1)] is +0.44, which is again

TABLE 3
THE RELATIONSHIP BETWEEN SHIFTS IN NICHE PARTY SUPPORTERS' LEFT–RIGHT POSITIONS, AND NICHE PARTIES' LEFT–RIGHT SHIFTS: SUPPLEMENTARY ANALYSES

							Errors-in-variables analyses (correlation between experts' perceptions and actual party shifts)			
	Basic model (1)		**Small niche parties included (2)**		**Communist parties omitted (3)**		**Correlation set to 0.8 (4)**		**Correlation set to 0.6 (5)**	
Experts' perception of party j's Left–Right shift (t)	0.05	(0.05)	−0.09	(0.13)	0.11	(0.09)	0.06	(0.12)	0.11	(0.15)
Experts' perception of party j's Left–Right shift (t − 1)	0.39**	(0.12)	0.36*	(0.18)	0.44**	(0.11)	0.49*	(0.18)	0.66**	(0.23)
Party j supporters' Left–Right shift (t − 1)	−0.26*	(0.13)	−0.28*	(0.13)	−0.26	(0.15)	−0.26*	(0.13)	−0.28*	(0.11)
Intercept	0.01	(0.01)	0.01	(0.01)	0.01	(0.01)	0.01	(0.00)	0.01	(0.00)
N	42		90		25		42		42	
R^2	0.23		0.10		0.28		0.27		0.33	

$^{**}p \leq 0.01$; $^{*}p \leq 0.05$; two-tailed tests.

Note: Standard errors are in parentheses. For these analyses the dependent variable was the change in the mean self-placement of the focal niche party's supporters on the Left–Right scale between the year of the current Chapel Hill expert survey and the year of the previous Chapel Hill expert survey, based on Eurobarometer respondents' self-placements. For the analyses reported in all columns except for columns 2–3, niche parties are defined as members of the communist, green, and nationalist party families, according to the party family codings of the Comparative Manifesto Project (CMP), and the analyses encompass all parties which had at least 50 supporters in the Eurobarometer surveys. Column 2 reports results when these analyses are expanded to encompass all niche parties which had at least 10 supporters in the Eurobarometer surveys. Column 3 reports results when communist parties are excluded from the definition of niche parties. Columns 4–5 report errors-in-variables (EIV) analyses, in which we specify correlations between the measured values of the experts' perceptions of the focal party's (current and lagged) Left–Right shifts, and the true values of these shifts. Column 4 reports the coefficient estimates when this correlation is specified as 0.8, and column 5 reports the coefficient estimates when this correlation is specified as 0.6.

substantively and statistically significant ($p < 0.01$).[10] These coefficient estimates thereby continue to support the Niche Parties Hypothesis and the Lagged Effects Hypothesis.

Finally, we explored the possible effects of errors in our measures of niche party elites' Left–Right shifts, which are based on over-time changes in the CHES respondents' mean party placements. Although the CHES experts' party placements have been extensively validated (see e.g. Hooghe *et al.* 2010) it is plausible that some experts are imperfectly informed about the parties' positions, and furthermore these experts may have differing interpretations of the Left–Right scales on which they placed the parties (see Budge 2000), a possibility that can lead to errors in the measures of party Left–Right shifts if the identities of the country CHES expert respondents change over time. For these computations we employed errors-in-variables (EIV) analysis, in which the analyst can specify the degree of reliability of the measured variable values, where reliability is defined as the correlation between the measured and the true or underlying values of the focal variables. Specifically, in EIV analysis the reliability of the measured value of each independent variable is specified on a 0–1 scale, where 1 denotes perfect reliability (i.e. that the correlation between the measured value and the true value of the variable is 1.0) and 0 denotes complete unreliability (i.e. that the measured and true values of the variable are uncorrelated).[11] To explore the effects of different degrees of measurement error on our substantive conclusions, we re-estimated the parameters of equation 1 on the set of niche parties while successively specifying the reliability of the [*Expert perceptions of j's Left–Right shift* (*t*)] variable, and the lagged version of this variable, to 0.9, 0.8, 0.7, and 0.6, where the reliability level 0.8, for instance, denotes that the correlation between the CHES experts' perceptions of niche parties' Left–Right shifts and the true or underlying values of these Left–Right shifts is 0.8. Columns 4–5 in Table 3 display the coefficient estimates when the reliability levels for the [*Expert perceptions of j's Left–Right shift* (*t*)] variable and the [*Expert perceptions of j's Left–Right shift* (*t* – 1)] variable were set to 0.8 (column 4) and to 0.6 (column 5).[12] These estimates continue to support the Niche Party Hypothesis and the Lagged Effects Hypothesis: the coefficient estimates on the [*Expert perceptions of j's Left–Right shift* (*t*)] variable remain near zero and are statistically insignificant, while the estimates on the lagged version of this variable, [*Expert perceptions of j's Left–Right shift* (*t* – 1)], remain positive and statistically significant ($p < 0.01$). Indeed, as we specify greater degrees of error in our measures of niche party elites' Left–Right shifts, the coefficient estimate on the [*Expert perceptions of j's Left–Right shift* (*t* – 1)] variable increases: this coefficient estimate is +0.39 when we specify no error in our measure of party Left–Right shifts (column 1), but the coefficient estimate increases to +0.49 when we specify a reliability measure of 0.8 for this variable (column 4), and the estimate increases to +0.66 when we specify a reliability measure of 0.6 for this variable (column 5). This latter estimate implies that when niche party elites shift their party's Left–Right position by one unit along the 0–1 scale, the mean Left–Right position of the niche party's supporters will shift by roughly two-thirds of one unit during the subsequent period, along an identical 0–1 scale. Thus when we specify realistic degrees of error in our measures of niche party elites' policy shifts, our coefficient estimates imply that these elite shifts will prompt (lagged) shifts of comparable magnitude in niche party supporters' Left–Right positions.

Finally, we note that we have replicated the analyses reported in Tables 2–3 using the Comparative Manifesto Project (CMP) codings of party Left–Right positions in place of the CHES experts' perceptions of these positions, and these analyses reveal no statistical association – for either niche or for mainstream party supporters – between shifts in the parties' Left–Right positions and shifts in their supporters' (current or lagged) Left–Right positions. These analyses thereby support the results reported in Adams *et al.* (2011), that rank-and-file voters do not perceive or react to shifts in the Left–Right tone of parties' election manifestos.

While it is beyond the scope of this study to parse out the causal processes that drive our findings of empirical support for the Niche Parties Hypothesis, Table 4 reports comparisons of the levels of political engagement among niche party supporters, mainstream party supporters, and political independents, which suggest that the stronger partisan sorting processes in the mass public with respect to niche parties may arise because niche party supporters are disproportionately engaged in politics. The table reports the proportions of Eurobarometer respondents across 1992–2002 who reported that they frequently discussed politics (row 1), along with the proportions of respondents who were classified as opinion leaders – i.e. those who reported that they discussed politics 'frequently' and that they attempted to persuade others to change their political viewpoints 'often' or 'from time to time' (row 2), stratified by the respondent's partisanship. These computations demonstrate that niche party supporters displayed substantially higher degrees of political engagement than did mainstream parties' supporters (and that both types of partisans were more engaged than were non-partisans).

TABLE 4
INCIDENCE OF POLITICAL DISCUSSION AND OPINION LEADERSHIP

	Niche party supporter	Mainstream party supporter	Independent
Frequently discusses politics	20.0%	15.4%	8.6%
Discusses politics and attempts to persuade others (opinion leader)	16.3%	12.1%	6.2%
N	3,876	26,549	3,288

Note: The percentages reported in the row labelled 'Frequently discusses politics' show the proportions of Eurobarometer respondents who chose the response category 'frequently' in answer to the question 'When you get together with friends, would you say that you discuss political matters frequently, occasionally, or never?' The percentages reported in the row labelled 'Discusses politics and attempts to persuade others (opinion leader)' show the proportions of Eurobarometer respondents who stated that they discussed politics 'frequently' and who also stated that they attempted to persuade friends 'often' or 'from time to time'. The percentages in the table are calculated over Eurobarometer survey data from Austria, Belgium, Britain, Denmark, Finland, France, Germany, Greece, Ireland, Italy, the Netherlands, Portugal, Spain, and Sweden, over the period 1992–2002 for all parties with at least 50 supporters, plus all respondents who did not identify with a party.

Conclusion

The linkage between the policy positions of party elites and rank-and-file citizens is central to representative democracy. We analyse whether citizens respond to shifts in the Left–Right ideologies of party elites in Western Europe. Our project is motivated by two recent studies: that of Adams *et al.* (2011), which reports analyses suggesting that rank-and-file citizens do not systematically perceive and react to the Left–Right tone of the policy statements that parties publish in their election manifestos, and a study by Fortunato and Stevenson (forthcoming), which presents remarkable evidence that citizens update their perceptions of parties' Left–Right positions in response to an important feature of party elites' behaviour – namely, parties' decisions to enter (or forgo) governing coalitions with particular sets of rival parties.

This set of findings motivated us to analyse partisan sorting in the electorate in response to parties' Left–Right policy shifts, as these shifts were perceived by political experts. Our reasoning was that because these experts plausibly weigh all relevant information when estimating parties' positions – including the content of party elites' speeches, interviews, and policy manifestos, along with elites' coalition bargaining behaviour and their roll-call votes – these experts' perceptions arguably provide reliable measures of the parties' Left–Right positions based on all relevant evidence. And hence, to the extent that we observe partisan sorting in the mass public that is consistent with these experts' perceptions of party positions, this will provide evidence that citizens react to the wider informational environment when updating their own Left–Right positions and their party support, even if citizens do not specifically cue off parties' election-year manifestos. Our empirical analyses suggest that this is indeed the case, at least with respect to mass–elite policy linkages between citizens and niche parties. Specifically, in situations where experts perceive that niche parties – namely green, communist, and radical right parties – have shifted their Left–Right positions, we observe large, substantively (and statistically) significant shifts in the mean Left–Right positions of these niche parties' supporters – a finding that supports our Niche Parties Hypothesis. Moreover, the timing of these niche party supporters' Left–Right shifts, specifically that these shifts are lagged relative to niche party elites' policy shifts, strongly implies a causal process whereby niche party supporters are reacting to niche party elites' shifts, not vice versa. Our finding of lagged effects supports our Lagged Effects Hypothesis. Our findings are robust to alternative definitions of niche parties (including definitions that include and those that exclude communist parties and ethno-territorial parties), to the inclusion or exclusion of very small niche parties in our data set, and to accounting for possible error in our (expert-based) measures of niche parties' policy shifts. By contrast, we find no evidence that citizens exhibit (current or lagged) reactions to mainstream parties' policy shifts, as these shifts are perceived by political experts.

Our findings raise the question of what individual-level processes explain the aggregate-level patterns that we identify, whereby we observe significant degrees of mass-level partisan sorting in response to niche parties' – but not mainstream parties' – Left–Right policy shifts. In this regard, the argument of Adams *et al.* (2006) – that in comparison to mainstream parties, niche parties tend to attract more policy-focused supporters – seems relevant here. To the extent this is the case, we might expect niche party supporters to be disproportionately sensitive to parties' policy shifts, and thus to abandon their party more quickly when it shifts its policies in ways of which these supporters disapprove, while supporting their party more enthusiastically when the party's policies mirror these supporters' beliefs. While we do not fully parse out this argument, we have reported preliminary support for this explanation in the Eurobarometer data, in that we find that the supporters of niche parties display markedly greater degrees of political engagement than do the supporters of mainstream parties.

We emphasise that our (non-)findings on partisan sorting in the mass public in response to mainstream parties' Left–Right shifts do not preclude other types of mass-level reactions to mainstream parties' policies. For instance Wlezien's (1995, 1996; see also Erikson *et al.* 2002; Soroka and Wlezien 2010) thermostatic model posits that citizens respond to government policy outputs by shifting their policy preferences in the opposite direction from the government's current policies – i.e. Wlezien concludes that aggregate citizen demand for government spending decreases when governments spend more, and vice versa. Note that such effects operate at the level of the mass public as a whole, not just the governing parties' current supporters, so that our (non-)findings on partisan sorting with respect to mainstream parties do not rule out this type of thermostatic effect. In addition, Ezrow and Xezonakis (2011) report evidence that parties' Left–Right positions influence citizens' satisfaction with democracy, a pattern that is unrelated to the types of partisan sorting analyses that we report here. Finally, both Meguid (2008) and Milazzo *et al.* (2012) conclude that mainstream political parties can, via their policy positions, influence the salience that citizens attach to different policy dimensions, i.e. that mainstream parties influence the 'terms of the debate' in the mass public via their policy positioning. *In toto*, this research suggests that both niche and mainstream parties' policy positions may prompt a variety of reactions from rank-and-file voters. Our contribution is to present analyses that imply that, with respect to partisan sorting processes relating to Left-Right policy debates, citizens react more strongly to niche parties' policy shifts than they do to the policy shifts of mainstream parties.

A further caveat to the present study is that we limit our analysis to the Left–Right dimension. Studies by Carmines and Stimson (1989) and de Vries (2007) suggest that voters are more likely to take cues from parties on new dimensions of political conflict, such as civil rights in the United States or on support for European integration in Western Europe. Whereas citizens may hold deeply embedded attitudes with respect to classic Left–Right debates (Tavits 2007), voter attitudes may be more malleable with respect to new and emerging dimensions of political debate. With respect to the countries in Western Europe in our study, conducting parallel analyses matching elite–supporter preferences for European integration would be worthwhile.

For now, however, we are left with the empirical pattern that there is little (or no) evidence of partisan sorting with respect to mainstream parties' Left–Right positions, regardless of whether these party positions are measured based on the codings of parties' election manifestos (as demonstrated by Adams *et al.* 2011), or whether parties' positions are measured based on the perceptions of political experts (as we document here). While we do not discount the possibility that alternative measures of mainstream parties' Left–Right positions – or alternative measures of their supporters' positions – may support different substantive conclusions, we believe these patterns raise important issues for future research on mass–elite policy linkages. By contrast, our finding that niche party supporters' (lagged) Left–Right shifts track experts' perceptions of elite-level shifts by niche parties, in combination with the earlier Adams *et al.* (2011) finding that this relationship does not hold when niche party elites' Left–Right shifts are measured based on their election manifestos, suggests that partisan sorting processes occur with respect to niche parties because their supporters respond to the wider informational environment that encompasses all relevant information pertaining to niche parties – including the content of party elites' speeches and interviews, along with elites' coalition bargaining behaviour and their actual roll-call votes – not simply the content of niche parties' election manifestos. This finding on niche parties supports the earlier thesis of Adams *et al.* (2006), that niche parties and their supporters are indeed fundamentally different from mainstream parties, in ways that have important implications for political representation.

Acknowledgements

An earlier version of this paper was presented at the annual meeting of the Midwest Political Science Association, Chicago, IL, 31 March–3 April 2011. We thank Elias Dinas, Michael McDonald, and the anonymous reviewers for very thoughtful comments. All three authors contributed equally to the paper.

Notes

1. Fortunato and Stevenson find that citizens perceive that parties that jointly participate in a governing coalition are more similar on Left–Right policy than is implied by these parties' manifesto-based policy statements alone, and that citizens' perceptions of party positions are also mediated by parties' past coalition behaviour.

2. As we discuss below, our conclusions are robust to alternative definitions of what constitutes a niche party, namely to the inclusion of ethno-territorial parties and also to the exclusion of communist parties (see e.g. Meguid 2008; Spoon 2011).
3. We note that we do not include the 2006 Chapel Hill expert survey in our analyses because our measures of party supporters' positions, described below, stops at 2002.
4. We note that Spain and Portugal were not included in the Eurobarometer surveys until 1981 and 1986, respectively. Finland was first included on the Eurobarometer survey in 1993, and Sweden and Austria were first included in 1994.
5. In each Eurobarometer survey respondents are asked to indicate their party support by answering the question: 'If there were a "general election" tomorrow, which party would you support?'
6. We also estimated the parameters of our model while omitting the lagged independent variable, and these estimates supported substantive conclusions that were identical to those we report below.
7. Since the Eurobarometer surveys typically feature approximately 1,000 respondents, the condition that at least 50 respondents support the focal party entails that the party command a minimum of roughly 5 per cent support.
8. We thank two anonymous reviewers for suggesting the analyses we report in this subsection of the paper.
9. We note that several additional definitions of niche parties exist. There are recent studies that classify niche parties based on their emphasis of non-Left–Right issues (Wagner forthcoming; see also Meyer and Wagner 2011). We do not employ this measure, because we are analysing responsiveness on the Left–Right dimension.
10. We note that we also estimated the parameters of our model for an expanded definition of niche parties that included ethno-territorial parties along with green, communist, and radical right parties, and that the parameter estimates continued to support our substantive conclusions.
11. In standard regression analysis the analyst implicitly specifies that all variables are accurately measured, i.e. the assumed reliability of each variable is set to 1.0.
12. The coefficient estimates with the reliability levels set to 0.9 and to 0.7 (available upon request) support identical substantive conclusions.

References

Adams, James, and Zeynep Somer-Topcu (2009). 'Moderate Now, Win Votes Later: The Electoral Consequences of Parties' Policy Shifts in 25 Postwar Democracies', *Journal of Politics*, 71:2, 678–92.

Adams, James, Michael Clark, Lawrence Ezrow, and Garrett Glasgow (2006). 'Are Niche Parties Fundamentally Different from Mainstream Parties? The Causes and Electoral Consequences of Western European Parties' Policy Shifts, 1976–1998', *American Journal of Political Science*, 50:3, 513–29.

Adams, James, Lawrence Ezrow, and Zeynep Somer-Topcu (2011). 'Is Anybody Listening? Evidence That Voters Do Not Respond to European Parties' Policy Statements During Elections', *American Journal of Political Science*, 55:2, 370–82.

Beck, Nathaniel, and Jonathan N. Katz (1995). 'What to Do (and Not to Do) with Time-Series Cross-Section Data', *American Political Science Review*, 89:3, 634–47.

Budge, Ian (2000). 'Expert Judgments of Party Policy Positions: Uses and Limitations in Political Research', *European Journal of Political Research*, 37:1, 103–13.

Budge, Ian, Hans-Dieter Klingemann, Andrea Volkens, Eric Tannenbaum, and Judith Bara (2001). *Mapping Policy Preferences: Estimates for Parties, Electors, and Governments 1945–1998*. Oxford: Oxford University Press.

Carmines, Edward G., and James A. Stimson (1989). *Issue Evolution: Race and the Transformation of American Politics*. Princeton, NJ: Princeton University Press.

Carsey, Thomas, and Geoffrey Layman (2006). 'Changing Sides or Changing Minds? Party Identification and Policy Preferences in the American Electorate', *American Journal of Political Science*, 50:2, 464–77.

Castles, Francis, and Peter Mair (1984). 'Left–Right Political Scales: Some Expert Judgments', *European Journal of Political Research*, 12:1, 73–88.

D'Alimonte, Roberto (1999). 'Party Behavior in a Polarized System: The Italian Communist Party and the Historic Compromise,' in Wolfgang Muller and Kaare Strom (eds.), *Policy, Office, or Votes? How Political Parties in Western Europe Make Hard Decisions*. Cambridge: Cambridge University Press, 141–71.

Dalton, Russell (1985). 'Political Parties and Political Representation', *Comparative Political Studies*, 18:3, 267–99.

De Vries, Catherine (2007). 'Sleeping Giant: Fact or Fairytale? How European Integration Affects National Elections', *European Union Politics*, 8:3, 363–85.

Erikson, Robert, Michael MacKuen, and James Stimson (2002). *The Macro Polity*. Cambridge: Cambridge University Press.

Ezrow, Lawrence, and Giorgios Xezonakis (2011). 'Citizen Satisfaction with Democracy and Parties' Policy Offerings', *Comparative Political Studies*, 44:8, 1152–78.

Ezrow, Lawrence, Catherine E. de Vries, Marco Steenbergen, and Erica E. Edwards (2011). 'Mean Voter Representation and Partisan Constituency Representation: Do Parties Respond to the Mean Voter Position or to their Supporters?', *Party Politics*, 17:3, 275–301.

Fortunato, David, and Randy Stevenson (forthcoming). 'Perceptions of Partisan Ideologies: The Effects of Coalition Participation', *American Journal of Political Science*.

Goren, Paul (2005). 'Party Identification and Core Political Values', *American Journal of Political Science*, 49:4, 881–96.

Highton, Benjamin, and Cindy Kam (2011). 'The Long-Term Dynamics of Partisanship and Issue Orientations', *Journal of Politics*, 73:1, 202–15.

Hix, Simon, and Christopher Lord (1997). *Political Parties in the European Union*. New York: St. Martin's.

Hobolt, Sara B., and Jae-Jae Spoon (2010). 'Motivating the European Voter'. PIREDEU Final Conference, Brussels.

Hooghe, Liesbet, Ryan Bakker, Anna Brigevich, Catherine de Vries, Erica Edwards, Jan Rovny, Marco Steenbergen, and Milada Vachudova (2010). 'Measurement Validity and Party Positioning: Chapel Hill Expert Surveys of 2002 and 2006', *European Journal of Political Research*, 42:4, 684 703.

Hsiao, Cheng (2003). *Analysis of Panel Data*, 2nd ed. Cambridge: Cambridge University Press.

Huber, John, and Ronald Inglehart (1995). 'Expert Interpretations of Party Space and Party Locations in 42 Societies', *Party Politics*, 1:1, 73–111.

Iversen, Torben (1994). 'Political Leadership and Representation in Western European Democracies: A Test of Three Models of Voting', *American Journal of Political Science*, 38:1, 45–74.

Kitschelt, Herbert (1994). *The Transformation of European Social Democracy*. New York: Cambridge University Press.

Klingemann, Hans-Dieter, Andrea Volkens, Judith Bara, Ian Budge, and Michael D. McDonald (2006). *Mapping Policy Preferences II: Estimates for Parties, Electors and Governments in Central and Eastern Europe, European Union and OECD 1990–2003*. Oxford: Oxford University Press.

Meguid, Bonnie (2008). *Competition between Unequals: Strategies and Electoral Fortunes in Western Europe*. Cambridge: Cambridge University Press.

Meyer, Thomas, and Markus Wagner (2011). 'Mainstream or Niche? Vote-seeking Incentives and the Programmatic Strategies of Political Parties'. ECPR General Conference, University of Iceland, Reykjavik.

Milazzo, Caitlin, James Adams, and Jane Green (2012). 'Are Voter Decision Rules Endogenous to Party Strategies? A Model with Applications to Elite Depolarization in Post-Thatcher Britain', *Journal of Politics*, 74:1, 262–76.

Pelizzo, Riccardo (2007). 'Party Direction and the Italian Case', unpublished paper, Singapore Management University.

Rogers, William H. (1993). 'Regression Standard Errors in Clustered Samples', *Stata Technical Bulletin*, 13, 19–23.

Sartori, Giovanni (1968). 'Representational Systems', *International Encyclopedia of the Social Sciences*, 13, 470–75.

Soroka, Stuart, and Christopher Wlezien (2010). *Degrees of Democracy: Politics, Public Opinion, Policy*. Cambridge: Cambridge University Press.

Spoon, Jae-Jae (2011). *Political Survival of Small Parties in Europe*. Ann Arbor: University of Michigan Press.

Tarrow, Sidney (1989). *Democracy and Disorder*. Oxford: Clarendon Press.

Tavits, Margit (2007). 'Principle versus Pragmatism: Policy Shifts and Political Competition', *American Journal of Political Science*, 51:1, 151–65.

Wagner, Markus (forthcoming). 'Defining and Measuring Niche Parties', *Party Politics*.

Wlezien, Christopher (1995). 'The Public as Thermostat: Dynamics of Preferences for Spending', *American Journal of Political Science*, 39:4, 981–1000.

Wlezien, Christopher (1996). 'Dynamics of Representation: The Case of U.S. Spending on Defence', *British Journal of Political Science*, 26:1, 81–103.

Zaller, John (1992). *The Nature and Origins of Mass Opinion*. Cambridge: Cambridge University Press.

APPENDIX
PARTIES INCLUDED IN ANALYSES

	Party name	Abbreviation	Years
Belgium			
	Socialist Party (Francophone)	PS	1988, 1992, 1996, 1999, 2002
	Socialist Party (Flemish)	SP	1992, 1996, 1999, 2002
	Ecologists (Francophone)	ECOLO	1988, 1992, 1996, 1999, 2002
	Ecologists (Flemish)	AGALEV	1988, 1992, 1996, 1999
	Christian Social Party (Francophone)	PSC	1988, 1992, 1996, 1999
	Christian People's Party (Flemish)	CVP	1988, 1992, 1996, 1999, 2002
	Flemish Bloc (Flemish)	VB	1988, 1992, 1996, 1999, 2002
Denmark			
	Social Democratic Party	SD	1988, 1992, 1996, 1999, 2002
	Radical Party	RV	1988, 1992, 1996, 1999, 2002
	Conservative People's Party	KF	1988, 1992, 1996, 1999, 2002
	Centre Democrats	CD	1988, 1992
	Socialist Peoples' Party	SF	1988, 1992, 1996, 1999, 2002
	Liberals	V	1988, 1992, 1996, 1999, 2002
	Progress Party	FP	1988, 1992
Germany			
	Christian Democratic Union	CDU	1988, 1992, 1996, 1999, 2002
	Social Democratic Party	SPD	1988, 1992, 1996, 1999, 2002
	Free Democratic Party	FDP	1988, 1992
	Republikaner	REP	1988, 1992
Greece			
	Pan Hellenic Socialist Movement	PASOK	1988, 1992, 1996, 1999, 2002
	New Democracy	ND	1988, 1992, 1996, 1999, 2002
	Progressive Left Coalition	SAP, SYN	1988, 1992, 1996, 1999
	Communist Party of Greece	KKE	1996, 1999
Spain			
	Spanish Socialist Workers' Party	PSOE	1988, 1992, 1996, 1999, 2002
	Popular Party	PP	1988, 1992, 1996, 1999, 2002
	United Left	IU	1988, 1992, 1996, 1999
	Convergence and Union (Catalan)	CiU	1988, 1992
France			
	French Communist Party	PCF	1988, 1992, 1996
	Socialist Party	PS	1988, 1992, 1996, 1999
	Ecologists	VERTS	1988, 1992
	Rally for the Republic (Gaullist)	RPR	1988, 1992, 1996, 1999
	National Front	FN	1988, 1992, 1996
	Union for French Democracy	UDF	1996, 1999
Ireland			
	Fianna Fail	FF	1988, 1992, 1996, 1999, 2002
	Fine Gael	FG	1988, 1992, 1996, 1999, 2002
	Labour Party	LP	1988, 1992, 1996, 1999
Italy			
	Christian Democrats/ Popular Party	DC/PP	1988, 1992

(continued)

APPENDIX
(*Continued*)

	Party name	Abbreviation	Years
	Newly Founded Communists	RC	1996, 1999
	Italian Socialist Party	PSI	1988, 1992
	Italian Social Movement-Right National/ National Alliance	MSI-DN, AN	1988, 1992
Netherlands			
	Christian Democratic Appeal	CDA	1988, 1992, 1996, 1999
	Labour Party	PvdA	1988, 1992, 1996, 1999
	Liberal Party	VVD	1988, 1992, 1996, 1999
	Democrats '66	D'66	1988, 1992, 1996, 1999
	Green League	GL	1996, 1999
United Kingdom			
	Conservative Party	TORY	1988, 1992, 1996, 1999, 2002
	Labour Party	LAB	1988, 1992, 1996, 1999, 2002
	Liberal Democratic Party	LDP	1988, 1992, 1996, 1999, 2002
Portugal			
	Portuguese Socialist Party	PSP	1996, 1999, 2002
	Popular Democratic Party/ Social Democratic Party	PPD/PSD	1996, 1999, 2002
Austria			
	Austrian People's Party	ÖVP	1996, 1999, 2002
	Socialist Party	SPÖ	1996, 1999, 2002
	Austrian Freedom Party/ Freedom Movement	FPÖ	1996, 1999, 2002
	Green Alternative/ Greens	GA	1996, 1999, 2002
Finland			
	Social Democratic Party	SSDP	1996, 1999, 2002
	National Coalition	KOK	1996, 1999, 2002
	Finnish Centre	KESK	1996, 1999, 2002
	Finnish People's Democratic Union/ Left Wing Alliance	SKDL/VL	1996, 1999, 2002
	Swedish People's Party	RKP/SFP	1996, 1999
	Green Union	VIHR	1996, 1999, 2002
	Christian League	SKL	1996, 1999
Sweden			
	Left Communists Party, Left Party	VK, V	1996, 1999, 2002
	Social Democratic Labour Party	SAP	1996, 1999, 2002
	Liberal People's Party	FPL	1996, 1999
	Moderate Coalition Party	MSP	1996, 1999, 2002
	Christian Democrats	KdS	1996, 1999, 2002
	Green Party, Green Ecology Party	GRONA, MP	1996, 1999

Note: Parties and Acronyms taken from Chapel Hill Expert Survey 1984–99 Codebook. The parties chosen overlap with both the Chapel Hill Expert Survey and Eurobarometer Surveys, are available for at least two waves of both the Chapel Hill Expert Survey and the Eurobarometer, and have at least 50 supporters in the Eurobarometer survey.

Intra-Party Democracy and Party Responsiveness

RON LEHRER

This study examines whether parties respond to their supporters or to the median voter position. Party leaders require the support of the 'selectorate', which is defined as the group that has influence in party leadership selection. Inclusive parties, which rely on rank-and-file membership to select their leaders, will respond to their members. Exclusive parties, which rely on office-seeking members for leadership selection, will respond to the median voter position. Thus, intra-party institutions that (dis)enfranchise party members are crucial for understanding whether a party responds to their supporters (or to the median voter position). Using data from 1975–2003 for six West European countries, this article reports findings that inclusive parties respond to the mean party supporter position. While there is evidence that exclusive parties respond to the median voter position in two-party systems, this finding does not extend to multiparty systems. This study has implications for the understanding of intra-party institutions and political representation.

It is one of modern democracies' principles that parties adapt their policy positions to public opinion and thus represent citizens' preferences. Also, parties represent their members whose policy ideals oftentimes strongly diverge from public opinion. In this article, I develop and test the hypotheses that the inclusiveness in intra-party leadership elections determines whether parties are responsive to the general electorate or their party members.

In particular, I argue that party leaders adopt positions that are consistent with the preferences of their selectorate, or the 'set of people who have an institutional say in choosing leaders' (Bueno de Mesquita *et al.* 2002: 560; see also Bueno de Mesquita *et al.* 2003: 41–3). Members of the selectorate value office and policy. However, office payoffs exceed policy payoffs.

Hence, candidates are motivated to respond to rank-and-file party members to the extent that these members have influence in selecting them.

If office-motivated party members dominate the leadership selection, then parties will respond to the median voter. By contrast, if the policy-motivated rank-and-file members dominate the party leadership selection, then parties will respond to shifts in their core supporters. Thus, intra-party institutions are decisive with respect to which groups they enfranchise in the leadership selection.

These hypotheses are tested employing data from six European countries between 1975 and 2003. The analysis reveals that inclusive parties – which rely on rank-and-file membership to select their leadership – are indeed different from exclusive parties – that rely on office-seeking members for leadership selection – in terms of responsiveness to its mean supporter. In addition, there is evidence that exclusive parties respond to mean voter opinion shifts in two-party systems, however, this finding does not extend to multiparty systems.

This article contributes to the literature in four important ways. First, it extends the general scholarship on intra-party institutions by evaluating the effects of the intra-party franchise. During the last 15 years, scholars have adopted an intra-party politics approach to address the question how parties adjust their positions (Budge *et al.* 2010; Meyer 2010; Schofield and Sened 2005; Strøm and Müller 1999). Strøm and Müller (1999: 18) introduce leadership accountability as a factor that may affect policy positions. Recently, Schumacher *et al.* (2011) have taken up the finding of Ezrow *et al.* (2011) that niche parties – i.e. parties from the Nationalist, Communist and Green party families – respond to the mean party supporter whereas mainstream parties respond to shifts in the mean voter. While Ezrow *et al.* (2011; see also Adams *et al.* 2006) propose that the crucial mainstream–niche distinction is based on attachments to ideology, Schumacher *et al.* (2011) argue that intra-party organisational strength matters, namely, that activist-dominated organisations induce responsiveness to the mean party supporter, and leadership-dominated parties are associated with responsiveness to the mean voter. To my knowledge, this article provides the first analysis of how intra-party institutions (i.e. intra-party franchise) affect parties' policy positions.

Second, this article's findings have important implications for the study of political representation. In general theories of democracy, citizen preferences are linked to public policy via a 'chain of responsiveness' (Powell 2004), although this 'chain' may be altered or distorted by institutional characteristics (e.g. majority-manufacturing electoral systems). For aggregating citizen preferences, the chain relies heavily on the delegation of interests within parties (Müller 2000). This article shows that whether parties represent their supporters depends on parties' internal institutions. Hence, we can add to the list of factors that attenuate the signal from citizens to representatives by pointing to the importance of institutions within parties.

Third, these findings have significant implications for coalition behaviour. For instance, exclusive parties should be more flexible to accept compromises and hence more likely to be members of a coalition government. Similarly, inclusive parties should be less forbearing with its leaders if they implement unpopular policies from the party members' point of view, and less likely to compromise their ideology to remain in a governing coalition. Hence, theories that combine intra-party politics and coalition politics (Giannetti and Benoit 2009) should analyse the effect of intra-party franchise too.

Fourth, this study extends previous work on niche and mainstream parties (Adams *et al.* 2006; Ezrow *et al.* 2011; Meguid 2005, 2008), and provides an additional step toward understanding the niche party phenomenon. What is it about niche parties that promotes responsiveness to their core supporters? The implication of this study is that it may be inclusiveness rather than attachments to ideology that promotes niche responsiveness to their supporters.

Hypotheses

Below, it is argued first that party members have office- and policy-seeking motivations, and that office-seeking motivations outweigh policy-seeking motivations. However, office motivations are important if a party member runs for office only. Whether a party member is office- or policy-motivated is decisive for the policy position that member prefers to be chosen by the party. Therefore, when deciding upon the party's policy, candidates for party leadership take into account to what extent the body that selects the party leader (i.e. the selectorate) is policy- or office-motivated. As shown below, the ratio of offices that a party leader commands to selectors proves to be crucial for the distribution of motives in the selectorate. Selectorates with many more selectors than offices are characterised by policy-motivated selectors that induce responsiveness to the median party member position. By contrast, selectorates with almost equally many selectors and offices incentivise responsiveness to the median voter position.

Individual Vote Choices: How Office Outweighs Policy

In the following, I assume that party members maximise utility by obtaining policy (Strøm and Müller 1999: 8; see also Wittman 1973, 1983) and office payoffs (Downs 1957: 30; see also Calvert 1985; Davis *et al.* 1970). On the one hand, everyone has a personal ideal position that is preferred over all alternatives. Moreover, the further the implemented policy is away from that ideal position, the less utility will be received. On the other hand and by contrast with policy payoffs, office payoffs are gained if a party member runs for office only. In the case of party members running for office, they face election. If they lose the election, they receive payoffs for policy and running for office. Moreover, the payoffs for running for office exceed the maximal amount of policy payoffs (Luebbert 1986: 46). Alternatively, they win the election, assume office, and obtain policy payoffs as well as office payoffs. Again, office is worthwhile enough to outnumber the maximal payoffs of policy and running for office together.

Provided there are two candidates for party leadership, three situations can evolve under these assumptions. First, if neither of the candidates for party leadership invites a party member to run for office, the vote decision is based on the candidates' policy offers. Thus, the party member is *policy-motivated.* Second, if the party member is invited to run for office by one candidate only, s/he will – even despite significant policy differences – vote for that candidate. The party member is then *office-motivated.* Third, if a party member is invited to run for office by both candidates for party leadership, s/he will prefer the candidate with the policy position that offers the greatest chance of assuming office in the electoral competition for office. I label this policy position the *office-seeking position.* Now we turn to how this pattern affects parties' policy positions via leadership elections.

Vote Choices and Intra-Party Franchise: Why Institutions Matter

For simplicity, I continue the example with two candidates for party leadership. Hence, a candidate is elected party leader if supported by a majority of the selectorate. Following Bueno de Mesquita *et al.*'s Selectorate Theory (2002, 2003), I define the selectorate as the subgroup of party members which takes part in the party leadership selection.

Since making party members office-motivated (i.e. inviting them to run for office) is an effective means to secure selectors' support, candidates for party leadership fully exploit this option. However, this strategy is constrained by the number of offices a candidate can distribute among selectors. Thus, the 'offices-to-selectors' ratio within the party is important. As this ratio decreases, the fewer selectors can be 'bribed' with office payoffs (i.e. they are office-motivated) and, in turn, the more selectors rely on policy considerations when making their vote choice (i.e. they are policy-motivated). Hence, the smaller the offices-to-selectors ratio, the closer a leadership candidate's winning policy position has to be to the median selector's ideal position. This situation typically evolves in parties that allow their rank-and-file members to participate in leadership selections. I label these parties *inclusive* and express the theoretical expectation about them in the Inclusiveness Hypothesis:

> *Hypothesis 1 (Inclusiveness Hypothesis):* Inclusive parties that are characterised by a relatively low offices-to-selectors ratio respond to shifts in the position of the median party member.

By contrast, *exclusive* parties' selectorates are primarily composed of office-holders (e.g. the parliamentary party). Due to mainly office-motivated selectors, these parties allow for more leeway from the median selector's ideal position. Since candidates for party leadership themselves are office-motivated – i.e. they try to maximise votes in elections to form a government or participate in it (Luebbert 1986) – they will use this leeway to move the party's policy position towards the office-seeking position.

The office-seeking position is somewhat complicated to derive. In a two-party framework, this position will be the position of the median voter (Downs 1957: 118). In a multi-party setting, scholars emphasise that parties have vote-seeking incentives to adopt distinctly non-centrist positions (i.e. they emphasise the role of centrifugal incentives) due to the existence of proportional electoral systems and more competitors (Adams and Merrill 2006; Cox 1990a, 1990b; Merrill and Adams 2002). On the other hand, the prospect of coalition formation exerts incentives for parties to adopt moderate or coalition-friendly policies (Schofield 1993) so that the median voter remains important in multi-party systems as well (Austen-Smith and Banks 1988; see also Ezrow 2008). Thus, it is reasonable to expect that exclusive parties orient towards the median voter in both types of systems. Hence,

> *Hypothesis 2a (Exclusiveness Hypothesis):* Exclusive parties that are characterised by a relatively high offices-to-selectors ratio respond to shifts in the position of the median voter.

Nevertheless, the incentives to respond to the median voter should be weaker in multi-party systems than in two-party systems because we expect that positioning effects of electoral rules and party system size slightly outweigh the incentives to present moderate policies to appeal to potential coalition partners. Thus,

> *Hypothesis 2b (Party System Hypothesis):* Exclusive parties are more responsive to shifts in the position of the median voter in two-party systems than in multi-party systems.

Data and Measurement

Testing these hypotheses requires developing measures of: parties' policy positions, offices-to-selectors ratios, median party member positions, the median voter position and the type of party system in a country election year.

Parties' Policy Positions

The academic debate on whether party positions are best measured by different types of text analysis (Budge *et al.* 2001; Laver *et al.* 2003; Slapin and Proksch 2008), mass surveys (Thomassen 2005; Bäck 2008), roll call data analysis (Hix *et al.* 2006), or expert surveys (Benoit and Laver 2006;

Huber and Inglehart 1995) is intense and ongoing (see also a special issue of *Electoral Studies* (Marks 2007) dedicated to this discussion). This paper relies on the data set on party positions provided by the Comparative Manifesto Project (CMP) (Budge *et al.* 2001; Klingemann *et al.* 2006). It places parties' election manifestos from all over the world on a left–right scale ranging from –100 for extreme left-wing parties to 100 for extreme right-wing parties. In order to obtain this scale, coders read each party's election manifesto and portion its content in 56 predefined quasi-sentence categories. Based on the relative frequency of categories defined as 'left' and 'right', each party's manifesto position on the left–right scale is computed. Consequently, the unit of observation is party election years.

Besides providing comparative results to other methods' estimates of party positions (Hearl 2001; Laver *et al.* 2003; McDonald and Mendes 2001), the CMP dataset also covers a large amount of countries, parties and elections which are needed to conduct the analysis.[1] Moreover, scholars argue (Inglehart 1990) and empirically show (Benoit and Laver 2006: 158) that the left–right dimension is dominant in West European politics. Since the CMP left–right measures and its counterpart for public opinion (see below) are not equivalently scaled, I linearly rescale the CMP left–right scale to 1–10.[2]

Offices-to-Selectors Ratio

Since it is very difficult to obtain the exact number of selectors for parties, I use an ordinal rather than an absolute scale. In particular, I utilise a scale that – similar to the theoretical classification above (i.e. inclusive and exclusive) – distinguishes, based on their formal institutions in party leadership selections, between two types of selectorates.

Data on formal procedures for electing the party leader can be found in Katz and Mair's (1992) *Data Handbook of Party Organizations* in which country experts compile institutional arrangements of various parties for the time period from 1960 until 1990. Since they only list and describe formal procedures, I apply a scheme developed by Kenig (2009) to classify parties according to their formal rules into inclusive or exclusive parties.

There are two scenarios that lead to a party being coded as inclusive. On the one hand, if all party members can elect the party leader – either because all members are entitled to vote in the party conference selecting the party leader or because there are grass-root elections ('Party Members' in Kenig's categorisation) – I categorise a party as 'inclusive'. On the other hand, parties that select their party leaders via delegates are also considered 'inclusive' if delegates to the party conference represent local party branches ('Selected Party Agency' according to Kenig). In either case, these parties are assigned the value 1 on the inclusiveness scale. Due to the size of modern parties it is obviously the corresponding category to the 'policy-motivated party' that is defined by its very small offices-to-selectors ratio. Thus, I expect the Inclusiveness Hypothesis to hold true for this party.[3]

By contrast, if the selection process is dominated – *ex officio* – by the parliamentary party (or 'Parliamentary Party Group' in Kenig's terms), I assign it the value 0 for the inclusiveness dummy and label it 'exclusive'. Considering that members of the parliamentary party hold electoral office and that these groups are – compared to the overall party membership – relatively small, they fit well with the theoretical definition of the 'office-motivated party' with its offices-to-selectors ratio greater than or equal to one half. Therefore, I expect the Exclusiveness Hypothesis as well as the Party System Hypothesis to hold for this type of party.

For some cases there was either no indication of how the party leader is elected in the *Data Handbook* (e.g. Labour and Conservatives in the UK; Katz and Mair 1992) or elections took place after 1991. In this event and if available, I use Kenig's data to assign inclusiveness scores.[4] This is a convenient strategy as the correlation between Kenig's and my coding is high ($r = 0.71$). Finally, 18 cases (8 per cent) rely on inclusiveness values adopted from Kenig (2009).

Median Voter Position

Following earlier research (Adams and Ezrow 2009; Adams *et al.* 2004; Ezrow *et al.* 2011; Schumacher *et al.* 2011), data on the electorate's position on the left–right scale is obtained from Eurobarometer surveys (Schmitt *et al.* 2008). From 1972 onwards, each year between 1,000 and 7,000 respondents in each member state of the European Union were asked for their self-placement on a 1–10 point left–right scale. Using this item, I compute for every country year the mean voter self-placement. In contrast to changes in the median voter self-placement, changes in the mean self-placement can be smaller than a unit change. This fact is especially important in this context since these statistics are computed from a large sample of respondents who place themselves on a 10-point scale. Moreover, the mean self-placement approximates the median self-placement as voters are on the whole normally distributed around one mode.

Median Party Member Position

Unfortunately respondents of the Eurobarometers have been asked if they were a member of a political party in 10 panels (1988–1991) only. Even though they were not asked what party they belonged to, they stated to which party they felt closest. Combining these pieces of information, I identify respondents who belong to a certain party and obtain – for the same reasons as above – their mean self-placement.

In order to use more than the 32 cases that party membership can be identified for, I have to rely on a proxy for party members' mean position.

Indeed, the mean party supporter's self-placement, defined as the mean self-placement on the left–right scale of all respondents who state that they intended to vote for a certain party if there was a general election next week, proves to be an excellent proxy for a party's mean member's self-placement. Their values are highly correlated ($r = 0.94$).

If values for the mean voter's or the mean supporter's position cannot be computed due to missing data, the preceding year's values are assigned. If this value is also not available, the following year's values are used.

Party System Type

All parties that compete in elections that lead to a party system whose effective number of parties in parliament is smaller or equal to 2.5 are classified as members of two-party systems. Data on effective party numbers in parliament are taken from Gallagher and Mitchell (2008).[5]

As a result, I obtain a data set including 33 panels of parties in six countries.[6] The time period covered is from 1975 through 2003. In total, there is a maximum of 228 cases of which 34 (15 per cent) represent exclusive parties. An exhaustive list of cases, election dates as well as categorisations of inclusiveness can be found in the appendix.

Model Specification and Estimation Techniques

Since it is reasonable to assume that parties respond consistently to any shift in public or their supporters' opinion, a linear model is the appropriate model to estimate. In order to evaluate the hypotheses, I specify a model of two interaction effects and their constitutive terms (Brambor *et al.* 2006). Therefore, the model reads:

$$
\begin{aligned}
&\textit{Change in party position}(t-1 \textit{ to } t) = \\
&\quad \beta_0 + \beta_1[\textit{Inclusiveness}(t)] \\
&\quad + \beta_2[\textit{Mean supporter's shift}(t-1 \textit{ to } t)] \\
&\quad + \beta_3[\textit{Inclusiveness}\,(t)x\,\textit{mean supporter's shift}\,(t-1 \textit{ to } t)] \\
&\quad + \beta_4[\textit{Mean voter's shift}\,(t-1 \textit{ to } t)] \\
&\quad + \beta_5[\textit{Inclusiveness}\,(t)x\,\textit{mean voter's shift}\,(t-1 \textit{ to } t)]
\end{aligned}
$$

where

Change in party position $(t-1$ *to* $t)$ = the change in a party's rescaled (10-point) CMP left–right score between elections at $(t-1)$ and (t).
Inclusiveness (t) = dummy equal unity if a party is inclusive at (t) and zero otherwise.

Mean supporter's shift (t – 1 to t) = the change in the mean self-placements between election years (*t* – 1) and (*t*) of respondents who state that they intend to vote for this party.
Mean voter's shift (t – 1 to t) = the change in the mean self-placement of all Eurobarometer respondents in this country between election years (*t* – 1) and (*t*).
For all variables expressing differences, positive values indicate policy shifts to the right and vice versa.

Due to the parties being observed at several consecutive elections, I treat the observation for parties as panels. Unfortunately, different estimation techniques for panel data suffer from econometrics' chronic trade-off between efficiency and bias. In order to use the full capacity of advantages and control for disadvantages, I employ two different models: an ordinary Fixed Effects (FE) set-up as well as a Fixed Effects Generalised Least Squares (FEGLS) approach (Wooldridge 2010: 312–15). The FE technique is the gold standard for applied panel analysis. However, it has some disadvantages compared to the FEGLS method, which I describe below.

I address auto-correlation since tests indicate the presence of first order auto-correlation.[7] In the FE set-up, I include a lagged dependent variable (LDV) to eliminate the serial correlation.[8] Three problems arise by employing an LDV. First, if included in an FE model, a bias is introduced (Judson and Owen 1999; Nickell 1981). Second, LDVs capture some of the theoretically motivated variables' effects in the estimation (Achen 2000; Plümper *et al.* 2005). Finally, since there is not always data on the last election's policy shifts some observations are lost.[9] The main advantage of FEGLS over FE models is that it allows for a transformation of the variance–covariance matrix that corrects coefficients and standard errors for first-order auto-correlation. Thus, it does not suffer from any of the mentioned problems.

An additional consideration is that a standard test detects heteroscedasticity in the error terms.[10] Again, the solutions by each estimation technique differ. For the FE set-up the well-known panel corrected standard errors can be used (Beck and Katz 1995, 1996). The FEGLS model allows us to estimate heteroscedasticity, and weight coefficients and the variance–covariance matrix by a corresponding factor to adjust for the disturbance. As a result, standard errors are often more accurate and smaller than their panel-specific counterparts.

Despite the striking advantages of FEGLS over FE, there is an important caveat. Its properties for a small to medium amount of panels (there are 33 in this analysis) may be poor (Wooldridge 2010: 298). Hence, I will present the findings of the more conservative FE model as well as the more desirable FEGLS model.[11]

With respect to the hypotheses, the Inclusiveness Hypothesis is supported to the extent that the joint coefficient on the [*Mean supporter's shift (t – 1 to t)*] and the [*Inclusiveness (t) x mean supporter's shift (t – 1 to t)*] variables exceeds zero and is statistically significant. Similarly, if the coefficient on the [*Mean voter's shift (t – 1 to t)*] variable is statistically significant and positive, the Exclusiveness Hypothesis is corroborated. The Party System Hypothesis is supported if the coefficient on [*Mean voter's shift (t – 1 to t)*] is significantly smaller in multi-party systems than in two-party systems.

Results

To ease substantive interpretation, note that except for [*Inclusiveness (t)*] and [*Niche*] all independent variables are on the same scale as the dependent variable. Also, positive coefficients on the [*Mean supporter's shift (t – 1 to t)*] and [*Mean voter's shift (t – 1 to t)*] variables indicate responsiveness to the mean supporter and the mean voter positions. Second, these coefficients are interpreted in terms of percentages. For example, if the coefficient for [*Mean supporter's shift (t – 1 to t)*] equals 0.7, the party will follow its mean supporter's movement by 70 per cent. Note, again, that this is to ease interpretation of the coefficients, and that it assumes that the public opinion data and the rescaled CMP data are on substantively equivalent scales. In the following, I discuss the general patterns of intra-party franchise and party responsiveness before turning to their differences between party systems.

General Effects of Intra-Party Franchise on Party Responsiveness

Table 1, column 1 contains the results of the baseline model described above, estimated with FEGLS.[12] Focusing on responsiveness to the mean party supporter first, the coefficient of –0.55 on the [*Mean supporter's shift (t – 1 to t)*] variable supports the finding that exclusive parties move, on average, in the opposite direction of their supporters. In particular, the 95 per cent confidence interval is between 22 per cent and 86 per cent of their mean supporter's movement in the opposite direction. This quite striking finding is reinforced by the FE estimate in Model 2, though the standard errors are larger.

Figure 1 consists of two columns of graphs. On the left-hand side, the effect of the mean supporter's shift is shown. On the right-hand side, the same is depicted for the mean voter. Y-axes always show the marginal effect of the opinion changes, *ceteris paribus*, on a party's policy position. In all figures, positive values on the y-axis indicate responsiveness and its values can be interpreted as percentages of responsiveness if multiplied by 100. The x-axes show the different types of parties. Finally, black circles indicate the estimated marginal effect of the FEGLS models and white circles the corresponding estimates of the FE model. In both cases, bars give the corresponding 95 per cent confidence intervals.

TABLE 1
ESTIMATED EFFECTS ON PARTIES' POLICY SHIFTS

	1	2	3	4	5	6	7	8
	Baseline model		**Two-party model**		**Multi-party model**		**Niche-party model**	
Inclusiveness (t)	−0.054 (0.10)	−0.33 (0.29)	−0.55*** (0.05)	−0.44** (0.16)	−0.00097 (0.11)	0.28** (0.13)	−0.0062 (0.06)	0.0064 (0.18)
Mean supporter's shift ($t-1$ to t)	−0.55*** (0.16)	−0.71** (0.34)	−0.74*** (0.07)	−1.00** (0.35)	−0.55*** (0.18)	−0.59 (0.38)	−0.39* (0.22)	−0.47 (0.30)
Inclusiveness (t) × Mean supporter's shift ($t-1$ to t)	0.90*** (0.19)	0.93** (0.35)	2.13*** (0.34)	2.43 (1.52)	0.89*** (0.21)	0.81** (0.38)	0.63** (0.25)	0.66** (0.30)
Mean voter's shift ($t-1$ to t)	0.69* (0.39)	−0.36 (0.77)	1.10*** (0.06)	0.80** (0.26)	−0.35 (0.37)	−1.63* (0.83)	0.44 (0.43)	−0.13 (0.71)
Inclusiveness (t) × Mean voter's shift ($t-1$ to t)	−0.87** (0.43)	0.52 (0.82)	−2.09*** (0.25)	−1.83* (0.80)	0.45 (0.43)	1.97** (0.86)	−0.37 (0.47)	0.30 (0.78)
Niche							−0.094 (0.07)	−0.14*** (0.05)
Niche × Mean supporter's shift ($t-1$ to t)							0.70*** (0.23)	0.69*** (0.17)
Niche × Mean voter's shift ($t-1$ to t)							−0.79** (0.35)	−0.91*** (0.32)
Change party position ($t-2$ to $t-1$)		−0.39*** (0.05)		−0.45** (0.18)		−0.33*** (0.06)		−0.35*** (0.06)
Observations	228	221	21	24	204	197	228	221
Model	FEGLS	FE	FEGLS	FE	FEGLS	FE	FEGLS	RE
Group	Party	Party	Party	Party	Party	Party	Country	Party
Group dummies	Yes	No	Yes	No	Yes	No	Yes	No
Number of parties	33	33	6	9	30	30	33	33

$*p < 0.1$; $**p < 0.05$; $***p < 0.01$, two-sided tests. Robust standard errors in parentheses. Party and country dummies are not shown.
FEGLS = Fixed Effects Generalised Least Squares, FE = Fixed Effects Least Squares, RE = Random Effects Least Squares.

FIGURE 1
MARGINAL EFFECTS OF OPINION CHANGES ON CHANGES IN PARTIES' POLICY POSITIONS IN THE BASELINE MODEL

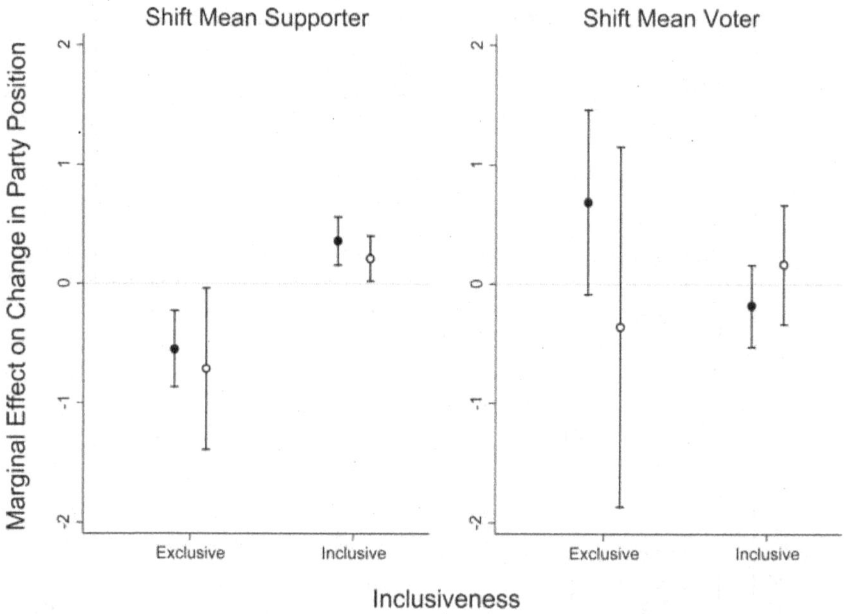

Note: Black circles indicate FEGLS estimates (Model 1), white circles FE estimates (Model 2). Bars give robust 95 per cent confidence intervals.

Turning now to inclusive parties, a first glance at the [*Inclusiveness (t) x mean supporter's shift (t* – 1 *to t)*] estimates in Model 1 and 2 in Table 1 are positively signed, demonstrates that inclusive parties are relatively more responsive to their supporters than exclusive parties. As clearly shown by the right pair of bars in the left panel of Figure 1, both estimation techniques provide strong support that inclusive parties are responsive to their mean supporter's opinion shifts. None of these intervals includes zero and hence they corroborate the Inclusiveness Hypothesis. Indeed, the average inclusive party is found to respond to 35 per cent to the mean supporter's policy shifts, and this estimate is statistically significant ($\beta_{23}=0.35$; $p<0.01$). Model 2 predicts a smaller effect, though this effect is still consistent with the general findings.

With respect to mean voters' opinion shifts, there is some evidence that exclusive parties are responsive to the mean voter position as shown by the estimates on [*Mean voter's shift (t* – 1 *to t)*] in Model 1, being positive and statistically significant ($\beta_4=0.69$; $p<0.10$). However, in Model 2 the corresponding coefficient is negative with a large standard error. These observations raise concern about evidence supporting the Exclusiveness Hypothesis. The null hypothesis that exclusive parties do not respond to the median voter cannot convincingly be rejected. Both of the left bars in the right panel in Figure 1 clarify this observation. The positive coefficient of the FEGLS model (not their standard errors) is consistent with the Exclusiveness Hypothesis. The FE results, on the other hand, indicate point estimates as well as standard errors that do not support the Exclusiveness Hypothesis.

Concerning mean voter responsiveness for inclusive parties, the estimation techniques return point estimates with different algebraic signs for [*Inclusiveness (t) x mean voter's shift (t* – 1 *to t)*] leading to opposed joint effects of the interaction terms ($\beta_{FEGLS45} = -0.18$; $\beta_{FE45} = 0.16$). And, in both cases, the confidence intervals clearly contain zero. Thus, one has to conclude that there is no clear pattern of responsiveness or anti-responsiveness for inclusive parties to the mean voter.

To summarise, the analysis reveals that inclusiveness in party leadership selections does indeed influence how parties shift their positions. In line with the Inclusiveness Hypotheses, I find that inclusive parties respond to opinion shifts of their mean supporters while exclusive parties do not show this pattern. Second, there is weak evidence that exclusive parties respond to the mean voter, but this evidence is very sensitive to the model specification (FEGLS or FE). Finally, there is no evidence that inclusive parties systematically respond to movements in the mean voter opinion. The next section evaluates whether these results hold in different party systems.

Party System Effects

The Party System Hypothesis states that exclusive parties will be more responsive to changes in the public opinion in two-party systems than their counterparts in multi-party systems. In order to test whether this statement holds, I stratify the sample and re-estimate the parameter estimates of Models 1–2 in Table 1. Estimates and standard errors for two-party systems appear in Models 3–4 and for multi-party systems in Models 5–6 in Table 1, respectively.

With respect to responsiveness to the mean voter in two-party systems, exclusive parties are – based on the coefficients on the [*Mean voter's shift (t* – 1 *to t)*] variable in Models 3 and 4 – responsive to shifts in the mean voter position which is consistent with the Exclusive Hypothesis. The confidence intervals of both approaches include an estimated effect of 1 which suggests 'one-to-one' responsiveness of the classical Downsian (1957) party in a two-party system.[13] Models 5–6 in Table 1 show the corresponding results for the multi-party case. In these party systems, it is striking that the FEGLS estimates are close to zero and that the standard errors are relatively large compared to the two-party set-up (Model 3) despite being based on significantly more observations.[14] A similar observation can be made for the FE estimates. Thus, neither model provides evidence to support the Exclusiveness Hypothesis in multi-party systems.

In order to evaluate the Party System Hypothesis, it is necessary to compare the estimates for two-party systems and multi-party systems. The hypothesis is supported if multi-party system estimates are significantly smaller than two-party system estimates. In the right-hand column of Figure 2, this comparison is depicted by the left-hand bars. Comparing FEGLS estimates (black) and FE estimates (white), respectively, it can be seen in Figure 2 that exclusive parties in multi-party systems display less responsiveness to the mean voter position than exclusive parties in two-party systems, and that this difference is statistically significant. This result is consistent with the Party System Hypothesis.

The results on party system size are also relevant for the Inclusiveness Hypothesis, and whether it is supported across the two types of party systems. Results in Models 3 and 4 reveal that in two-party systems, evidence for the Inclusiveness Hypothesis depends on the model specification. As shown by the right bars in the upper left panel of Figure 2, inclusive parties respond positively to their mean supporter's policy shifts according to the FEGLS estimates. The estimated marginal effects of the FE model are rather similar to the FEGLS estimates, however, the FE standard errors are significantly larger. Thus, the Inclusiveness Hypothesis is not clearly

FIGURE 2
MARGINAL EFFECTS OF OPINION CHANGES ON CHANGES IN PARTIES' POLICY POSITIONS IN THE TWO-PARTY AND MULTI-PARTY MODELS

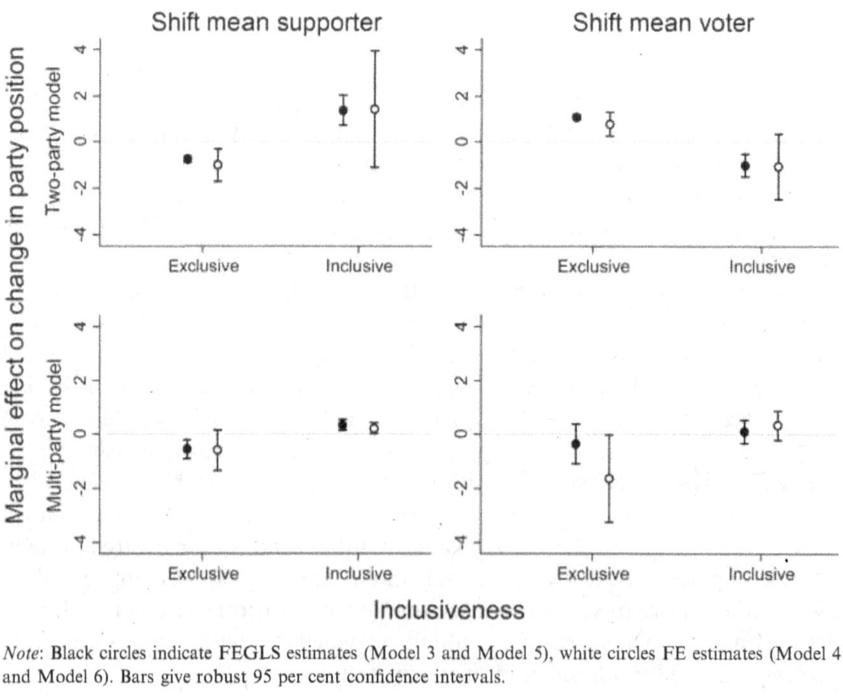

Note: Black circles indicate FEGLS estimates (Model 3 and Model 5), white circles FE estimates (Model 4 and Model 6). Bars give robust 95 per cent confidence intervals.

corroborated by the FE model. Nevertheless, these results are suggestive. Given the few observations present in the sample in two-party systems (21 and 24 cases,[15] respectively), it is not surprising that standard errors are slightly inflated.

The findings for responsiveness to the mean party supporter in multi-party systems are very similar to the baseline model which is not surprising as only roughly 10 per cent of the baseline model's cases are excluded. The right pair of bars in the lower left panel in Figure 2 still support the Inclusiveness Hypothesis.

In sum, the two-party cases support the Inclusiveness Hypothesis and the Exclusiveness Hypothesis (although these conclusions are based on a limited set of observations). While the evidence does not support the Exclusive Hypothesis in multi-party settings – which, in turn, is in line with the Party System Hypothesis – there is strong evidence for the Inclusiveness Hypothesis in this context.

Robustness Tests

This section tests to what extent the results are robust to alternative model specifications and whether they are biased by other potential problems.

Niche Parties

Ezrow *et al.* (2011; see also Adams *et al.* 2006) have recently argued that niche parties, or parties that belong to the Communist, Nationalist or Green party families, are more responsive to their supporters than mainstream parties.[16] In order to test the results' robustness to this alternative explanation, I include a dummy variable which equals 1 if a party is among one of the mentioned groups in the CMP data set (Budge *et al.* 2001; Klingemann *et al.* 2006) and 0 otherwise. Moreover, I interact [*Niche*] with each variable, [*Mean supporter's shift (t* – 1 *to t)*] and [*Mean voter's shift (t* – 1 *to t*)]. Table 2 shows the relation between nicheness and inclusiveness. It reveals that in fact all niche parties in the sample are inclusive parties.

Before turning to the estimation results, there is one more problem to address that arises from this procedure. [*Niche*] is constant over time and hence will necessarily be dropped if a fixed-effects model with party-specific effects is estimated. Ezrow *et al.* (2011) circumvent this fact by shifting to a higher level, namely countries instead of parties, as panels. I adopt their approach because it proves to eliminate most of the party-specific effects.[17]

In order to show that the results are not driven by the fact that country-specific effects differ from party-specific effects, I estimate the model specification as FEGLS, FE and Random Effects (RE) model. The first two models eliminate country-specific heterogeneity, the latter estimates party-specific heterogeneity. Since FE and RE model return almost the same results that differ only in their standard errors, I report only the results of

TABLE 2
DISTRIBUTION OF SELECTORATE TYPES AND PARTY TYPES

	Selectorate type					
	Exclusive		Inclusive		Total	
Party type	**No.**	**Col. %**	**No.**	**Col. %**	**No.**	**Col. %**
Mainstream	34	100.0	179	87.6	204	89.5
Niche	0	0.0	20	12.4	24	10.5
Total	34	100.0	194	100.0	228	100.0

Sources: Katz and Mair (1992) and Kenig (2009) for Selectorate Type; Budge *et al.* (2001) and Klingemann *et al.* (2006) for Party Type.

the RE model in Model 8 in Table 1 because its standard errors are larger in most cases and thus conclusions are more conservative.

If the pattern of responsiveness is driven by parties' (missing) nicheness, the coefficient on [*Mean voter's shift (t – 1 to t)*] should be significantly positive. Moreover, the joint effect of [*Mean supporter's shift (t – 1 to t)*] and its interaction with [*Niche*] should be positive and statistically significant. By contrast, if the conclusions drawn from the baseline models persist, the Inclusiveness Hypothesis is corroborated whereas the Exclusiveness Hypothesis is not.[18]

Regarding Models 7–8 in Table 1 and comparing them to Models 1–2 respectively, although the coefficients and significance levels change, the substantive conclusions concerning the hypotheses do not change when controlling for niche parties. In both model specifications, responsiveness to the mean supporter is strictly positive for inclusive parties. This corroborates the Inclusiveness Hypothesis. Again, neither model finds exclusive parties to be responsive to the mean voter. Hence, the Exclusiveness Hypothesis is not supported by the data.

Furthermore, the second row in Figure 3 reveals that the observation Ezrow *et al.* (2011) made, namely that niche parties differ from mainstream parties in terms of responsiveness to the mean voter and the mean supporter, cannot be replicated by the RE or the FEGLS model while controlling for inclusiveness. However, the FE model succeeds to perform this task.[19] Therefore, the conclusion for the hypotheses has to be that even if one controls for niche parties, inclusiveness remains decisive in whether parties respond to their mean supporter. These findings support the Inclusiveness Hypothesis. Recalling that all niche parties in the sample are inclusive parties, the analysis provides indication that niche parties may be 'fundamentally different from mainstream parties' (Adams *et al.* 2004) because they happen to be inclusive.

Alternation

Another possibility is that parties naturally alternate their positions in between elections. As Budge (1994; see also Budge *et al.* 2010) argues,

FIGURE 3
MARGINAL EFFECTS OF OPINION CHANGES ON CHANGES IN PARTIES' POLICY POSITIONS IN THE NICHE-PARTY MODEL

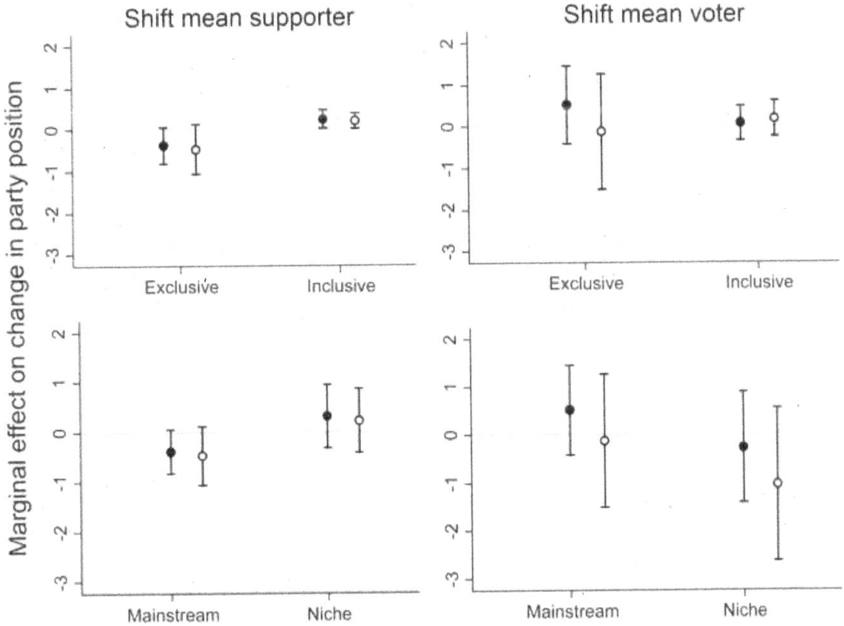

Note: Black circles indicate FEGLS estimates (Model 7), white circles RE estimates (Model 8). Bars give robust 95 per cent confidence intervals.

parties may shift their positions back and forth because of uncertainty. To address this possibility the lagged dependent variable was included in Models 2, 4, 6 and 8. If parties alternate, the coefficient on [*Change party position (t* – 2 *to t* – 1*)*] should be equal to –1. As Table 1 shows, in fact [*Change party position (t* – 2 *to t* – 1*)*] is statistically significant and negative whenever included in a model. However, its effect size is far from 1, which suggests that it is auto-correlation in the error terms that drives the result. More importantly, including the lagged dependent variable does not change the substantive results reported above.

Endogeneity

In order to rule out endogeneity (i.e. that party position shifts cause opinion shifts), I perform a Durbin–Wu–Hausman test (Ezrow *et al.* 2011: 287). I compute the residuals from regressing mean voter opinion shifts and mean party supporter opinion shifts on its lagged values, respectively. Both types of residuals are used to model parties' policy shifts. If opinions are *not* endogenous with respect to party policy shifts, their coefficients are *in*significant. Indeed, these results hold up clearly.[20]

Outliers

With regard to whether outliers drive the results reported above, I re-estimate the baseline models (i.e. Model 1 and Model 2, respectively) without those cases whose residual is more than two standard deviation from the mean residual away. However, results do not substantially change any of the conclusion drawn.[21]

Conclusion

This study derives a model of intra-party competition for party leadership. Since candidates need the support of the selectorate, which is defined as the group of all party members who are entitled to vote in the party leadership selection (Bueno de Mesquita *et al.* 2002, 2003), they are generally responsive to the median selector's ideal policy position. However, if selectors are offered office benefits, they compromise their policy ideals for office. Thus the share of office candidates in the selectorate determines how close the party's position has to be to the median selector's position. Since institutions are crucial for enfranchising party members and thereby determine the denominator of the offices-to-selectors ratio by setting the selectorate's size, they are decisive for parties' policy positions.

The empirical analysis evaluates these expectations against 228 cases from six countries from 1975–2003. Inclusive parties that choose their leader based on widespread membership (e.g. grass-root dominated party conferences or grass-root elections) respond to shifts in the mean party supporter position. This finding holds across two-party and multi-party systems. Moreover, this result holds controlling for niche parties and policy alternation. In contrast, exclusive parties whose leadership selection is based on a few members are not responsive to their supporters. Finally, the evidence reported indicates that exclusive parties do not respond to shifts in the mean voter position in multi-party systems. However, in two-party systems they do.

Besides providing the first analysis of the effect of intra-party institutions (i.e. intra-party franchise in leadership selections) on party positions and party responsiveness, this article has three important implications for future research. First and with respect to coalition behaviour (Giannetti and Benoit 2009), exclusive parties should be more flexible to accept compromises and hence more likely to be members of a coalition government. Similarly, inclusive parties should be less forbearing with its leaders if they implement unpopular policies from the party members' point of view, and less likely compromise their ideology to remain in a governing coalition. Hence, theories that combine intra-party politics and coalition politics should analyse the effect of intra-party democracy on parties' willingness to join coalitions as well as their inclination to terminate them.

Second, an obvious implication of this study is that countries that produce legislation that affects intra-party institutions will affect patterns of party responsiveness. Powell (2004) highlights the delegation of interests in democracies via a 'chain of responsiveness'. Müller (2000) points to the crucial role of parties in these delegation processes. This paper adds to this knowledge the insight that intra-party institutions affect whose preferences dominate a party's policy. Hence, political systems that impose inclusive party structure on parties by law (e.g. Germany) should have different patterns of responsiveness to the mean voter than political systems without these restrictions.

Third, Schumacher *et al.* (2011) raise doubt about the explanation that niche parties (i.e. parties from Communist, Nationalist or Ecologist party families) respond to their mean supporters rather than the mean voter because of 'ideological' aspects (Adams *et al.* 2006; Ezrow *et al.* 2011). In this paper, I not only make their argument more specific by pointing out the importance of enfranchising institutions in leadership selections, yet I also control for the alternative niche-party approach. As a result, I find strong indication that niche parties are responsive to their mean supporters because they are internally democratic parties. Nevertheless, this does not prove that the ideological explanation is false. It rather raises the question whether certain party ideologies lead to specific internal institutions which, in turn, lead to responsiveness to the mean voter or the mean supporter.

Acknowledgements

I thank Lawrence Ezrow, Hugh Ward, Thomas Plümper, the two anonymous reviewers and the special issue's editors for very valuable comments on previous versions of this paper. Moreover, I thank Ofer Kenig for kindly sharing his data. Research on this project was supported by the Economic and Social Science Research Council (Grant ID: ES/J500045/1).

Notes

1. For Italy data is available, yet, there is massive doubt about the validity of the CMP left–right scale (Pelizzo 2003). Thus, like Meyer (2010) and Schumacher *et al.* (2011) I exclude Italy from the analysis.
2. To do so, I use the formula: ([*CMP value*] × (9/200)) + 5.5.
3. Within the 194 cases of the inclusive category, 187 cases (96 per cent) originate from Kenig's category 'Selected Party Agency'.
4. Kenig's (2009) data is collected in party leadership election years only. However, these do not always coincide with the general election years that are the unit of analysis here. Therefore, I assign Kenig's inclusiveness values not only in the year for which they were coded, yet, also in the following four years. If a party, for instance, had a leadership election coded in 2000 its inclusiveness value from the year 2000 is used until 2004. Of course, if the party is coded again in 2002, this new value is used.
5. In Germany, CDU and CSU are treated as one party since they always form a 'Fraktion' together and do not run against each other in the electoral competition.
6. These countries are: Denmark (1975–2001), Belgium (1977–2003), the Netherlands (1977–1998), Germany (1976–2002), the United Kingdom (1979–2001) and Ireland (1977–2002).

7. Regressing the residuals of the FE model on its prosecutors results in a negative and statically highly significant coefficient ($\beta = -0.32$, $p = 0.000$).
8. Indeed, this eliminates auto-correlation. The corresponding coefficient (see last footnote) reduces to $\beta = -0.01$, $p = 0.831$).
9. Here, seven observations are dropped.
10. A likelihood-ratio test of the given model specification estimated by generalised least squares for panel data with and without controlling for panel heteroscedasticity clearly indicates that panel specific heteroscedasticity exists ($p = 0.004$).
11. Both estimation techniques may have problems if party supporter and public opinion shifts are highly correlated. However, the corresponding coefficient is found to be $r = 0.34$. Moreover, in 36 per cent of all cases the opinions move even to opposite directions. Thus, the estimation techniques are appropriate.
12. Party-specific intercepts are not shown.
13. Surprisingly, Model 3 as well as Model 4 report statistically significant and strong effects in the opposite direction for responsiveness to the mean supporter for exclusive parties, as shown by the negative coefficient on the [*Mean supporter's shift* $(t-1$ *to* $t)$] variable. These observations of almost perfect responsiveness to the mean voter combined with almost perfect anti-responsiveness to the mean supporter may be interpreted as indication of a trade-off between these two types of responsiveness.
14. Explaining whether the huge variation within multi-party systems expressed by the standard errors can be traced back to certain variables is beyond the scope of this study.
15. Even though 63 per cent of the cases represent British there also German and Irish parties in this sample.
16. For alternative approaches to niche parties see Meguid (2005, 2008) and Wagner (forthcoming).
17. To draw this conclusion, I estimate the baseline model with party fixed effects and compute the party-specific heterogeneity that the model isolates. Subsequently, I use the same model specification while grouping cases according to different criteria to obtain other types of heterogeneity. Looking for the best predictor of party specific heterogeneity, I model it using one of the other types of heterogeneity in each estimation. Among decade-specific, party family-specific and country-specific heterogeneity, the latter proves to be the best predictor of party-specific heterogeneity.
18. There are no niche parties in two-party systems in the sample, therefore, the Party System Hypothesis cannot be tested.
19. The FE model finds the marginal effect of the mean supporter's policy shift on a party's policy movement to be positive. Moreover, this result is significant with 95 per cent confidence intervals.
20. The p-value for the coefficient on the residuals of mean party supporters' shifts is 0.404. The corresponding value for mean voter position shifts is 0.656.
21. The only observable difference is that the marginal effect for exclusive parties and their response to party supporter opinion shifts in the FE model is no longer statistically significant with 95 per cent confidence intervals, yet with 90 per cent confidence intervals. All results are available from the author upon request.

References

Achen, Christopher H. (2000). 'Why Lagged Dependent Variables Can Suppress the Explanatory Power of Other Independent Variables', unpublished paper, University of Michigan.

Adams, James, and Lawrence Ezrow (2009). 'Who Do European Parties Represent? How Western European Parties Represent the Policy Preferences of Opinion Leaders', *Journal of Politics*, 71:1, 206–223.

Adams, James, and Samuel Merrill III (2006). 'Why Small, Centrist Third Parties Motivate Policy Divergence by Major Parties', *American Political Science Review*, 100:3, 403–417.

Adams, James, Michael Clark, Lawrence Ezrow, and Garrett Glasgow (2004). 'Understanding Change and Stability in Party Ideologies: Do Parties Respond to Public Opinion or to Past Election Results?', *British Journal of Political Science*, 34, 589–610.

Adams, James, Michael Clark, Lawrence Ezrow, and Garrett Glasgow (2006). 'Are Niche Parties Fundamentally Different from Mainstream Parties? The Causes and the Electoral Consequences of Western European Parties' Policy Shifts, 1976–1998', *American Journal of Political Science*, 50:3, 513–529.

Austen-Smith, David, and Jeffrey Banks (1988). 'Elections, Coalitions, and Legislative Outcomes', *American Political Science Review*, 82:2, 405–422.

Bäck, Hanna (2008). 'Intra-Party Politics and Coalition Formation: Evidence from Swedish Local Government', *Party Politics*, 14:1, 71–89.

Beck, Nathaniel, and Jonathan N. Katz (1995). 'What to do (and not to do) with Time-Series Cross-Section Data', *American Political Science Review*, 89:3, 643–647.

Beck, Nathaniel, and Jonathan N. Katz (1996). 'Nuisance vs. Substance: Specifying and Estimating Time-Series-Cross-Section Models', *Political Analysis*, 6:1, 1–36.

Benoit, Kenneth, and Michael Laver (2006). *Party Policy in Modern Democracies*. London and New York: Routledge.

Brambor, Thomas, William R. Clark, and Matt Golder (2006). 'Understanding Interaction Models: Improving Empirical Analyses', *Political Analysis*, 14:1, 63–82.

Budge, Ian (1994). 'A New Spatial Theory of Party Competition: Uncertainty, Ideology and Policy Equilibria Viewed Comparatively and Temporally', *British Journal of Political Science*, 24, 443–467.

Budge, Ian, Dieter Klingemann, Andrea Volkens, Judith Bara, and Eric Tanenbaum, eds. (2001). *Mapping Policy Preferences. Estimates for Parties, Electors, and Governments 1945–1998*. Oxford: Oxford University Press.

Budge, Ian, Lawrence Ezrow, and Michael D. McDonald (2010). 'Ideology, Party Factionalism and Policy Change: An Integrated Dynamic Theory', *British Journal of Political Science*, 40, 781–804.

Bueno de Mesquita, Bruce, James D. Morrow, Randolph M. Siverson, and Alastair Smith (2002). 'Political Institutions, Policy Choice and the Survival of Leaders', *British Journal of Political Science*, 32, 559–590.

Bueno de Mesquita, Bruce, Alastair Smith, Randolph M. Siverson, and James D. Morrow (2003). *The Logic of Political Survival*. London: The MIT Press.

Calvert, Randall L. (1985). 'Robustness of the Multidimensional Voting Model: Candidate Motivations, Uncertainty, and Convergence', *American Journal of Political Science*, 29:1, 69–95.

Cox, Gary W. (1990a). 'Multicandidate Spatial Competition', in James Enelow and Melvin Hinich (eds.), *Advances in the Spatial Theory of Voting*. Cambridge: Cambridge University Press, 179–198.

Cox, Gary W. (1990b). 'Centripetal and Centrifugal Incentives in Electoral Systems', *American Journal of Political Science*, 34:4, 903–935.

Davis, Otto A., Melvin J. Hinich, and Perter C. Ordeshook (1970). 'An Expository Development of a Mathematical Model of the Electoral Process', *American Political Science Review*, 64:2, 426–448.

Downs, Anthony (1957). *An Economic Theory of Democracy*. New York: Harper & Row.

Ezrow, Lawrence (2008). 'Parties' Policy Programmes and the Dog that Didn't Bark: No Evidence that Proportional Systems Promote Extreme Party Positioning', *British Journal of Political Science*, 38, 479–497.

Ezrow, Lawrence, Catherine De Vries, Marco Steenbergen, and Erica Edwards (2011). 'Mean Voter Representation and Partisan Constituency Representation: Do Parties Respond to the Mean Voter Position or to Their Supporters?', *Party Politics*, 17:3, 275–301.

Gallagher, Michael, and Paul Mitchell (2008). *The Politics of Electoral Systems*. Oxford: Oxford University Press.

Giannetti, Daniela, and Kenneth Benoit, eds. (2009). *Intra-party Politics and Coalition Governments*. London: Routledge.

Hearl, Derek J. (2001). 'Checking the Party Policy Estimates: Reliability', in Ian Budge, Dieter Klingemann, Andrea Volkens, Judith Bara, and Eric Tanenbaum (eds.), *Mapping Policy Preferences. Estimates for Parties, Electors, and Governments 1945–1998*. Oxford: Oxford University Press, 111–126.

Hix, Simon, Abdul Noury, and Gérald Roland (2006). 'Dimensions of Politics in the European Parliament', *American Journal of Political Science*, 50:2, 494–520.

Huber, John, and Ronald Inglehart (1995). 'Expert Interpretations of Party Space and Party Locations in 42 Societies', *Party Politics*, 1:1, 73–111.

Inglehart, Ronald (1990). *Culture Shift in Advanced Industrial Society*. Princeton, NJ: Princeton University Press.

Judson, Ruth A., and Ann L. Owen (1999). 'Estimating Dynamic Panel Data Models: A Guide for Macroeconomists', *Economics Letters*, 65, 9–15.

Katz, Richard S., and Peter Mair, eds. (1992). *Party Organizations: A Data Handbook on Party Organizations in Western Democracies, 1960–90*. London: Sage.

Kenig, Ofer (2009). 'Classifying Party Leaders' Selection Methods in Parliamentary Democracies', *Journal of Elections, Public Opinion and Parties*, 19:4, 433–447.

Klingemann, Hans-Dieter, Andrea Volkens, Judith L. Bara, Ian Budge, and Michael D. McDonald (2006). *Mapping Policy Preferences II. Estimates for Parties, Electors, and Governments in Eastern Europe, European Union, and OECD 1990–2003*. Oxford: Oxford University Press.

Laver, Michael, Kenneth Benoit, and John Garry (2003). 'Extracting Policy Positions from Political Texts Using Words as Data', *American Political Science Review*, 97:2, 311–331.

Luebbert, Gregory M. (1986). *Comparative Democracy. Policy Making and Governing Coalitions in Europe and Israel*. New York: Columbia University Press.

Marks, Gary (2007). 'Special Issue: Comparing Measures of Party Positioning: Expert, Manifesto and Survey Data', *Electoral Studies*, 26:1, 1–234.

McDonald, Michael D., and Silvia M. Mendes (2001). 'Checking the Party Policy Estimates: Convergent Validity', in Ian Budge, Dieter Klingemann, Andrea Volkens, Judith Bara, and Eric Tanenbaum (eds.), *Mapping Policy Preferences. Estimates for Parties, Electors, and Governments 1945–1998*. Oxford: Oxford University Press, 127–142.

Meguid, Bonnie M. (2005). 'Competition Between Unequals: The Role of Mainstream Party Strategy in Niche Party Success', *American Political Science Review*, 99:3, 348–359.

Meguid, Bonnie M. (2008). *Party Competition between Unequals. Strategies and Electoral Fortunes in Western Europe*. New York: Cambridge University Press.

Merrill III, Samuel, and James F. Adams (2002). 'Centrifugal Incentives in Multi-Candidate Elections', *Journal of Theoretical Politics*, 14:3, 275–300.

Meyer, Thomas (2010). *Party Competition Over Time: How Voters and Intra-party Structure Constrain Party Policy Shifts*. MADOC, available at http://madoc.bib.uni-mannheim.de/madoc/volltexte/2010/2938/ (accessed 17 March 2011).

Müller, Wolfgang C. (2000). 'Political Parties in Parliamentary Democracies: Making Delegation and Accountability Work', *European Journal of Political Research*, 37, 309–333.

Nickell, Stephen (1981). 'Biases in Dynamic Models with Fixed Effects', *Econometrica*, 49:6, 1417–1426.

Pelizzo, Riccardo (2003). 'Party Positions or Party Direction? An Analysis of Party Manifesto Data', *West European Politics*, 26:2, 67–89.

Plümper, Thomas, Vera E. Troeger, and Phillip Manow (2005). 'Panel Data Analysis in Comparative Politics: Linking Method to Theory', *European Journal of Political Research*, 44:2, 327–354.

Powell, G. Bingham (2004). 'The Chain of Responsiveness', *Journal of Democracy*, 15:4, 91–105.

Schmitt, Hermann, Eva Scholz, Iris Leim, and Meinhard Moschner (2008). *The Mannheim Eurobarometer Trend File 1970–2002. 2.0.1*. Leibniz: GESIS – Leibniz Institute for the Social Sciences.

Schofield, Norman (1993). 'Political Competition and Multiparty Coalition Governments', *European Journal of Political Research*, 23, 1–33.

Schofield, Norman, and Itai Sened (2005). 'Modeling the interaction of Parties, Activists and Voters: Why is the Political Center so Empty?', *European Journal of Political Research*, 44, 335–390.

Schumacher, Gijs, Catherine De Vries, and Barbara Vis (2011). 'Why Political Parties Change Their Position: Environmental Incentives and Party Organization'. MPSA General Conference, Chicago.

Slapin, Jonathan B., and Sven O. Proksch (2008). 'A Scaling Model for Estimating Time-Series Party Positions from Texts', *American Journal of Political Science*, 52:3, 705–722.

Strøm, Kaare, and Wolfgang C. Müller (1999). 'Political Parties and Hard Choices', in Wolfgang C. Müller and Kaare Strøm (eds.), *Policy, Office, or Votes? How Political Parties in Western Europe Make Hard Decisions*. Cambridge: Cambridge University Press, 1–35.

Thomassen, Jacques (2005). *The European Voter. A Comparative Study of Modern Democracies*. Oxford: Oxford University Press.

Wagner, Markus (forthcoming). 'Defining and Measuring Niche Parties', *Party Politics*, published online: doi: 10.1177/1354068810393267.

Wittman, Donald (1973). 'Parties as Utility Maximizers', *American Political Science Review*, 67:2, 490–498.

Wittman, Donald (1983). 'Candidate Motivation: A Synthesis of Alternative Theories', *American Political Science Review*, 77:1, 142–157.

Wooldridge, Jeffrey M. (2010). *Econometric Analysis of Cross Sectional and Panel Data*. Cambridge, MA: MIT Press.

APPENDIX

LIST OF PARTIES' INCLUSIVENESS IN ELECTION YEARS

Country	Name of party	Election year										
Denmark		**1975**	**1977**	**1979**	**1981**	**1985**	**1987**	**1988**	**1990**	**1994**	**1998**	**2001**
	SF – Socialist People's Party	1	1	1	1	1	1	1	1	1	1	1
	SD – Social Democratic Party	1	1	1	1	1	1	1	1	1	1	1
	CD – Centre Democrats	–	1	1	1	1	1	1	1	1	1	–
	RV – Radical Party	1	1	1	1	1	1	1	1	1	1	1
	V – Liberals	1	1	1	1	1	1	1	1	1	1	1
	KrF – Christian People's Party	–	1	1	1	1	1	1	1	1	1	1
	KF – Conservative People's Party	1	1	1	1	1	1	1	1	1	1	1
	FP – Progress Party	0	1	1	1	1	1	1	1	1	1	–
Belgium		**1977**	**1978**	**1981**	**1985**	**1987**	**1991**	**1995**	**1999**	**2003**		
	ECOLO – Francophone Ecologists	–	–	–	1	1	1	1	1	1		
	SP – Flemish Socialist Party	–	–	0	0	0	0	0	0	–		
	PS – Francophone Socialist Party	–	–	0	1	1	1	1	1	1		
	PVV – Party of Liberty and Progress	–	1	1	1	1	1	–	–	–		
	PRL – Francophone Liberals	–	–	1	1	1	1	1	–	–		
	CVP – Christian People's Party	–	1	1	1	1	1	1	1	1		
	PSC – Christian Social Party	1	1	1	1	1	1	1	1	1		
	Flemish Christian People's Union	1	1	1	1	–	–	–	–	–		
	VU – People's Union	–	–	–	–	1	1	1	–	–		
Netherlands		**1977**	**1981**	**1982**	**1986**	**1989**	**1998**					
	PPR – Radical Political Party	–	1	1	1	–	–					
	PvdA – Labour Party	1	1	1	1	1	1					
	D'66 – Democrats 66	1	1	1	1	1	–					
	VVD – People's Party for Freedom and Democracy	1	1	1	1	1	–					
	CDA – Christian Democratic Appeal	–	1	1	1	1	–					

(continued)

APPENDIX
(*Continued*)

Country	Name of party	Election year							
Germany		**1976**	**1980**	**1983**	**1987**	**1990**	**1994**	**1998**	**2002**
	90 and Greens – Alliance '90 and Greens	–	–	–	1	1	1	1	1
	SPD – Social Democratic Party	1	1	1	1	1	1	1	1
	FDP – Free Democratic Party	1	1	1	1	1	1	1	1
	CDU and CSU – Christian Democratic Union and Social Union	1	1	1	1	1	1	1	1
United Kingdom		**1979**	**1983**	**1987**	**1992**	**1997**	**2001**		
	Labour Party	0	1	1	1	1	1		
	Liberal Party	1	1	1	–	–	–		
	Conservative Party	0	0	0	0	0	1		
Ireland		**1977**	**1981**	**1982**	**1987**	**1989**	**1992**	**1997**	**2002**
	WP – Workers' Party	–	–	–	1	1	–	–	–
	LP – Labour Party	0	0	0	0	1	1	0	–
	PD – Progressive Democrats	–	–	–	–	0	0	–	–
	Fine Gael	0	0	0	0	0	0	–	0
	Fianna Fail	0	0	0	0	0	0	–	–

0 = Exclusive; 1 = Inclusive; – = not in sample.
Sources: Katz and Mair (1992) and Kenig (2009).

Institutional Context and Representational Strain in Party–Voter Agreement in Western and Eastern Europe

ROBERT ROHRSCHNEIDER and STEPHEN WHITEFIELD

Theories of electoral institutions and representation suggest that majoritarian and proportional systems will produce distinct patterns of party–voter congruence, with the centripetal incentives of the former pulling parties to the ideological centre and reducing, by comparison with the latter, congruence with voters to the right and left. Recent scholarship, however, has found little contemporary empirical evidence for this pattern but no satisfactory explanation has been advanced to account for these non-findings. This paper develops a new theoretical account of the impact of electoral institutions on congruence that takes into account the increasingly dealigned character of voters. The central argument is that the impact of institutions is conditional on the balance between partisans and independents in the electorate. It is this conditional nature of the influence that seems to account for the absence of the anticipated relationship of institutions to congruence nowadays. This theory is tested using a unique data set of party positions in 24 European states and its consequences are drawn out for the relative representational effectiveness of electoral systems in contemporary conditions.

How do institutional contexts influence the extent of party–voter agreement in Western democracies? The answers, until recently, seem to have been settled. For much of the post-war decades, political representation and political institutions seemed to be inextricably intertwined. Much of the available evidence suggests that majoritarian institutions produce less overlap between the preferences of parties, governments, and citizen than proportional regimes (Dalton 1985; Lijphart 1999; Powell 2000), with consequences for our view of the relative effectiveness of each system in achieving democratic representation (Norris 2004).

In the past few years, however, this conventional wisdom has been set aside by several studies that reveal the declining influence of regime type on congruence (Ezrow 2010; Golder and Stramski 2010). This fact was acknowledged recently by one of the foremost analysts of political representation (Powell 2009), who reports that political institutions no longer seem to affect the ideological distance between governments and median voters.

No explanation exists for this surprising finding, which questions not only the relevance of institutions for representation research nowadays but even puts the previously found effect under the spot light: why would institutions have had an effect on congruence in the past if, without change in the institutions, that effect has now disappeared?

This paper tries to answer this question on the basis of the following intuition. Institutions do not affect representation in a societal vacuum. Instead, we begin by assuming that the congruence effect of institutions depends on the characteristics of voters, in particular their degree of partisanship. Our argument, in brief, is as follows. Consider the impact of institutions when electorates are highly partisan, as they were during the 'Golden Era' of political parties (Mair 1997). In this context, where partisan voters tend to be spread across the ideological spectrum, we argue that majoritarian institutions are at a congruence disadvantage as these institutions provide incentives for parties to converge fairly close to the ideological centre even though voters are spread out. However, in a highly dealigned electorate, where many voters are more concentrated ideologically, our argument predicts that majoritarian institutions may actually enjoy a congruence *advantage* because the concentration of voters near the ideological centre maps more neatly onto the institutional incentives for parties to position themselves near the ideological centre. In short, our central argument is that the impact of institutions depends on the degree of electorates' partisanship. To develop this argument, and to provide some empirical evidence for it, is the purpose of this paper.

Theorising the Impact of Institutions on Congruence

To better get at the issue of the impact of institutional effects on party–voter agreement, we will situate the problem in a broader context of party representation and party competition. The achievement of representation, we argue, may vary not only depending on the institutional context but also on the characteristics of voters themselves and how they are linked to parties. The cornerstone of our argument is that voters – and party–voter linkages – have changed considerably over the last decades, and that this change interacts with the institutional environment. In short, we have moved from a partisan model of party–voter linkages, where the bulk of the electorate is closely attached to a party, to a much more dealigned model in which there are many more independents (Dalton *et al.* 1984; Franklin *et al.* 1992). The balance between partisans and independents in national electorates clearly varies across countries. But we note that in almost all party systems nowadays, in order to win elections parties must deal with the challenge of representing diverse voters – both partisans and independents – simultaneously. This follows from the arithmetical fact that electorates these days are generally evenly divided between partisan and independent voters. How in these circumstances can parties represent partisan and independent voters equally well? This difficulty we refer to as representational strain (Rohrschneider and Whitefield 2012: chapter 2).

To understand the representational strain created by these two types of voters, let us consider the different character of independents and partisans. A classical statement on the psychological origins of partisanship can be found in the US literature which assumes that 'many people associate themselves psychologically with one or the other of the parties, and that this identification has predictable relationships with their perceptions, evaluations, and actions' (Campbell *et al.* 1954: 90; see also Budge *et al.* 1976). This perspective argues that voters with partisan loyalties differ in significant ways from independent voters. To start with, partisans are likely to agree with the issue positions of parties because these formulate issues based on the interests of its social base. In other words, the shared social origins of parties and voters entail that partisan constituencies probably hold ideological views that resemble the policy stances of parties. Psychological mechanisms also help to reduce the perceived distance between parties and voters with partisan loyalties, as when partisans are predisposed to accept the messages from party leaders. Independents, in contrast, lack characteristics that aid in reducing the opinion distance between parties and voters. By definition, they lack a close psychological connection to a party and thus their perceptions are not influenced by distance-reducing mechanisms. For instance, independents are less likely to look for partisan cues when forming issue positions, less likely to project their own views onto those of parties, and less likely to agree with parties on the basis of shared social roots.

From a representational perspective, all of this means that mainstream parties face trade-offs that will probably shape their policy choices and programmes, which in turn influences the degree of opinion agreement with partisans and independents. We can highlight the representational consequences through two mechanisms of representation. At one polar end, we see a partisan mode of representation. This mode predominates when the large majority of electorates consist of loyal party supporters connected to parties through socially grounded pillars. In this scenario, voter ideologies tend to be spread out across the ideological spectrum. At the other polar end is a dealignment mode of representation. Here, the overall ideological orientations tend to be concentrated nearer the ideological centre because in this scenario electorates mostly consist of independents.[1] Therefore, parties must compete in very different ways for voters given their characteristics and given that what counts is to attract the largest number of possible voters.

We view these two mechanisms as ideal-typical models that can be superimposed on reality in order to determine where party systems stand nowadays. Given the relative size of partisans and independents in current European electorates, which often approach a 50–50 split between partisans and independents, neither mode fully captures any party system in Europe. But thinking about them helps to sharpen our expectation about how representation occurs given the relative numerical size of partisans and independents. This, then, creates the representational strain for parties: they must compete for both types of voters which creates difficulties for parties to be ideologically close to both of them simultaneously. In some cases, they may be drawn towards their partisan supporters, which will tend to reduce the congruence of their positions with their supporters who are independents. In other cases, the opposite might apply. In short: the *way parties compete for these voters nowadays affects the degree of representation of groups*.

To get at how institutional design might affect congruence given the current electoral context, we next consider the ways that institutions may mediate the representation of different voter groups.

The Influence of Institutions on Congruence

The research literature clearly sets up the expectation that institutions influence the degree of ideological agreement between parties and voters (Dalton 1985; Ezrow 2010; Lijphart 1999; Powell 2000; Thomassen 1994). Put simply, it is often argued theoretically that parties in majoritarian electoral systems with mechanical restrictions on the number of effective parties will have greater incentives to compete near to the median voter. From this simple Downs/Duverger perspective, therefore, parties in majoritarian systems *should* be close to the median voter (Powell 2000). However, in the past, this expectation has not been met empirically because governments in majoritarian institutions are usually further away from the median voter than under proportional regimes. The central thrust of explanations for this unexpected empirical pattern is that parties may be pulled away from the median voter by party activists (Garrett and Lange 1989; Kitschelt 1994; Powell and Vanberg 2000). In turn, in proportional systems, there are more parties (because of the lower thresholds to enter legislatures) distributed along the ideological spectrum which initially leads one to predict that parties here, too, are on average removed from the median voter. This theoretical logic alone might suggest an empirical 'wash' regarding the predicted influence of institutions on congruence. However, empirically, it turns out that if the median legislative party is included in post-election negotiations, then proportional regimes are, on average, closer to the median voter than in majoritarian regimes (Powell 2000). Theoretically, then, there is no clear basis on which to predict the impact of institutions on levels on congruence, at least not conceptually, though empirically it turned out to be the case in the past that proportional regimes enjoyed a congruence advantage.

More recently, however, one prominent proponent of this approach actually suggests that, despite the fact that institutions themselves have changed little, the majoritarian character of institutions no longer affects party–voter agreement (Powell 2009: 1493) and concludes that this is 'an area that will require further investigation. At the moment we do not know if the 1996–2004 decade represents a random fluctuation (of the few SMD elections), the outcome of short-term global or ideological context, or a trend'.

Our own theoretical and empirical focus may provide a basis to address this puzzle about the changing relationship between institutions and congruence. Our argument begins with the question: what happens to the impact of institutions in conditions of *diverse* voters? Does the potential for representational strain attenuate the effect of institutions on congruence? There may be good reasons to believe that this will be the case.

The emphasis of the extant research literature on national institutions assumes that the main variation in ideological voter–party agreement occurs across countries. That is to say, this perspective assumes that national institutions push *entire* electorates (often represented by the median voter) towards agreement with parties (or governments), or away from it. Indeed, this is the way that Downs (1957: 123–5) explained cross-national differences in party–voter agreement. However, our argument about representational strain assumes that there are two different sets of voter distributions *within* countries that affect the degree of representation: partisans and independents. Each of these types of voters holds a different set of interests, and a different way of viewing the choices offered by parties (as we argued above). And parties compete for these voters in significantly different ways. Crucially, therefore, we argue that institutions may affect congruence in different ways, depending on which segment of the electorate we are talking about.

Imagine (again) that parties must appeal both to more centrist independents and more polarised partisans in order to win an election. In other words, their voters will be located at different parts of the distribution, whatever the electoral system under which they are operating. Given this, proportional systems may have the edge in a highly partisan electorate where parties communicate with voters that are (relatively) ideologically polarised. Here, the larger number of parties that proportional systems permit and the fact that they tend to be more spread out ideologically may help them to be, on average, closer to their own voters. In addition, proportional regimes may have a chance, on average, to be closer to the median independent voter as well.[2]

However, this congruence advantage may vanish when a large majority of voters is independent because here voters tend to be more ideologically centrist. At the same time, not all parties can locate themselves near the ideological centre given the incentives of proportional institutions for divergence. Thus, keeping constant proportional institutions, our argument predicts that a declining level of partisanship over time puts parties increasingly under strain to be ideologically proximate to voters, especially independent ones.

The consequences for majoritarian systems are the reverse given specific assumptions about levels of partisanship in electorates. In highly partisan electorates, the incentive structures can produce a congruence disadvantage because parties have an incentive to be near the median voter even though most partisan voters are located away from the ideological centre. This means they face difficulties to be as close to partisan voters as they might be under proportional regimes; and they cannot exactly occupy the ideological centre either because their partisan voters and activists may then defect (as we discussed above). This is the more so because voters typically adjust their voting preferences rather than their issue positions.

However, if we now assume that electorates are largely dealigned, and therefore ideologically centrist, this may give parties under majoritarian institutions a congruence advantage. Under these circumstances, institutions provide incentives to compete for the median independent voter which, in a highly dealigned electorate, is the location where the majority of voters tends to be located. Thus, from the dealignment model of representation, one expectation is that if electorates are highly partisan, proportional regimes are better in providing overall congruence between parties and voters; but in a highly dealigned electorate, majoritarian systems may be better equipped to bring about ideological congruence between parties and independent voters (hypothesis 1).

In short, our argument is that we are better able to understand party–voter congruence if we move away from a static understanding of institutional effects towards a more dynamic one where institutional effects are conditional on the balance of partisans and independents in electorates.

Data

In order to collect party-level information, we conducted an expert survey in Central Eastern and Western Europe. For Central Eastern Europe (CEE) in the autumn of 2007, the analyses presented here are based on 70 parties from 10 CEE countries (see columns 1–3 in Appendix Table A1 for the parties and countries in this study).[3] Nearly simultaneously with the survey in CEE, we also conducted an expert survey in the early spring of 2008, covering 104 parties in 14 democracies in Western Europe (WE).

For each country, we first assembled a master list of experts whom we considered sufficiently qualified to be an expert for our study. First, the most important requirement was that an expert had to have published an article on a party system in the past 10 years. We also required that a scholar published this article in English in a peer-reviewed journal. This demand may seem unnecessarily stringent but assures us that experts had the detailed knowledge about a given party system necessary to answer our long questionnaire in the English language. Second, we canvassed our own contacts for recommendations. If these recommendations met the first requirement (which they nearly always did), we included them in our master list of experts. In total, we assembled a list of 504 names. For each country, we aimed to have 10 completed questionnaires. While there is no fixed number that one should achieve with an expert survey, Huber and Inglehart (1995) suggest that one should obtain a minimum of five experts per country; a strategy that was empirically supported by Huber and Gabel (2000) who show that various expert surveys converge on their estimates for parties' overall ideological orientation. As column 1 in Table 1 makes plain, we have a sufficient number of experts for each country, with many countries meeting the goal of 10, and all coming close to it.

What is more, we achieved an excellent overall response rate for CEE and WE which we attribute in no small part to the fact that we were able to pay experts an honorarium of £50 for a completed questionnaire.[4] If we take as a base the number of experts we approached (regardless of whether they responded to our initial request for participation in the survey) and relate it to how many completed questionnaires we actually obtained, the response

TABLE 1
THE INFLUENCE OF INSTITUTIONAL AND SOCIO-ECONOMIC FACTORS ON IDEOLOGICAL DISTANCE BETWEEN PARTIES AND DIVERSE CONSTITUENCIES

Variables	All constituents	Independent constituents	Partisan constituents	Median IV
Class–vote linkage	–0.18	–0.09	–0.07	–0.23
	(0.216)	(0.226)	(0.204)	(0.240)
Ideological range	0.03	0.01	0.01	0.08
	(0.083)	(0.086)	(0.078)	(0.091)
District magnitude	0.00	0.00	0.00	–0.01
	(0.000)	(0.000)	(0.000)	(0.000)
Proportion of partisans	0.02	0.04	–0.02	0.05
	(0.107)	(0.111)	(0.100)	(0.117)
HDI	0.92***	0.66**	1.12***	0.89**
	(0.282)	(0.287)	(0.286)	(0.352)
Constant	–1.20**	–1.01*	–0.97	–0.99
	(0.572)	(0.560)	(0.626)	(0.805)
N parties	147	146	144	144
N countries	24	24	24	24

Note: Entries are unstandardised regression coefficients in the first row; entries in parentheses are standard errors. $***p = 0.01$; $**p = 0.05$; $*p = 0.10$ significance level. Coefficients were estimated using the xtmixed procedure in Stata 11. All analyses include the following variables at the party level: mass party organisation, party age, governing party status, economic policies (main and squared terms), electoral support. At the constituency level, it includes indicators about voters' class status (working, middle, and upper class status); religious denomination (Protestants and Catholics) and constituents' average age and education).

rate is 52 per cent in CEE and 54 per cent in WE. If we only consider experts who actually responded to our initial request, either by confirming or declining their participation, then the response rate in CEE and WE is 73 per cent and 77 per cent, respectively.[5]

To these data, we added information about party supporters from the European Social Surveys (round 2), including whether they identify with a party or not. We used the ESS because of its large sample size and the high quality fieldwork.[6] We then computed the ideological distance between parties and all voters, as well as the distance of parties to their partisan and independent voters. We counted every partisan of party constituencies as a partisan of a party constituency, including 'incorrect' partisans who voted for a party that does not reflect their party identification.[7] If we exclude these incorrect partisans from the analyses, we receive identical results so we decided to include them. Our decision has the advantage that we do not lose those parties that otherwise would have to be dropped because the number of constituents would have fallen below $N = 20$ – our decision criterion for a minimum number of cases within party constituencies. Finally, a fourth measure captures the distance of parties to the median independent voter. To this end, we computed the median ideology score of voters without partisanship.

Empirical Analysis

We begin the analyses by presenting bivariate relationships between key institutional and societal predictors. At the institutional side, we rely on a country's index of disproportionality as a widely used indicator for the character of electoral systems. This indicator gauges the degree of distortion produced by the electoral laws when votes are translated into seats (Benoit 2007; Cox 1997; Gallagher and Mitchell 2005). This measure correlates with the dispersion of power within a political system (Lijphart 1999), affects the decisions of voters (Cox 1997), and structures the choices offered by parties. We therefore use a party system's index of disproportionality to gauge the incentives for parties and voters to be ideologically close to each other.

Bivariate Analyses

The absence of any relationship is depicted in Figure 1, and confirms recent studies that found little influence of institutions on ideological congruence (Blais and Bodet 2008; Golder and Stramski 2010; Powell 2009). The three graphs display a country's disproportionality index on the x-axis. The y-axis contains the distance of parties to independent supporters, partisan supporters, and the median independent voter, averaged by countries. The Figures 1(a) and 1(b) indicate no relationship at all between disproportionality and party–voter distances. A side-by-side comparison of the two charts

FIGURE 1
THE LINKAGE BETWEEN THE GALLAGHER INDEX AND AVERAGE DISTANCE BETWEEN PARTIES AND DIVERSE VOTERS. (a) PARTY DISTANCE TO PARTISAN VOTERS (b) PARTY DISTANCE TO INDEPENDENT VOTERS (c) PARTY DISTANCE TO INDEPENDENT MEDIAN VOTERS

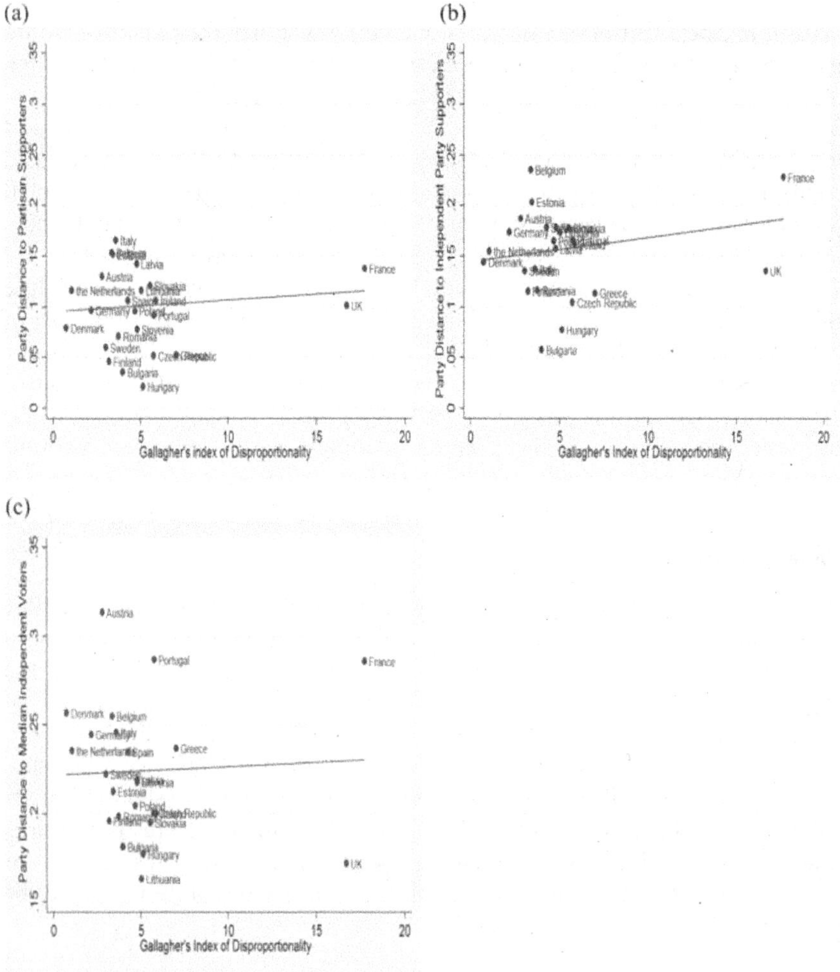

shows that parties are a bit more removed from independents than partisans (as the higher fit line in the graph for independents indicates). Figure 1(c) suggests the same pattern for parties' distance to the median voter: there is very little effect of majoritarian regimes on ideological distance. More formally, when we regress party distances on disproportionality,[8] none of the coefficients for district magnitude is statistically significant. These initial patterns are broadly consistent with the recent reports in the research literature noting the absence of any institutional effects on party–voter congruence.

It is noteworthy that the same general patterns emerge when we use other measures of electoral laws. First, we estimated all models using a country's district magnitude (Benoit 2007) but both the bivariate and multivariate patterns parallel those presented here (Rohrschneider and Whitefield 2012: chapter 8). Second, we used a simple dichotomy distinguishing between regimes with proportional electoral laws and those with other types. Importantly, the results lead to the same substantive conclusions reported here. Of course, one shortcoming of these analyses is that there only two clear instances of majoritarian regimes in Europe (France and Great Britain); all other electoral laws are a bit closer to the proportional polar end. For that reason, we also estimated comparable models using data from the Comparative Study of Electoral Systems data set (round two) and added to it Benoit/Laver and party manifesto data. We were therefore able to compute the distance between parties and voters in two different ways: first we used Benoit/Laver ideology scores; then we employed the ideology score from the party manifesto data set. We then checked whether majoritarian institutions with a broader range of variation of the electoral systems variable has a greater effect on congruence. Happily, the results of these additional analyses are nearly identical to those presented here.

Multivariate Analyses

In order to comprehensively estimate the effects of majoritarian electoral laws on party–voter agreement, we conducted several multivariate analyses. Our aim is to unpack the influence of theoretically relevant institutional variables, controlling for characteristics of parties, their constituencies, and other variables measuring national context.[9] We therefore control for: at the party level, an indicator for mass party organisations, governing status, policy extremism, and electoral success; at the constituency level, indicators measuring the class composition of constituencies, along with their religious orientations, as well as the average age and education levels of constituents; and at the national level, we include a measure of the Human Development Index (HDI).

The two central indicators of theoretical interests are Gallagher's index of disproportionality (measuring the majoritarian character of institutions) and the levels of partisanship in national electorates as the critical mediating variable. We also included a measure of ideological range because it stands to reason that a broader choice-set at the party level affects the distance between parties and voters (Wessels and Schmitt 2008). It is unclear, however, whether it increases the distance between parties and voters because small parties tend to be further away from their constituents than larger parties (Adams *et al.* 2006), or decreases it because more parties articulate the ideological preferences of voters (Dalton 2008). The effect can go either way so we remain agnostic about it in our analyses. We included a measure of the class–vote linkage from each party system as measured by Cramer's V because one study found that stronger linkages reduce the ideological distance between parties and their voters (Dalton 1985). Finally, we incorporated the proportion of partisans at the national level in the analyses because the size of partisanship within electorates in their entirety may affect the ideological distance between parties and their constituents.

The results are straightforward (Table 1).[10] We first note that none at the national level save one is statistically significant. In fact, they are not even close to passing conventional thresholds of significance. This pattern is consistent with the growing number of recent studies that finds no influence of institutions on congruence. Instead, a country's position on the HDI indicator is the *only* significant predictor of party–voter distances at the country level. The coefficients are positive and highly significant for all voter groups, indicating that the distance between parties and various constituencies is larger in the socio-economically more advanced nations. Remarkably, none of the other contextual characteristics comes even close to reaching statistical significance. Institutional characteristics do not directly influence the distance, and neither does the range of choices offered by parties[11] or the size of partisans in national electorates.

Why is the effect of socio-economic affluence so important? While it goes beyond the scope of this paper to fully answer the question here, we speculate that parties have greater difficulties in being equally close to a range of voter groups when the issue space in which they compete is multi-dimensional – as it is in nations that are socio-economically advanced (Kriesi *et al.* 2008; Rohrschneider and Whitefield 2012: chapter 4).

The Conditional Influence of Institutions on Congruence

The analyses thus far suggest that institutions do not directly influence the congruence of parties and voters, in contrast to socio-economic affluence. Despite this result for institutions, and the growing evidence in the research literature that institutions currently do not affect the ideological distance between parties and voters (e.g. Ezrow 2010; Powell 2009), we believe it is too early to dismiss institutional explanations. As we argued above, institutional effects do not necessarily have to be direct because other conditions can mediate the influence of national institutions on party–voter distances. We hypothesised that the effect of institutions on congruence may depend on the level of electorates' partisanship and which voter group we consider.

As a preliminary test of our argument, we computed an interaction term between disproportionality and the number of partisans in national electorates, and then added this term to each of the models presented in Table 1, and re-estimated the models. The goal is to test whether the influence of institutions on congruence to partisans and independents is indeed mediated by the number of partisans in the electorate. Recall that the two alternative hypotheses on the table are that institutions, mediated by the degree of partisanship in electorates, may either affect the distance to partisans (H1) or to independents (H2).

On the whole, based on statistical significance alone, we would have to reject the argument about the mediating role of the size of partisans in electorates as none of the interaction effects passes the conventional threshold of statistical significance ($p=0.05$). However, we note that we have a fairly small sample at the macro-level ($N=24$) which constitutes the number of cases for the computation of standard errors in multi-level models for country effects. We therefore focus on the potentially substantive implications of marginal effects as reflected in the solid lines because we think that these hold potentially far-reaching implications.

An intuitively accessible way to display the conditional influence of the disproportionality index on party–voter agreement is provided by Figure 2, which depicts the conditional influence of disproportionality on congruence for different levels of partisanship in electorates. The solid line in each figure displays the marginal effects; the broken line displays the confidence intervals. If the 0 line of the y-axis is included, it denotes that an effect is statistically insignificant.

The most important result is that the sign of the marginal effects changes in the predicted way: as the degree of partisanship is high, parties in majoritarian systems are further away from various voter groups. However, where the degree of partisanship is low, parties in majoritarian systems are actually a bit closer to their partisan voters (as the negative coefficient indicates). A second empirical observation is that the marginal effects line for the disproportionality index is considerably steeper regarding the distance between parties and independent voters. Indeed, for this distance, the multivariate analyses indicate that the interaction term between disproportionality and the proportion of partisans almost reaches conventional thresholds of significance ($p=0.07$) despite the small number of countries in the analyses. Overall, what is remarkable is that the sign of the coefficients change in precisely the direction that our argument predicts. Majoritarian institutions in highly partisan electorates increase the ideological distance to independent voters whereas majoritarian regimes in highly dealigned electorates tend to *decrease* the distance to independent voters. What is more, this pattern emerges for both independent party constituencies (Figure 1(b)) and the distance of parties to the median independent voter (Figure 1(c)). In other words, this evidence suggests that majoritarian regimes are *actually better at diminishing the distance between parties and independent voters when a large proportion of electorates lack a party identification.* Empirically, then, institutional effects are conditional upon the degree to which electorates are dealigned – especially for the distance between parties and independent voters.

FIGURE 2
MARGINAL EFFECTS OF GALLAGHER'S INDEX OF DISPROPORTIONALITY ON PARTY–VOTER DISTANCE, BY PROPORTION OF VOTERS WITH A PARTY IDENTIFICATION IN ELECTORATES. (a) PARTY DISTANCE TO PARTISAN VOTERS (b) PARTY DISTANCE TO INDEPENDENT VOTERS (c) PARTY DISTANCE TO MEDIAN INDEPENDENT VOTERS

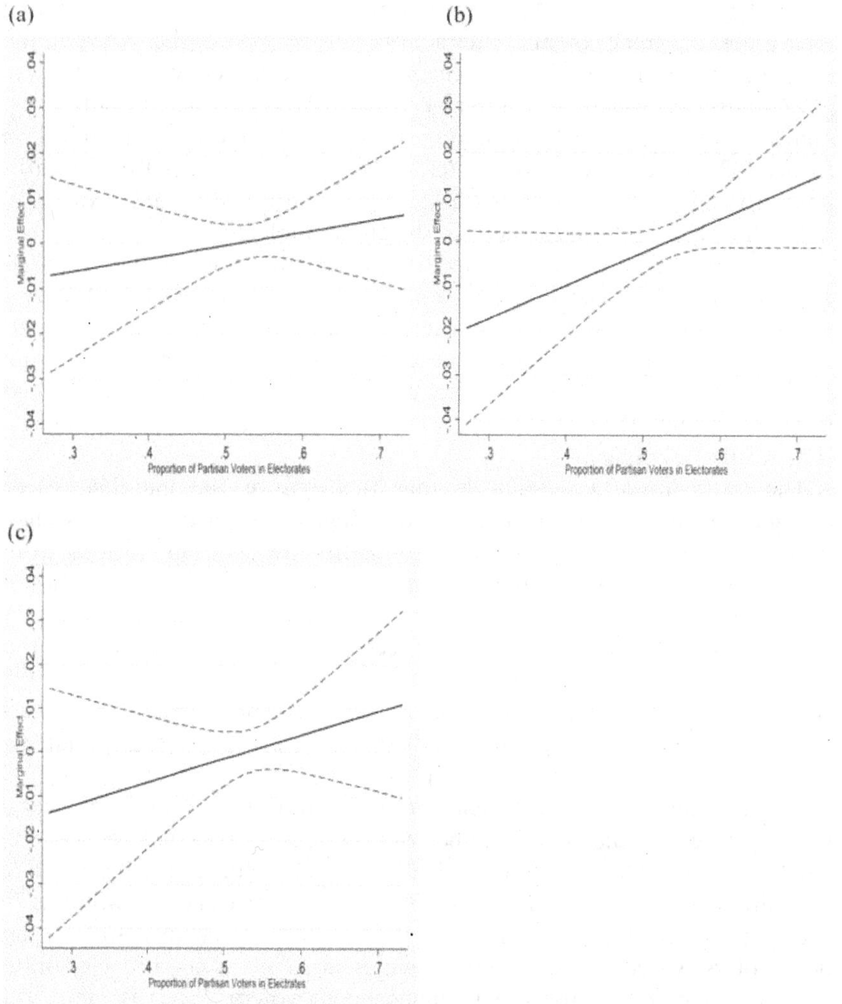

Conclusions

This paper has considered the impact of one of the most centrally important explanatory factors in the political science literature – electoral institutions. It is widely held to structure how parties position themselves and thus how well they can represent voters. No work to date, however, has systematically considered the conditional effect of institutions on congruence. How do parties make their positions congruent with the increasingly diverse and dealigned voters that rising affluence tends to produce? Do institutions matter directly to the representation of diverse voters? And do institutions have differential effects on parties' capacities to represent diverse voters depending on how affluent a country is?

To summarise our results:

(1) Partisan voters and parties line up more closely than parties and independent constituents regardless of the electoral institutional conditions. In short, in line with other recent evidence, proportional systems have no inherent advantage in representing voters, particularly partisans, over majoritarian systems. To account for this, we have suggested a need to reconsider theories of party representation that account for the different characteristics of partisan and independent voters, and how parties compete for them.
(2) The strain of representation, however, is clearly greater in more affluent societies where the issue space is more complex and where, on average, the distance between parties and various constituencies is largest. Thus, while strain emerges everywhere, it becomes *especially* noticeable in more affluent contexts. While we cannot fully explain this finding here, we link it to the greater complexity of the issue space in socio-economically advanced societies (Rohrschneider and Whitefield 2012).
(3) While the effects of institutions vary little by levels of partisanship so far as partisans are concerned, in less partisan aligned societies the centrifugal pressures of proportional systems appear to lead parties further away from representing the centrist independent voter.

An important implication of our argument is that it may help explain why institutions mattered to congruence in the past but exert less influence nowadays. Our argument and evidence point to the possibility that the past impact of institutions was due, in large part, to the distance of parties to independent voters under conditions of highly partisan electorates. This possibility emerges because we find that institutions have little effect on the ideological distance of parties to their partisan voters. Crucially, then, the conditional influence of institutions depending on the size of partisans in an electorate becomes the key. When the proportion of unaligned voters is small, proportional regimes have the advantage; when the proportion of unaligned voters is very large, then majoritarian regimes have an advantage. And, for a transitional period, when both groups are of about equal size, neither regime has an advantage. If this reasoning is correct, then the impact of institutions in the past was largely due to the small number of independent voters. And one reason why Powell and others find no institutional effect nowadays is because most party systems are about equally divided between partisans and independents.

We recognise the tentative character of our argument, but we believe it points to a worthwhile research agenda. In addressing these questions and suggesting these possible solutions, we believe we recast traditional discussions about factors generating party behaviour in quite new ways and reset them for contemporary socio-economic conditions. Moreover, our theoretical approach, supported by the results of our analysis, helps resolve some odd puzzles in the representation literature and points in some quite unexpected directions that should stimulate further research. Finally, the paper highlights again a central problem for contemporary party systems, which face strains in representing diverse voters. If recent research showing that differing electoral institutions had little effect on voter congruence appeared to take the normative sting out of the old debate about the relative effectiveness of electoral institutions in representation, then our findings raise the issue again in a new way. For in conditions of diverse voters and in particular of growing numbers of independents in the electorate, it is now majoritarian institutions that may hold a representational advantage.

Acknowledgements

This article is based on our study *The Strain of Representation. How Parties Represent Diverse Voters in Western and Eastern Europe* (Oxford: Oxford University Press, 2012). We are grateful to Bing Powell for insightful comments on an earlier version of the paper; and seminar participants at the Center for Democracy, UC Irvine, for helpful comments.

Notes

1. See Rohrschneider and Whitefield (2012: chapter 5) for empirical evidence on this point.
2. In this situation, parties can compete for voters near the moderate left, moderate right and at centrist ideological locations, whereas parties in majoritarian regimes only compete at the moderate left and moderate right but not in the centre. This increases the odds that parties, on average, are closer to the median voter. Although this logic does not have to play out in reality with mathematical necessity, it is a statement of odds.
3. The second wave CEE expert survey was undertaken thanks to the support of an EU FP7 grant, 'Social Inequality and Why It Matters for the Economic and Political Development of Europe and Its Citizens: Post-Communist Central and Eastern Europe in Comparative Perspective' (EUREQUAL).
4. The Nuffield Foundation supported our surveys so we were able to provide respondents with this incentive. In addition, each expert received the party-level data set for her/his country.
5. In order to assess the validity of our expert surveys, we merged the ideology indicators from our 2007–2008 surveys with those from the Chapel Hill group as well and the ideology estimates from Benoit and Laver's expert survey (2006) and the Comparative Manifesto data. Various analyses indicate that all surveys produce nearly identical estimates for parties' overall ideological position. The relationship between the Rohrscheider/Whitefield (RW) survey and the Chapel Hill surveys, for 132 shared parties, is $r = 0.91$; and the relationships are of comparable magnitude in CEE and WE. We find similarly strong relationships between our ideology indicators and that generated by the Bennoit/Laver expert survey ($r = 0.95$ in the pooled data; and $r = 0.93$ and $r = 0.96$ in CEE

and WE, respectively). The relationships are a bit lower for the Comparative Manifesto data but are still respectable ($r = 0.69$ in WE and $r = 0.49$ in CEE). These results and other analyses (Rohrschneider and Whitefield 2012) suggest that the currently available expert surveys tend to produce comparable estimates of parties' overall ideological position.

6. For 20 countries, we use data from the third round of the ESS (conducted in 2006 and 2007). For the Czech Republic, Greece, and Italy, we use the data from round 2 conducted in 2004 because these nations were excluded in ESS 3. While there is about a three year interval between the collection of public opinion and party-level data, this is less than the five year yardstick Powell (2000: 272–3, n.22) reasonably applies in his study
7. This proportion is very small: 12.5 per cent of voters in the ESS, with nearly identical proportions in CEE (11.6 per cent) and WE (13.5 per cent).
8. We conducted several multi-level analyses, with the distance measures at the party level as the dependent variable, and district magnitude at the independent level.
9. A full description of conceptual underpinnings, empirical results can be found in Rohrschneider and Whitefield (2012).
10. All other variables are presented and discussed in detail in Rohrschneider and Whitefield (2012).
11. We also used an indicator of range weighted by party size, on the grounds that what really matter is the range offered by larger parties (Dalton 2008) but the results are identical to those presented here.

References

Adams, J.M.C., Lawrence Ezrow, and Garrett Glasgow (2006). 'Are Niche Parties Fundamentally Different from Mainstream Parties? The Causes and the Electoral Consequences of Western European parties' Policy Shifts, 1976–1998', *American Journal of Political Science*, 50:3, 513–29.

Benoit, K. (2007). 'Electoral Laws as Political Consequences: Explaining the Origins and Change of Electoral Institutions', *Annual Review of Political Science*, 10, 363–90.

Blais, A., and M.A. Bodet (2008). 'Does Proportional Representation Foster Closer Congruence Between Citizens and Policy Makers?', *Comparative Political Studies*, 39:10, 1243–62.

Budge, I., I. Crewe, and D.J. Fairlie (1976). *Party Identification and Beyond: Representations of Voting and Party Competition*. London and New York: Wiley.

Campbell, A., G. Gurin, and W.E. Miller (1954). *Voter Decides*. Evanston, IL: Row, Peterson.

Cox, G. (1997). *Making Votes Count*. New York: Cambridge University Press.

Dalton, R.J. (1985). 'Political Parties and Political Representation. Party Supporters and Party Elites in Nine Nations', *Comparative Political Studies*, 18:3, 267–99.

Dalton, R.J. (2008). 'The Quantity and the Quality of Party Systems. Party System Polarization, its Measurement, and Its Consequences', *Comparative Political Studies*,41:7, 899–920.

Dalton, R.J., S.C. Flanagan, P.A. Beck, and J.E. Alt, eds. (1984). *Electoral Change in advanced Industrial Democracies: Realignment or Dealignment?* Princeton, NJ: Princeton University Press.

Downs, A. (1957). *An Economic Theory of Democracy*. New York: Harper & Row.

Ezrow, L. (2010). *Linking Citizens and Parties*. Oxford: Oxford University Press.

Franklin, M., T. MacKie, H. Valen, and C. Bean (1992). *Electoral Change: Responses to Evolving Social and Attitudinal Structures in Western Countries*. Cambridge and New York: Cambridge University Press.

Gallagher, M., and P. Mitchell, eds. (2005). *The Politics of Electoral Systems*. Oxford: Oxford University Press.

Garrett, G., and P. Lange. (1989). 'Government Partisanship and Economic Performance: When and How does "Who Governs" Matter?', *Journal of Politics*, 51:3, 676–93.

Golder, M., and J. Stramski (2010). 'Ideological Congruence and Electoral Institutions', *American Journal of Political Science*, 54:1, 90–106.

Huber, J., and M. Gabel (2000). 'Putting Parties in their Place: Inferring Party Left-Right Ideological Positions from Manifestos Data', *American Journal of Political Science*, 44:1, 94–103.

Huber, J., and R. Inglehart (1995). 'Expert Interpretations of Party Space and Party Locations in 42 Societies', *Party Politics*, 1:1, 73–111.

Kitschelt, H. (1994). *The Transformation of European Social Democracy*. New York: Cambridge University Press.

Kriesi, H., E. Grande, R. Lachat, M. Dolezal, S. Bornschier, and T. Frey, eds. (2008). *West European Politics in the Age of Globalization*. Cambridge: Cambridge University Press.

Lijphart, A. (1999). *Patterns of Demcoracy*. New Haven, CT: Yale University Press.

Mair, P. (1997). *Party System Change: Approaches and Interpretations*. Oxford: Oxford University Press.

Norris, P. (2004). *Electoral Engineering: Voting Rules and Political Behaviour*. Cambridge: Cambridge University Press.

Powell, G.B. (2000). *Elections as Instruments of Democracy*. New Haven, CT: Yale University Press.

Powell, G.B. (2009). 'The Ideological Congruence Controversy: The Impact of Alternative Measures, Data, and Time Periods on the Effects of Election Rules', *Comparative Political Studies*, 42:12, 1475–97.

Powell, G.B., and G.S. Vanberg (2000). 'Election Laws, Disproportionality, and Median Correspondence: Implications for Two Visions of Democracy', *British Journal of Political Science*, 30:3, 383–411.

Rohrschneider, R., and S. Whitefield (2012). *The Strain of Representation: How Parties Represent Diverse Voters in Western and Eastern Europe*. Oxford: Oxford University Press.

Thomassen, J. (1994). 'Empirical Research into Political Representation: Failing Democracy or Failing Models?', in M.K. Jennings and T.E. Mann (eds.), *Elections at Home and Abroad: Essays in Honor of Warren Miller*. Ann Arbor: University of Michigan Press, 237–65.

Wessels, B., and H. Schmitt (2008). 'Meaningful Choices, Political Supply, and Institutional Effectiveness', *Electoral Studies*, 27, 19–30.

APPENDIX

TABLE A1
COUNTRIES AND PARTIES INCLUDED IN THE RW SURVEYS ARE LISTED IN THE FIRST AND SECOND COLUMN, WITH THE NUMBER OF COMPLETED QUESTIONNAIRES OBTAINED FOR EACH COUNTRY LISTED IN PARENTHESES IN COLUMN 1. THE FOURTH COLUMN INDICATES WHETHER A PARTY IS ALSO INCLUDED IN THE EUROPEAN SOCIAL SURVEY (WAVES 2 AND 3)

Country	Party name in RW survey	Label	ESS
Central Eastern Europe:			
Bulgaria (11)	Bulgarian Socialist Party	CfB	Yes
Bulgaria	Citizens for European Development of Bulgaria	CEDB	
Bulgaria	National Movement for Stability and Progress	NMSS	Yes
Bulgaria	Movement for Rights and Freedoms	MrF	Yes
Bulgaria	Union of Democratic Forces	UDF	Yes
Bulgaria	National Union Attack	NUA	Yes
Bulgaria	Democrats for a Strong Bulgaria	DSB	Yes
Czech Republic (10)	Civic Democratic Party	ODS	Yes
Czech Republic	Czech Social Democratic Party	CSSD	Yes
Czech Republic	Communist Party of Bohemia and Moravia	KSCM	Yes
Czech Republic	Christian and Democratic Union	KDU-CSL	Yes
Czech Republic	Green Party	SZ	Yes
Estonia (10)	Estonian Reform Party	RF (RE)	Yes
Estonia	Estonian Centre Party	EK	Yes
Estonia	Pro Patria and Res Publica Union	IrL	
Estonia	Social Democratic Party	SDE	Yes
Estonia	Estonian Greens	Er	
Estonia	Estonian People's Union	RL	Yes
Hungary (9)	Hungarian Socialist Party	MSZP	Yes
Hungary	Fidesz - Hungarian Civic Union	FIDESZ	Yes
Hungary	Union of Free Democrats	SZDSZ	Yes
Hungary	Hungarian Democratic Forum	MDF	Yes
Hungary	Christian Democratic People's Party	KDNP	
Latvia (10)	People's Party	TP	Yes
Latvia	Union of Greens and Peasants	ZZS	Yes
Latvia	New Era	JL	Yes
Latvia	Harmony Centre	SC	Yes
Latvia	Latvia's First Party/Latvia's Way	LPP	Yes
Latvia	Fatherland and Freedom	TB/LNNK	Yes
Latvia	For Human Rights in United Latvia	PCTVL	Yes
Latvia	Latvian Social Democratic Workers' Party	LSdSP	
Lithuania (10)	Lithuanian Social Democratic Party	LSDP	
Lithuania	Fatherland Union	TS-LK	
Lithuania	New Union - Social Liberals	NS	
Lithuania	Order and Justice - Liberal Democrats	TiT	
Lithuania	Liberals' Movement of the Republic of Lithuania	LrLS	
Lithuania	Labour Party	DP	
Lithuania	Liberal and Centre Union	LCS	
Lithuania	Lithuanian Peasant Popular Union	LVLS	
Lithuania	Lithuanian Poles' Electoral Alliance	LrA	
Lithuania	Civic Democratic Party	PDP	
Poland (9)	Law and Justice	PIS	Yes

(*continued*)

TABLE A1
(*Continued*)

Country	Party name in RW survey	Label	ESS
Poland	Civic Platform	PO	Yes
Poland	Left and Democrats	LiD	
Poland	Self-Defense of the Republic of Poland	SrP	Yes
Poland	League of Polish Families	LPr	Yes
Poland	Polish People's Party	PSL	Yes
Romania (8)	Social Democratic Party	PSD	Yes
Romania	Democratic Party	PD	
Romania	National Liberal Party	PNL	Yes
Romania	Great Romania Party	PrM	Yes
Romania	Conservative Party	PC	
Romania	Democratic Alliance of Hungarians in Romania	UDMr	Yes
Romania	New Generation Party	PNG	
Romania	Liberal Democratic Party	PLD	
Romania	Christian Democratic National Peasant's Party	PNTCD	
Romania	National Iniziative Party	PIN	
Slovakia (10)	Christian Democratic Movement	KDH	Yes
Slovakia	People's Party - Movement for a Democratic Slovakia	HZDS	Yes
Slovakia	Slovak Democratic and Christian Union	SDKU	Yes
Slovakia	Direction - Social Democracy	Smer	Yes
Slovakia	Party of the Hungarian Coalition	SMK	Yes
Slovakia	Slovak National Party	SNS	Yes
Slovenia (9)	Liberal Democracy of Slovenia	LDS	Yes
Slovenia	Slovenian Democratic Party	SDS	Yes
Slovenia	Social Democrats	SD	Yes
Slovenia	Slovenian People's Party	SLS	Yes
Slovenia	New Slovenia - Christian People's Party	NS	Yes
Slovenia	Slovenian National Party	SNS	Yes
Slovenia	Democratic Pensioners' Party of Slovenia	DSUS	Yes
Western Europe:			
Country	Party Name in RW survey		
Austria (10)	Social Democratic Party of Austria	SPO	Yes
Austria	Austrian People's Party	OVP	Yes
Austria	The Greens	GRUNE	Yes
Austria	Freedom Party of Austria	FPO	Yes
Austria	Alliance for the Future of Austria	BZO	Yes
Belgium (10)	Christian-Democratic & Flemish	CDV	Yes
Belgium	New Flemish Alliance	N-VA	Yes
Belgium	Reform Movement	MR	Yes
Belgium	Flemish Interest	VB	Yes
Belgium	Flemish Liberals and Democrats	VLD	Yes
Belgium	Socialist Party	PS	Yes
Belgium	Socialist Party. Different	SPA	Yes
Belgium	Humanist Democratic Centre	CDH	Yes
Belgium	Ecologists	ECOLO	Yes
Belgium	List Dedecker	LDD	
Belgium	The Flemish Greens	GROEN	Yes
Belgium	National Front	FN	Yes
Denmark (9)	Denmark's Liberal Party	V	Yes
Denmark	Social Democracy	S	Yes

(*continued*)

TABLE A1
(*Continued*)

Country	Party name in RW survey	Label	ESS
Denmark	Danish People's Party	DF	Yes
Denmark	Socialist People's Party	SF	Yes
Denmark	Conservative People's Party	KF	Yes
Denmark	Radical Liberals	RV	Yes
Denmark	Unity List - The Red-Greens	EL	Yes
Finland (9)	Finnish Centre	KESK	Yes
Finland	National Coalition Party	KOK	Yes
Finland	Finnish Social Democratic Party	SDP	Yes
Finland	Left Alliance	VAS	Yes
Finland	Green Alliance	VIHR	Yes
Finland	Finnish Christian Democrats	KD	Yes
Finland	Swedish People's Party in Finland	SFP	Yes
Finland	True Finns	PS	Yes
France (10)	Union for a Popular Movement	UMP	Yes
France	Socialist Party	PS	Yes
France	Democratic Movement	MoDem	Yes
France	French Communist Party	PCF	Yes
France	National Front	FN	Yes
France	The Greens	VERTS	Yes
France	Movement for France	MPF	Yes
Germany (10)	Christian Democracy Union	CDU	Yes
Germany	Christian Social Union	CSU	
Germany	Social Democratic Party of Germany	SPD	Yes
Germany	Free Democratic Party	FDP	Yes
Germany	The Left (Party of Democratic Socialism, PDS)	DIE LINKE	Yes
Germany	Alliance 90/The Greens	GRUNE	Yes
Greece (10)	New Democracy	ND	Yes
Greece	Panhellenic Socialist Movement	PASOK	Yes
Greece	Communist Party of Greece	KKE	Yes
Greece	Coalition of the Left, the Movements and the Ecology	SYN	Yes
Greece	Popular Orthodox Rally	LAOS	Yes
Ireland (10)	Fianna Fáil	FF	Yes
Ireland	Fine Gael	FG	Yes
Ireland	Labour Party	LAB	Yes
Ireland	Sinn Fein	SF	Yes
Ireland	Green Party	GP	Yes
Ireland	Progressive Democrats	PD	Yes
Ireland	Communist	SP	
Italy (10)	Left Democrats	Left_Dem	Yes
Italy	Communist Refoundation Party	PRC	Yes
Italy	Italian Democratic Socialists	SDI	
Italy	Party of Italian Communists	PdCI	Yes
Italy	Italy of Values	IdV	Yes
Italy	Green Federation	VERDI	
Italy	National Alliance	AN	Yes
Italy	Union of Christian and Centre Democrats	UDC	Yes
Netherlands (9)	Christian Democratic Appeal	CDA	Yes
Netherlands	Labour Party	PvdA	Yes
Netherlands	Socialist Party	SP	Yes
Netherlands	People's Party for Freedom and Democracy	VVD	Yes

(*continued*)

TABLE A1
(Continued)

Country	Party name in RW survey	Label	ESS
Netherlands	Freedom Party	PVV	
Netherlands	Green Left	GL	Yes
Netherlands	Christian Union	CU	Yes
Netherlands	Democrats 66	D66	Yes
Netherlands	Party for the Animals	PvdD	
Netherlands	List Rita Verdonk	VERDONK	
Netherlands	Reformed Political Party	SGP	
Portugal (10)	Socialist Party	PS	Yes
Portugal	Social Democratic Party	PSD	Yes
Portugal	Portuguese Communist Party	PCP	Yes
Portugal	Ecological Party The Greens	PEV	
Portugal	Democratic Social Centre	CDS-PP	Yes
Portugal	Left Bloc	BE	Yes
Spain (10)	Spanish Socialist Workers' Party	PSOE	Yes
Spain	People's Party	PP	Yes
Spain	United Left	IU	Yes
Spain	Convergence and Union of Catalonia	CiU	Yes
Spain	Republican Left of Catalonia	ERC	Yes
Spain	Basque National Party	EAJ-PNV	Yes
Spain	Aragonese Council	CHA	Yes
Spain	Navarre Yes	Na-Bai	Yes
Sweden (10)	Social Democratic Workers' Party	SAP	Yes
Sweden	Moderate Rally Party	M	
Sweden	Centre Party	C	Yes
Sweden	Liberal People's Party	FP	Yes
Sweden	Christian Democrats	KD	Yes
Sweden	Left Party	VP	Yes
Sweden	Environment Party The Greens	MP	Yes
Sweden	Sweden Democrats	SD	
UK (10)	Labour Party	LAB	Yes
UK	Conservative Party	CON	Yes
UK	Liberal Democrats	LD	Yes
UK	Scottish National Party	SNP	Yes
UK	Plaid Cymru	PC	Yes

Source: Rohrschneider and Whitefield (2012).

Parties' Positions on European Integration: Issue Congruence, Ideology or Context?

CHRISTINE ARNOLD, ELIYAHU V. SAPIR and CATHERINE DE VRIES

This paper models the correlates of parties' positions on the issue of European integration, asking why some parties are in favour of European integration, while others are less favourable or even opposed to it. The paper builds on existing work which has identified three sets of explanatory factors predicting parties' positions on integration: the electorate, parties and party system characteristics. By employing multilevel modelling using data on over 220 parties in 14 Western EU member states for the years 1984 to 2006, the effects of party- and context-level predictors of parties' positions on EU integration are assessed. The findings demonstrate that parties' positions are primarily influenced by EU preferences of the general electorate, parties' left–right ideological extremes and incumbency status. The results also show that the impact of party characteristics is moderated by the electoral context in which parties operate. Moreover, the interaction between both levels offers further insights as to the nature of these associations. Specifically, party size is a robust predictor of integration position only when accounting for the levels of party system's fractionalisation and polarisation. Additionally, parties oriented towards the centre of the ideological spectrum are even more likely to favour European integration within highly polarised systems.

The issue of European integration is turning out to be a force that polarises both public opinion and political elites across Europe. At present, we are witnessing increased public contention over European Union matters in referenda, party competition and media reporting (de Vries 2007, 2009; de Vries and Edwards 2009; Hobolt 2009; Hooghe *et al.* 2002; Kriesi *et al.* 2006, 2008; Steenbergen and Marks 2007; Tillman 2004; van der Eijk and Franklin 2004). The significance of European integration forces parties increasingly to take a position on the deepening and widening of the European project. Despite the growing public interest in the dynamics underlying the integration process, the scholarly debate is still ongoing, and to date there is little agreement on the question of what explains why some parties are in favour of integration, while others are less favourable or even opposed to it. The importance of this question increases further when considering that many political commentators believe that current democratic institutions in Europe are facing severe challenges, which are further exacerbated by the present economic turbulences.

This study revisits the debate on the forces that shape parties' positions on European integration. Previous work has resulted in different findings. Some scholars highlighted the influence of voter positions in defining parties' positions on Europe (Carrubba 2001; Ray 2003; Steenbergen *et al.* 2007), while others suggested that party characteristics such as ideological stances, party size and incumbency status are crucial (Hooge *et al.* 2002; Marks and Wilson 2000). Notwithstanding the importance of these findings, we argue that the party system characteristics, such as the levels of fractionalisation and polarisation, shape and condition both the interaction of parties and the parties' strategic considerations. These characteristics have, by and large, received insufficient research attention, and most analyses do not consider their effect on parties' positions. In order to fully understand parties' position on European integration, we posit that it is imperative to account for the context parties operate in, namely the respective party systems, and its interactions with fractionalisation and polarisation.

The present study unfolds as follows. In the first section, we briefly review the literature on the dynamics of parties' positions on European integration. We focus our theoretical scope on the importance of voter, party and party system characteristics in understanding the dynamics of parties' positions on European integration. Here we build on existing work and develop our hypotheses to be tested in our analysis. Subsequently, we discuss the data and methods we employed and, ultimately, we discuss our findings and reflect on the insights these results provide above and beyond what we already know from prior research on the determinants of parties' positions on EU integration. Finally, we conclude by stressing the broader implications of our findings and outlining possibilities for future research.

Determinants of Parties' Positions on European Integration

What are the factors that explain the positions parties take on a policy issue? This question has occupied the minds of many scholars for decades now. Three groups of explanatory factors stand out in this literature. In many studies, it has been observed that voter positions matter. Building on the work of Miller and Stokes (1963), studies of substantive representation have examined the dyadic correspondence between the preferences of voters and elected representatives' policy positions (Powell 2004). This correspondence is a key mechanism which influences the policy positions parties adopt. Consistent with Downs' (1957) observation that voters tend to prefer parties that best represent their policy preferences in order for them to maximise their electoral utilities, party positions tend to converge to the median voter[1] (see also Enelow and Hinich 1984; Iversen 1994; McDonald and Budge 2005). A second strand of literature highlights the role of party characteristics such the incumbency status and ideological position (Hooghe *et al.* 2002). Yet another line of research directs attention to the importance of the electoral environment in which parties strategise. The classic work of Sartori (1976) for example highlights the role of party systems characteristics, such as party polarisation and fractionalisation.

The importance of the characteristics of party systems for understanding parties' policy positions on EU integration has received far less scholarly attention. In the present analysis, we aim to explore the relevance of the electorate, party and party system characteristics in order to sharpen our understanding of the determinants of parties' positions on European integration. In doing so, we will test existing theoretical perspectives, and will attempt to develop these perspectives further by focusing on the role of party system context.

Party Positions on European Integration: The Role of the Electorate

Much of the general literature on why parties change their policy positions focuses on the role of the electorate (see for example Adams *et al.* 2006; Budge 1994; Ezrow *et al.* 2011). Party responsiveness to changes in the policy mood of the electorate is a cornerstone of dynamic representation and ensures the proper functioning of a democratic system as party elites are likely to follow public preferences when crafting legislation (Erikson *et al.* 2002; Stimson *et al.* 1995).

The evidence concerning the congruence between preferences of the electorate and political parties when it comes to European integration has been mixed. While many studies found evidence of a representative connection on European integration whereby party positions reflect, by and large, the electorate's general preferences for European integration (Carrubba 2001; Rohrschneider and Whitefield 2007; van der Eijk and Franklin 1991), other analyses focusing on party–voter congruence across specific policy areas revealed that in many respects, parties and the public favour a different kind of Europe (Hooghe 2003; Thomassen and Schmitt 1997).[2] Although parties and the public may differ on the exact *content* of the European integration process, it seems reasonable that party elites as rational agents aim to stay largely in tune with public preferences. This seems especially likely in recent years given that increasingly voters utilise their European attitudes when deciding whom to vote for in national and European elections (de Vries 2007, 2010; Tillman 2004). In order to capture the dynamics of the link between parties and the electorate on EU integration, we assess the degree of issue congruence in terms of the correlations between the mean voter and the party positions on European integration. Specifically, we hypothesise that:

> H_1: *The more favourable the electorate is to EU integration, the more likely a party will be to have a positive position on it.*

Party Positions on European Integration: The Role of Party Characteristics

Alongside the positions of the electorate, the literature on party position on European integration highlights the role of several party characteristics. Three factors stand out: party ideology, incumbency and party size. It has been shown that an important predictor of a party's position on EU integration is the ideological stance of the party. Socio-economic issues which are the basis for the classification on the ideological left–right spectrum facilitate the salience of issues for parties (Pierce 1999). Partisan structuring of the left–right continuum partly overlaps with the distribution of support for European integration. In a seminal paper explaining parties' positions on European integration, Hooghe *et al.* (2002) highlight the role of left–right ideology and demonstrate that the further a party leans to the right, the more it tends to favour European integration. In line with this research we hypothesise:

> H_2: *The further a party is to the ideological right, the more likely it is that it will be in favour of EU integration.*

An alternative approach in the literature considers those aspects of European integration that cannot easily be incorporated into the left–right axis as a function of their ideological extremity. Some observers noted that the further a party was towards both extreme ends of the left–right spectrum, the less likely it was to be positive on EU integration. This is the case for parties both on the left and on the right (Hooghe *et al.* 2002). Parties more oriented towards the centre, such as Social Democrats, Christian Democrats, Liberal and Conservative parties, are more supportive of European integration on average (van der Eijk and Franklin 2004). We therefore offer a second hypothesis about ideology and position on EU integration:

> H_3: *The further a party's ideological position is from the centre, the less likely it is that it will be positive on EU integration.*

Another important characteristic of parties is their government experience. Scholarly work suggests that parties' incumbency in government is a key factor in explaining their positions on European integration. Notwithstanding the gradual increase in the power of the European Parliament over the years, which in turn allowed a range of parties to participate in EU decision-making, it is well recognised that national incumbent parties hold a privileged position of influence on EU-level decision-making, through the Council of the European Union and the direct involvement of member states' chief executives (Ray 2003). Given the visibility of incumbent parties in regular decision-making of the EU, and the deep involvement these parties have in the process of EU integration, many of them are being seen as accountable for EU decision-making outcomes in general, and the integration they have advanced over the years in particular. Opting for anti-EU stances may now not be credible for most incumbent parties in light of their deep involvement earlier in the decision-making processes (de Vries and Hobolt 2012; Hooghe *et al.* 2002; Jensen and Spoon 2010). Using this reasoning, we expect that parties' position on EU integration will be influenced by their incumbency status so that:

> H_4: *Incumbent parties will be more likely to be in favour of European integration.*

Finally, party size is likely to matter for the positions parties take on European integration. In this respect, it has been observed that smaller parties have an added incentive to emphasise non-centrist, sometimes even extreme positions (Wagner 2012). The rationale for these parties is that such a strategy may allow them to sharpen their ideological distinctiveness from other parties (Kitschelt 1994; Spoon 2009) and ultimately to develop an issue ownership on European integration (Petrocik 1996). Similar dynamics were found in studies discussing the electoral strategies of the non-mainstream, also sometimes referred to as niche parties (Meguid 2005). These parties often reject the traditional class-based orientation of party competition and were putting forward alternative issues that often do not coincide with existing lines of political division. Conversely, mainstream parties often have an incentive to collude and to not politicise the issue of European integration (Mair 2007). Van der Eijk and Franklin (2004) suggested that in some countries, parties' strategies to differentiate themselves from other parties on EU terms may prove utility maximising (cf. de Vries and Hobolt 2012). Thus, smaller parties that cater towards an electoral niche may benefit electorally from holding extreme positions and conversely get penalised when they moderate their policy programmes. In line with these findings we hypothesise:

> H_5: *The larger a party is, the more likely it is that it will be in favour of EU integration.*

Party Positions on European Integration: The Role of the Party System

Finally, we consider the effect party system context has on parties' position on European integration. Although this factor is often overlooked in studies that examine the determinants of party stances on European integration, the centrality of party systems in organising and aggregating voters' preferences is well noted in the literature (Kim *et al.* 2010). The characteristics of the party systems shape and condition both the interaction of parties and the parties' strategic considerations on issue salience and ownership (Arnold and Pennings 2009). In order to understand parties' position on EU integration we need to account for the context parties operate in. Our understanding of party systems is building on works that highlight the importance of inter-party competition (Lijphart 1999; Sartori 1976). In an effort to better understand the strategic choices parties make regarding the issue of EU integration, we focus our attention on the system characteristics in terms of power sharing. Specifically, we account for the systems' levels of fractionalisation and polarisation.

Fractionalisation, which is often measured in terms of the effective number of parties (Laakso and Taagepera 1979) in the system, was found to be closely associated with higher degrees of issue congruence, since voters have more supply of parties to choose from, and their choice is guided by the match between these parties' positions and their own policy preferences (Downs 1957; Huber and Powell 1994). Building on this work, we expect the level of fractionalisation to have some effect on parties' positions on EU integration.

There is, however, some ambiguity in the literature whether this effect would make parties more likely to take a positive position or negative one on EU integration. On the one hand, building on the work on mainstream and niche parties, discussed above, one can expect party system fractionalisation to influence parties to take an overall negative position on the EU. A higher degree of fractionalisation means that there are more parties competing for votes. This, in turn, is likely to lead to an increase in the anti-EU sentiments within the political system as this strategy allows parties to differentiate themselves from the political mainstream which is largely pro-EU (de Vries and Hobolt 2012; Hooghe *et al.* 2002). On the other hand, these dynamics may very well work in the opposite direction. Given the increase in the effective number of parties, one may expect that the sharpening of these distinctions over the EU issue will result in parties taking sides on the matter (Bardi and Mair 2008). Since the more electorally successful parties are expected to be in favour of the EU, we can expect that a system characterised by higher degrees of fractionalisation will also have more enthusiastic supporters of it (Daalder and Mair 1983). These competing expectations are highlighted in hypotheses 6A and 6B:

> H_{6A}: *The more fractionalised a political system is, the more likely it is that parties within it will be in favour of EU integration.*
> H_{6B}: *The more fractionalised a political system is, the less likely it is that parties within it will be in favour of EU integration.*

Finally, there is a rich body of work that focuses on party system polarisation (Capoccia 2002; Freire 2008; Mair 2003). Polarisation captures how the legislator is divided between parties representing the entire political spectrum, and as such is complementary to the information we receive from the measure of fractionalisation, which provides the number of parties competing for support, and thus is not directly a measure of their ideological leaning (Dalton 2008). Sartori classifies polarised systems as exhibiting a centrifugal force, making parties more dispersed along the political spectrum, as opposed to centripetal forces in less-polarised systems, where parties converge to the centre and compete for the median voter. Recent work suggests another possible link between polarisation and parties' EU positions. Wessels and Schmitt (2008) observed that the greater the degree of party system polarisation, the more differentiated the ideological electoral supply for voters will be. This, in turn, increases the likelihood that parties will be congruent with their voters (Wessels and Schmitt 2008). Due to the fact that recent work suggests that the general electorate is increasingly sceptical about the European project, we expect parties to become less supportive of European integration when party polarisation increases. Consequently, we hypothesise:

> H_7: *The more polarised a political system is, the less likely it is that parties within it will be in favour of EU integration.*

Data and Methods

In order to test our hypotheses and understand the multifaceted dynamics of party positions on the EU, we created a multi-level dataset capturing information on parties, the electorate of eligible voters and political systems in 14 West European EU member states, for the years 1984–2006. In the first stage, we collected and computed annual data points for all our study indicators. Next, we aggregated our information on citizens to the country level, so that it will represent the average positions within the country for each of the years. Finally, we linked the different data components using sampling year, country and party ID as our primary linking keys (van der Eijk and Sapir 2010). The linked dataset was multi-level, and pertained to the characteristics of some 2,458 parties nested within political systems over 22 years.

Party-Level Data: Positions on EU and Left–Right, and Electoral Success

Our source of data on party positions was the Chapel Hill Expert Survey (CHES) on party positioning regarding European integration (Ray 1999; Steenbergen and Marks 2007). The CHES data are longitudinal, and offer expert evaluations of 227 national political parties' positions in 24 EU member states over seven time-points[3] on the issue of EU integration. These data are ideal for our purposes as they include estimates of party positions on both the EU and the left–right dimensions.

Our dependent variable in this analysis was party position on EU integration. This variable was based on CHES experts' rating of each party's overall leadership orientation to European integration, using a seven-point scale. A score of 1 indicated strong opposition to integration, and a score of 7 indicated a strongly favoured position. In order to derive a dynamic measure of these positions over time, we interpolated the CHES data to estimate party positions for the years between the seven CHES waves.

Party positions on the left–right dimension were measured in terms of their stance on economic issues. This metric was based on a 10-point scale ranging from 0 (extreme left) to 10 (extreme right). To obtain the ideological extremity of parties, we calculated their left–right position's distance from the centre point (5). Since theory emphasises ideological extremity with no relation to its direction, we used the absolute values of these distances. To assess parties' electoral success, we employed two further variables. Firstly, we used a binary variable differentiating between parties participating in the national government at the sampling time (1) and for parties that were not part of government at the time (0). Secondly, we used an indicator of party size, which was operationalised by CHES as the vote share each party received in the elections prior to the data year.

Finally, another measure of parties' EU leaning in the CHES dataset was the degree of salience each party attributed to the EU as an issue. We include this variable as a control in the analysis. Issue salience of European integration was measured using a five-point scale ranging from 'European integration is of no importance, never mentioned by the party' (1) to 'European integration is the most important issue for the party' (5).

Political System-Level Data: The Electorate and the Electoral System

Since theory suggests that a certain degree of issue congruence around the issue of EU integration exists (Rohrschneider and Whitefield 2007; van der Eijk and Franklin 1991), and since parties, as rational agents, aim at maximising their vote shares by attracting new voters (Downs 1957; Riker 1982), we were interested in the extent to which parties adjust their EU positions in line with policy preferences of citizens, indicating their vote intention in the coming elections. Furthermore, considering the mixed results discussed earlier as to the importance of left–right position in explaining parties' stance on EU issues, we needed to control for the general left–right leaning in the electorate (Hooghe *et al.* 2002).

To obtain these measures, we utilised data from the Eurobarometer (EB) surveys for the years 1984 to 2006. In each of the years, EB respondents placed themselves on a 10-point left–right scale. Additionally, in each of these years respondents reported whether they thought that their country's membership in the EU was a good thing, a bad thing or neither good nor bad. To account for the electorate's position on these issues, we aggregated the EB data by calculating the averages for all respondents in all countries for all study years. The resulting measures were indices of the mean voter EU membership position and the mean voter left–right placement.

Our information on the electoral system was derived from the World Bank's Database on Political Institutions (DPI) (Beck *et al.* 2001). These data provided rich information on dozens of institutional variables since the early 1970s, and covers 177 countries, including all 14 considered in this analysis. We utilised two DPI institutional variables in our investigation: the levels of fractionalisation and polarisation. The former was calculated as the probability that two deputies picked at random from the legislature will be of different parties (so that 1 would indicate a single-party legislature).[4] Fractionalisation scores ranged from a low average probability of 0.54 in the UK, corresponding with an average effective number of 2.2 parties, to a high probability of 0.81 on average in Finland, corresponding with an effective number of 5.2 parties on average. Our measure of polarisation was composed as the maximum difference, in ideological terms, between the Chief Executive's party, the three largest government parties and the largest opposition party (Beck *et al.* 2001; Keefer and Stasavage 2003). A maximum difference of 0 indicated that all four parties belonged to the same ideological bloc (left, centre or right), and a maximum difference of 2 indicated that the two most distant parties are on the two opposing sides of the ideological spectrum.

Methods

The analysis proceeded in three stages. We began by examining the longitudinal trends in our study variables, in order to assess the degree of variance in both the dependent variable and its model predictors. Next, we examined the bivariate associations between each of the independent variables and perceived party position on EU integration using the Pearson's correlation coefficient for the party-level data and independent sample t-tests to replicate previous associations between the study variables and to verify that all associations are statistically significant. Finally, we employed a multi-level OLS regression to predict parties' positions on EU integration. Noting the high autocorrelation in this variable over time, we opted against nesting party data within countries within years (or within years within countries), and created a new level 2 unit of analysis, interacting the two higher level units of analysis, namely political system for sampling year. This strategy of nesting parties within system × year resulted in removing the autocorrelations in our data, and consequently the stationary R-square dropped to less than 1 per cent.

In the multilevel analysis we regressed parties' positions on EU integration in three bloc-recursive models. In the first we loaded only the party-level predictors, attempting to test our hypotheses at baseline, with no complementary contextual information. In the second model we added our information on the electorate and political system. The aim in this model was to assess the study hypotheses accounting for context, and test the associations between the contextual factors and the outcome variable. In the final model we added cross-level interaction terms, in an attempt to determine if the associations between predictors at one level and parties' positions on EU integration were independent of the associations of predictors from the other level with this outcome.

Results

In the theoretical section we posited that parties' positions on European integration are most likely a function of three sets of factors: the position of the electorate, party characteristics (ideology, incumbency and party size) and party system characteristics (fractionalisation and polarisation). In this analysis we test our study hypotheses by means of a presentation of the longitudinal trends in our dependent, independent and control variables, by testing the bivariate associations between our explanatory factors and study outcome, and by employing a multivariate model in order to assess the relative importance of our three different groups of predictors.

Longitudinal Trends in Study Variables

Our analysis commences with an inspection of the longitudinal trends in our study's variables. These trends, displayed in Figure 1, are the OLS unstandardised estimated annual average values for each of the study variables. Each of these averages, which pertain to all countries in each of the study years, was regressed against the sampling year. Looking at this figure we observe that our dependent variable, the level of parties' support for EU integration, has increased over the years by an annual average increase of a little over 3 per cent. Other party characteristics have also changed significantly over the years. The salience parties give to the issue of European integration increased by an annual average of 3.5 per cent, and a similar increase was noted for the number of incumbent parties in the electoral system. More substantial changes were noted with regard to parties' ideological positions. Party average left–right score increased, it moved to the right, by slightly under 7 per cent annually, while party extremism dropped by a staggering 11 per cent annually. The contextual variables, the electorate left–right and EU leaning and the electoral system fractionalisation and polarisation levels, however, did not change substantially over the years. The annual increase for each of these factors was 1 per cent or less for every year.

FIGURE 1
STUDY VARIABLES ANNUAL AVERAGES FITTED OVER TIME: OLS REGRESSION UNSTANDARDISED PREDICTED VALUES, 1984–2006 (N = 2,458)

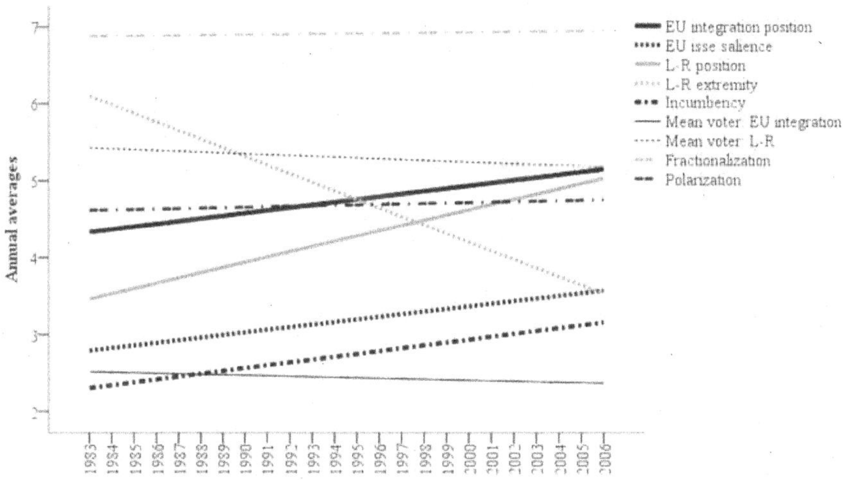

Note: Annual averages for incumbency and fractionalization were multiplied by 10; 1 was added to the annual averages for polarisation, and the outcome was then multiplied by 2.

Bivariate Analyses

In a next step, we test the bivariate associations between our explanatory factors and the outcome variable, aiming at replicating previous research findings. We correlated party position on EU integration with the five party-level predictors, capturing party ideological leaning and extremity, their electoral utilities and incumbency status, and the degree of salience of EU integration for the parties in our sample. The results of this analysis are presented in Figure 2.

Our first observation is that all five factors were significantly associated with parties' position on EU integration. Although all these associations were statistically significant, each of these explanatory factors' individual power of prediction was modest, ranging from 9 per cent explained variance by means of parties' EU issue salience to 13 per cent by means of party size. Left–right extremity had the highest associations and has accounted for a noteworthy 30 per cent of the total variance in the outcome variable. As we have expected, ideological extremity and parties' EU integration stand were inversely associated, indicating that less extreme parties are more pro-EU and vice versa. The left–right score variable was weakly, yet significantly associated with this outcome, indicating that right-wing parties were slightly more pro-EU compared with their counterparts on the left.

In an effort to understand the associations of both measures of ideology, namely party ideological stand and extremity, we followed up on Hooghe *et al.* (2002), and tested the bivariate associations between these two and the

FIGURE 2
PEARSON'S CORRELATION COEFFICIENTS FOR THE ASSOCIATIONS BETWEEN THE MODEL EXPLANATORY FACTORS PERTAINING TO PARTIES AND PARTY EU INTEGRATION POSITION IN 14 EU MEMBER STATES, 1984–2006 ($N = 2{,}458$)

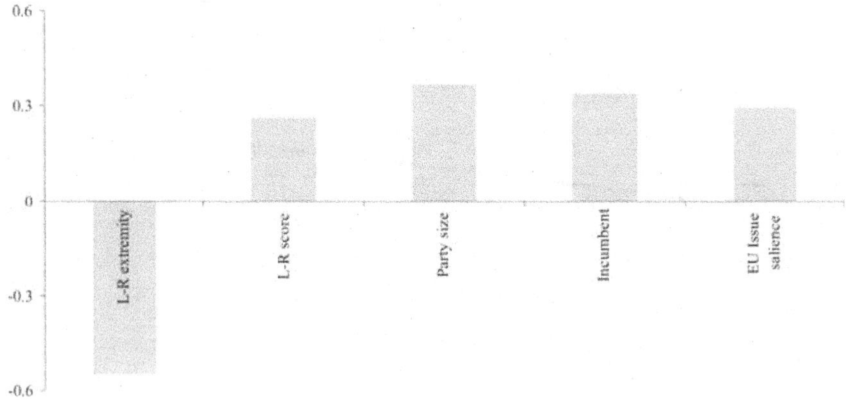

Note: All coefficients are statistically significant ($p < 0.01$).

outcome variable, without constraining them by linear assumptions. In Figure 3 we plot the scatter points for both ideological variables against the party EU integration metric, and fit the best lines to describe these associations. Looking at this figure, we note that the associations between a party's left–right position and its position on the EU exhibited an inverted U-curve trend, while ideological extremity was almost linearly associated with the outcome. Both these associations had a quadratic R-square of 0.25, suggesting that the strength of the relationship between both predictors and the outcome variable, without assuming linearity, were similar. Considering the inverse U-shape of the associations between left–right and EU positions, we did not expect the former to be strongly and linearly associated with the latter in our multivariate multi-level model. However, as it reached statistical significance, indicating that parties on the right were substantially different than those on the left on the issue of integration, we opted for controlling for it in our multivariate models.

To determine the bivariate associations of our macro explanatory factors with the parties' EU position, we classified each of the measures into two discrete categories, and calculated the independent sample t-values for each predictor and the outcome. The cutoff points for the electorate's left–right and EU leaning and the level of fractionalisation were the sample average (5.3, 2.5 and 0.7, respectively). Our polarisation variable was transformed to reflect systems with low and high levels of polarisation. The associations between the macro predictors and parties' position on EU integration are displayed in Figure 4. It is notable that all four context variables returned statistically significant t-values. The highest t-test score was obtained from

FIGURE 3
SCATTERPLOT FOR PARTY LEFT–RIGHT POSITION AND PARTY LEFT–RIGHT EXTREMITY AND PARTY EU INTEGRATION POSITION, 14 EU MEMBER STATES, 1984–2006 ($N = 2{,}458$)

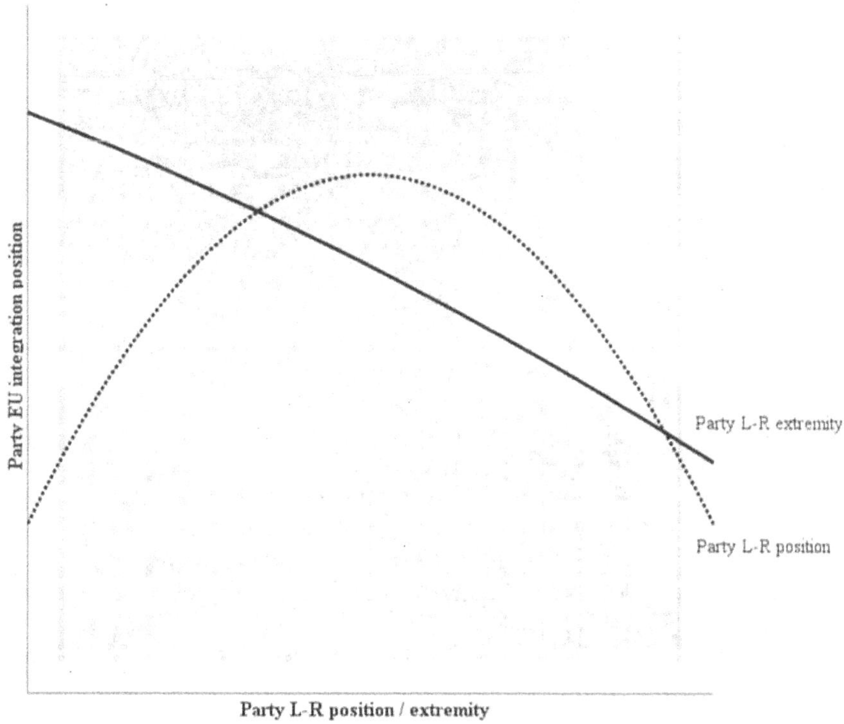

Note: R^2-quadratic = 0.25 for both ideology measures

crossing the mean voter on the EU and the parties' EU positions, indicating a high degree of issue congruence. In other words, parties were very much in line with the mood in the general electorate regarding the issue of EU integration. The electorate's mean left–right position was also significantly associated with this outcome, and its direction suggests that parties will favour EU integration in the context of having an electorate which is leaning towards the ideological left. The associations between polarisation and fractionalisation with the outcome were both positive and significant, indicating that parties operating in highly polarised and fractionalised political systems are more prone to favour EU integration.

Multivariate Analyses

In the final stage of the empirical analysis, we integrate the different predictors to identify their net contribution to an explanation of parties' EU

FIGURE 4
INDEPENDENT SAMPLE T-TEST FOR POLITICAL SYSTEM FACTORS EFFECTS ON PARTY EU INTEGRATION POSITION IN 14 EU MEMBER STATES, 1984–2006 ($N = 2{,}458$)

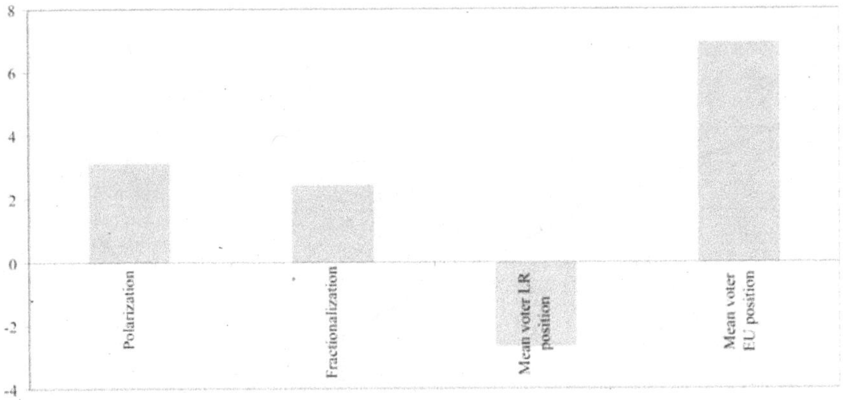

Note: All coefficients are statistically significant ($p < 0.01$); t-test scores were calculated assuming equal distributions (in all cases Levene's F test gained statistical significance).

position, holding all other variables constant. This will also allow us to inspect the robustness of the findings presented in previous work, while controlling for the different explanations provided by researchers. In addition, by estimating a multilevel model, we are able to add an additional layer of complexity, which has often been ignored in previous work, namely accounting for the context within which parties operate. This context in itself might be important for understanding parties' EU positions, since it can have direct associations with the outcome variable, but it may also prove to have indirect effects by moderating some of our other predictors, and thus help us to better understand the bivariate associations we discussed earlier.

Our multivariate analysis is conducted in three stages. First, we predict the outcome employing only variables which provide information about parties. Next, we add contextual variables, providing complementary information on the political system and the characteristics of the electorates. Finally, we introduce interaction terms to sharpen the multilevel associations discovered in the first two stages. By assessing the multilevel explanatory factors' coefficients and their consistency across models, we can test our hypotheses in a more robust way.

In the first model we test the associations between parties' characteristics and their EU integration positions, holding the other characteristics constant. The findings, reported in Table 1, are by and large consistent with the findings reported in the literature and corroborated in our bivariate analyses. Specifically, we note that incumbent parties are more likely to hold positive views on EU integration, as are parties that exhibit higher salience levels on

TABLE 1
BLOC-RECURSIVE MULTI-LEVEL MODEL FOR PARTY POSITION ON EU INTEGRATION, 14 EU MEMBER STATES, 1984–2006 ($N = 2,458$)

	Model 1		Model 2		Model 3	
Explanatory variables	**B**	**S.E.**	**B**	**S.E.**	**B**	**S.E.**
Constant	3.490	0.185	3.914	0.907	3.689	0.949
Party information						
Incumbent	0.443	0.069	0.456	0.073	0.383	0.073
EU issue salience	0.645	0.051	0.420	0.055	0.510	0.102
Party size	0.015	0.011	0.021	0.003	−0.073	0.019
L–R score	0.096	0.011	0.019	0.011	0.019	0.011
L–R extremity	−0.485	0.021	−0.513	0.022	−0.416	0.035
Political system information						
Mean voter EU position	–	–	0.875	0.166	0.863	0.170
Mean voter LR position	–	–	−0.548	0.100	−0.449	0.101
Fractionalisation	–	–	2.138	0.571	1.001	0.676
Polarisation	–	–	−0.256	0.059	−0.073	0.231
Interaction terms						
Fractionalisation * Party size	–	–	–	–	0.127	0.033
Polarisation * Party size	–	–	–	–	0.010	0.004
Polarisation * L–R extremity	–	–	–	–	−0.063	0.022
Polarisation * salience	–	–	–	–	−0.049	0.063
σ^2_{u0}	0.359	0.046	0.133	0.029	0.147	0.030
σ^2_e	1.806	0.051	1.782	0.054	1.699	0.051
−2*log likelihood	9945.3	–	8534.2	–	8434.2	–
VPC	0.166	–	0.069	–	0.079	–

Note: Cell entries represent multilevel OLS regression coefficients and standard errors.

the issue. This finding suggests that we should reject the null hypothesis for H_4. Both measures of ideology, left–right score and extremity, were also significantly associated with this outcome. As the effect of extremity on the outcome variable remains significant in models 2 and 3, we can reject the null hypothesis for H_3. Conversely, the significant effect we found for left–right leaning in model 1 is not consistent in the following models, so at this stage we hold our judgement regarding the validity of H_2. As in the bivariate analyses, the directions of these associations were in line with our theoretical expectations, which suggest that considering only party characteristics, we find support for all the aforementioned theoretical approaches. Finally, we note that parties' electoral success did not significantly predict their stance on EU integration.

Looking at the summary statistics we note that parties' positions on EU integration possess statistically significant variance components at both party and party-system levels. Overall some 17 per cent of the total variance in the outcome variable is a result of contextual differences independent of party characteristics.

In the next model we add our party system and electorate metrics, in an attempt to disentangle the influence of political context on the dynamics captured in model 1. Accounting for these contextual factors increases our ability to assess these dynamics more accurately and, interestingly, we note that parties' left–right score, which was identified as a predictor of parties' EU position, has lost its statistical significance. Conversely, the regression coefficient for ideological extremity has slightly increased. These findings lead us to reject H_2. These results, coupled with the results from the bivariate analysis on the correlates between parties' ideological and EU positions discussed in Figure 2, lead us to conclude that the effect parties' left–right position may have on their EU positions is non-linear.

All contextual factors in model 2 were significantly associated with the outcome variable. As we expected, we found that party system fractionalisation fosters an a priori positive position regarding EU integration, while higher levels of party system polarisation lead to the opposite result, namely less favourable positions regarding EU integration. These associations too were inconsistent with the ones we found in model 3, and this makes us hold our judgement regarding the validity of H_{6a}, H_{6b} and H_7. Looking at the electorate, we note that having an overall positive attitude regarding European integration increases the likelihood of parties being positive on the EU as well. Additionally, when electorates are left-leaning, on average parties are significantly more likely to be positive on EU integration. These findings suggest that the electorate's mood is a valid predictor of parties' positions on EU integration, and we therefore reject the null hypothesis for H_1. Overall the variance for both components substantially decreased after adding the political system information and the share of the variance in the outcome variable that is attributed to contextual factors dropped by more than half to a little under 7 per cent.

In our final model we attempt to identify associations between party characteristics and position on EU integration, conditioned by contextual factors. This model employs variables from both levels as well as cross-level interaction terms. In this analysis we have employed four such terms. Party size was interacted with fractionalisation and polarisation, and additionally we have interacted polarisation with issue salience and extremity.

The findings suggest that left–right extremity, which maintained its direct relations with the outcome variable, was also part of an interaction term that significantly predicted parties' EU integration position. Thus, non-extreme parties which were more likely to support this outcome were even more likely to do so in relatively polarised systems. Finally, party size was positively associated with parties' EU integration position in party systems that are characterised by relatively high fractionalisation levels. By deduction, smaller parties in party systems with lower levels of fractionalisation are expected to exhibit higher levels of support for EU integration. Party size gained significant results when interacted with polarisation as well. However the significant effect party size had in model 3 is in the opposite direction to our theoretical expectations, and we therefore reject H_5. We further found that larger parties in relatively polarised systems tended to be more supportive of EU integration compared with smaller parties in such systems. Both indicators of electoral system, namely the levels of fractionalisation and polarisation, did not yield direct significant associations with the outcome variable on top of the conditioning effect they had on the party-level predictors. We can therefore reject hypotheses H_{6a}, H_{6b} and H_7. As we have noted, the importance of these variables in predicting parties' positions on EU integration is evident. Though theory leads us to hypothesise that there will be a direct effect between these contextual factors and the outcome variable, our analyses revealed that this effect is limited to indirect associations.

Switching to the party information variables, we note one major change. Party size, which was positively associated with the outcome in models 1 and 2 (insignificantly in the former), is now inversely associated with it. After accounting for party size in the interaction terms, we find that smaller parties are in fact more in support of EU integration. This change of direction is a result of accounting for the context that defines the electoral competition. Finally, looking at the political system predictors, we note that after accounting for the interaction terms, the level of both fractionalisation and polarisation did not retain their statistical significance.

These findings suggest that previous studies, which found party size, fractionalisation and polarisation to be directly associated with party position on the EU have overlooked the interplay between party's electoral lot and the overall electoral result, manifested by means of the system levels of fractionalisation and polarisation. Put differently, parties' positions on EU integration are not just functions of the party size, system fractionalisation and polarisation, but rather a combination of parties' electoral returns and context.

Discussion and Conclusions

European integration has increasingly gained salience over the years and, consequently, political parties all over Europe are progressively forced to carve out a position on this issue. This raises the question why some parties hold favourable positions on European integration, while others are more negative? To date, tremendous scholarly efforts have been made to understand which factors explain parties' positions on European integration. This paper revisits this debate by examining the factors highlighted in previous research as well as party characteristics such as ideology and incumbency. In addition, we move beyond the current state-of-the-art by drawing explicit attention to the institutional structure in which parties operate, while focusing specifically on the levels of polarisation and fractionalisation of the party system. These factors have by and large been sub-optimally utilised in scholarship on party positions on European integration, but have been a key consideration for explaining parties' stances and activities concerning other policy issues (for recent examples, see Ezrow 2007; Kim *et al.* 2010).

Modelling parties' positions on European integration by employing longitudinal data from CHES, linked with other data pertaining to parties, such as the electorates' position and party system characteristics, our multilevel analyses allowed examining the validity of existing theory. In addition, we could inspect the robustness of these results as we consider the different factors simultaneously in a multivariate analysis. Overall, our results corroborate much of the existing work explaining party positions on European integration. In line with the work by Carrubba (2001) suggesting that an 'electoral connection' exists in European politics, we find evidence that parties' positions on European integration are indeed affected by the preferences of the general electorate. This finding resonates with the ongoing debates in the study of issue congruence on the EU. Over the years, many observers have argued that political elites are out of touch when it comes to representing voters on European integration. Our analysis contributes to this ongoing debate by reaffirming that, overall, parties are indeed responsive to voters' preferences in the realm of European integration.

Next, we also find that the characteristics of parties themselves are important to our understanding of their EU positions. In line with Hooghe *et al.* (2002), our results indicate that left–right extremity is a strong predictor of parties' EU positions. Parties with extremist positions to the left or right are negative about European integration, while parties representing the political mainstream are far more positive.[5]

Our analyses contribute to the ongoing scholarship on the determinants of parties' policy positions by highlighting the importance of party system characteristics. While we found no evidence of direct effects of polarisation and fractionalisation on parties' EU positions, our results do point to the existence of indirect effects. That is to say, the impact of party characteristics, such as ideology or incumbency, is moderated by the institutional context in which parties operate. For example, parties that are ideologically closer to the centre are even more likely to favour European integration within highly polarised systems. Additionally, it is evident that bigger parties in systems with higher levels of fractionalisation exhibit higher levels of support for EU integration.

These findings indicate that an electorally successful party, and/or a party with a centrist left–right position, that is operating in a competitive political system is more likely to provide an even clearer pro-EU position. Parties behave in this fashion in order to distinguish themselves from their competitors. Overall, our findings suggest that while contextual characteristics do not have a direct effect on parties' positions on EU integration, they nevertheless condition parties' behaviour. Specifically, we note that parties' left–right ideological position, as well as their electoral success, interacting with information about the electoral system, results in varying levels of support for EU integration. Consequently, future work on party positions or issue congruence regarding European integration will benefit from examining the extent to which parties' behaviour is a function of the context in which they operate.

Despite these insights, this study has two limitations. First, when testing the effect of voter preferences on party positions on European integration, we only focused on the mean voter position. This is largely in line with the notion that parties respond to the general electorate, in terms of the positions of the mean voter (see Downs 1957; Erikson *et al.* 2002; Powell 2004). An equally compelling vision of party behaviour emphasises party responsiveness to the mean party supporter (Adams *et al.* 2006; Ezrow *et al.* 2011; Wessels 1999). However, data on the mean partisan voter is not available after 2002, as respondents' vote intentions were no longer asked in Eurobarometer surveys. Additionally, we note a high correlation between the mean and partisan-mean voters' position (on both EU and their left–right position) which means that if one were to model them simultaneously this would result in high levels of multicollinearity. Finally, our aim has not been to deliver the best possible predictions of a party's support for or opposition to European integration; rather we set out to test and expand existing results by being sensitise to temporal and contextual dynamics. Consequently, we acknowledge that there are still substantial variance components left to be explained at both the party and contextual level. It may be a promising line for future research to further theoretically develop and empirically substantiate the exact way in which context matters for party positions on European integration.

Notes

1. Assuming parties offer coherent choices, citizens have clearly defined preferences on policy dimensions and they base their voting choices on these policy preferences (Mair 2008; Miller *et al.* 1999; Thomassen and Schmitt 1997, 1999).
2. An extensive literature on party cueing, especially within the field of EU studies, has evolved, demonstrating the importance of elites in shaping public opinion, and vice versa (Gabel and Scheve 2007; Steenbergen and Jones 2002; Steenbergen and Marks 2007). These studies focus on the debate regarding the nature of cueing effects, i.e. top-down or bottom-up. In other words, the research focuses on the question: who is cueing whom? Although we acknowledge the centrality of this question, we assume that the relationship between public opinion and the positions of political parties is bottom-up. On studying the research on public opinion and mass behaviour in the context of the left–right and EU dimensions, this assumption seems reasonable, as strong support can be found for public cueing on integration issues (Adams *et al.* 2006; Steenbergen *et al.* 2007).
3. The CHES data was created for all EU member states excluding Cyprus, Luxembourg and Malta, for the years 1984, 1988, 1992, 1996, 1999, 2002 and 2006. Data was collected for all parties that secured a minimum of 2 per cent of the valid votes and/or one seat in the lower house of the national legislature. For the full study documentation, see Hooghe *et al.* (2010).
4. This measure of fractionalisation is a linear transformation of another popular measure of this construct, the Effective Number of Parties (ENP). Specifically, ENP = 1/(1 − Fractionalisation).
5. It is worth noting that although ideological extremity seems to be linearly correlated with parties' positions on EU integration, there may well be different mechanisms defining both

the extreme right's and extreme left's anti-EU dispositions. While the extreme right opposes European integration in defence of national community and sovereignty, the extreme left rejects the European project on the basis of its neoliberal character, which may undermine existing welfare state provisions (de Vries and Edwards 2009).

References

Adams, James, Michael Clark, Lawrence Ezrow, and Garrett Glasgow (2006). 'Are Niche Parties Fundamentally Different from Mainstream Parties? The Causes and Consequences of Western European Parties' Policy Shifts, 1976–1998', *American Journal of Political Science*, 50:3, 513–29.

Arnold, Christine, and Paul Pennings (2009). 'Party Positions on the European Constitution during the 2004 Parliament Elections', *Journal of Contemporary European Research*, 5:1, 24–42.

Bardi, Luciano, and Peter Mair (2008). 'The Parameters of Party Systems', *Party Politics*, 14:2, 147–66.

Beck, Thorsten, George Clarke, Alberto Groff, Philip Keefer, and Patrick Walsh (2001). 'New Tools in Comparative Political Economy: The Database of Political Institutions', *World Bank Economic Review*, 15:1, 165–76.

Budge, Ian (1994). 'A New Spatial Theory of Party Competition: Uncertainty, Ideology and Policy Equilibria Viewed Comparatively and Temporarily', *British Journal of Political Science*, 24, 443–67.

Cappoccia, Giovanni (2002). 'Anti-system Parties: A Conceptual Reassessment', *Journal of Theoretical Politics*, 14:1, 9–35.

Carrubba, Clifford J. (2001). 'The Electoral Connection in European Union Politics', *Journal of Politics*, 63:1, 141–58.

Daalder, Hans, and Peter Mair (1983). *The West European Party System*. London: Oxford University Press.

Dalton, Russell (2008). 'The Quantity and Quality of Party Systems: Party System Polarization, its Measurement, and its Consequences', *Comparative Political Studies*, 41:7, 899–920.

De Vries, Catherine E. (2007). 'Sleeping Giant: Fact or Fairytale? How European Integration Affects Vote Choice in National Elections', *European Union Politics*, 8:3, 363–85.

De Vries, Catherine E. (2009). 'The Impact of EU Referenda on National Electoral Politics: Evidence from the Dutch Case', *West European Politics*, 32:1, 142–71.

De Vries, Catherine E. (2010). 'EU Issue Voting: Asset or Liability? How European Integration Affects Parties' Electoral Fortunes', *European Union Politics*, 11:1, 89–117.

De Vries, Catherine E., and Erica E. Edwards (2009). 'Taking Europe to its Extremes: Extremist Parties and Public Euroskepticism', *Party Politics*, 15:1, 5–28.

De Vries, Catherine E., and Sara B. Hobolt (2012). 'When Dimensions Collide: The Electoral Success of Issue Entrepreneurs', *European Union Politics*, 13:2, 246–68.

Downs, Anthony (1957). *An Economic Theory of Democracy*. Belmont, CA: Thompson Wadsworth.

Enelow, James M., and Melvin J. Hinich (1984). *The Spatial Theory of Voting: An Introduction*. Cambridge: Cambridge University Press.

Erikson, Robert S., Michael MacKuen, and James Stimson (2002). *The Macro Polity*. Cambridge: Cambridge University Press.

Ezrow, Lawrence (2007). 'The Variance Matters: How Party Systems Represent the Preferences of Voters', *Journal of Politics*, 69:1, 182–92.

Ezrow, Lawrence, Catherine E. de Vries, Marco R. Steenbergen, and Erica E. Edwards (2011). 'Mean Voter Representation and Partisan Constituency Representation: Do Parties Respond to the Mean Voter or Their Supporters?', *Party Politics*, 17:3, 275–301.

Freire, Andre (2008). 'Party Polarization and Citizens' Left–Right Orientations', *Party Politics*, 14:2, 189–209.

Gabel, Matthew, and Kenneth Scheve (2007). 'Estimating the Effect of Elite Communications on Public Opinion Using Instrumental Variables', *American Journal of Political Science*, 51:4, 1013–28.

Hobolt, Sara B. (2009). *Europe in Question: Referendums on European Integration*. Oxford: Oxford University Press.

Hooghe, Liesbet (2003). 'Europe Divided? Elite vs. Public Opinion on European Integration', *European Union Politics*, 4:3, 281–305.

Hooghe, Liesbet, Gary Marks, and Carole J. Wilson (2002). 'Does Left/Right Structure Party Positions on European Integration?', *Comparative Political Studies*, 35:8, 965–89.

Hooghe, Liesbet, Ryan Bakker, Anna Brigevich, Catherine E. de Vries, Erica E. Edwards, Gary Marks, Jan Rovny, and Marco R. Steenbergen (2010). 'Reliability and Validity of Measuring Party Positions: The Chapel Hill Expert Surveys of 2002 and 2006', *European Journal of Political Research*, 49:5, 687–703.

Huber, John D., and Bingham G. Powell (1994). 'Congruence between Citizens and Policy Makers in Two Visions of Liberal Democracy', *World Politics*, 46, 291–326.

Iversen, Torben (1994). 'Political Leadership and Representation in West European Democracies: A Test of Three Models of Voting', *American Journal of Political Science*, 38:1, 45–74.

Jensen, Christian B., and Jae-Jae Spoon (2010). 'Thinking Locally, Acting Supranationally: Niche Party Behaviour in the European Parliament', *European Journal of Political Research*, 49:2, 174–201.

Keefer, Philip, and David Stasavage (2003). 'The Limits of Delegation: Veto Players, Central Bank Independence, and the Credibility of Monetary Policy', *American Political Science Review*, 97:3, 407–23.

Kim, HeeMin, Bingham G. Powell, and Richard C. Fording (2010). 'Electoral Systems, Party Systems, and Ideological Representation: An Analysis of Distortion in Western Democracies', *Comparative Politics*, 42:2, 167–85.

Kitschelt, Herbert (1994). *The Transformation of European Social Democracy*. Cambridge: Cambridge University Press.

Kriesi, Hanspeter, Edgar Grande, Romain Lachat, Martin Dolezal, Simon Bornschier, and Timotheos Frey (2006). 'Globalization and the Transformation of the National Political Space: Six European Countries Compared', *European Journal of Political Research*, 45, 921–56.

Kriesi, Hanspeter, Edgar Grande, Romain Lachat, Martin Dolezal, and Simon Bornschier (2008). *West European Politics in the Age of Globalization*. Cambridge: Cambridge University Press.

Laakso, Markku, and Rein Taagepera (1979). 'Effective Number of Parties: A Measure with Application to West Europe', *Comparative Political Studies*, 12:1, 3–27.

Lijphart, Arend (1999). *Patterns of Democracy: Government Forms and Performance in Thirty-Six Countries*. New Haven, CT: Yale University Press.

Mair, Peter (2003). 'Comparing Party Systems', in Lawrence LeDuc, Richard G. Niemi, and Pippa Norris (eds.), *Comparing Democracies 2: New Challenges in the Study of Elections and Voting*. London: Sage Publications, 88–107.

Mair, Peter (2007). 'Political Parties and Party Systems', in Paolo Grazioano and Maarten Vink (eds.), *Europeanization: New Research Agenda*. Basingstoke: Palgrave Macmillan, 154–66.

Mair, Peter (2008). 'The Challenge to Party Government', *West European Politics*, 31:1–2, 211–34.

Marks, Gary, and Carole J. Wilson (2000). 'The Past in the Present: A Cleavage Theory of Party Response to European Integration', *British Journal of Political Science*, 30, 433–59.

McDonald, Michael, and Ian Budge (2005). *Elections, Parties, Democracy: Conferring the Median Mandate*. Oxford: Oxford University Press.

Meguid, Bonnie (2005). 'Competition between Unequals: The Role of Mainstream Party Strategy and Niche Party Success', *American Political Science Review*, 99:3, 347–60.

Miller, Warren E., and Donald E. Stokes (1963). 'Constituency Influence in Congress', *American Political Science Review*, 57:1, 45–56.

Miller, Warren E., Roy Pierce, Jacques Thomassen, Richard Herrera, Sören Holmberg, Peter Esaiasson, and Bernhard Wessels (1999). *Policy Representation in Western Democracies*. Oxford: Oxford University Press.

Petrocik, John R. (1996). 'Issue Ownership in Presidential Elections, with a 1980 Case Study', *American Journal of Political Science*, 40:3, 825–50.

Pierce, Roy (1999). 'Mass–Elite Issue Linkages and the Responsible Party Model', in Warren E. Miller, Roy Pierce, Jacques Thomassen, Richard Herrera, Sören Holmberg, Peter Esaiasson, and Bernhard Wessels, *Policy Representation in Western Democracies*. Oxford: Oxford University Press, 9–32.

Powell, Bingham G. (2004). 'Political Representation in Comparative Perspective', *The Annual Review of Political Science*, 7, 273–96.

Ray, Leonard (1999). 'Measuring Party Positions on European Integration: Results from an Expert Survey', *European Journal of Political Research*, 36, 283–306.

Ray, Leonard (2003). 'Reconsidering the Link between Incumbent Support and Pro-EU Opinion', *European Union Politics*, 4:3, 259–79.

Riker, William (1982). *Liberalism against Populism. A Confrontation between the Theory of Democracy and the Theory of Social Choice*. Long Grove, IL: Waveland Press.

Rohrschneider, Robert, and Stephen Whitefield (2007). 'Political Parties, Public Opinion and European Integration in Post-Communist Countries', *European Union Politics*, 7:1, 141–60.

Sartori, Giovanni (1976). *Parties and Party Systems: A Framework for Analysis*. Cambridge: Cambridge University Press.

Spoon, Jae-Jae (2009). 'Holding their Own: Explaining the Persistence of Green Parties in France and the UK', *Party Politics*, 15:5, 615–34.

Steenbergen, Marco R., and Brian S. Jones (2002). 'Modelling Multilevel Data Structures', *American Journal of Polititical Science*, 46:1, 218–37.

Steenbergen, Marco R., and Gary Marks (2007). 'Evaluating Expert Surveys', *European Journal of Political Research*, 46:3, 347–66.

Stimson James, Michael MacKuen, and Robert S. Erikson (1995). 'Dynamic Representation', *American Political Science Review*, 89, 543–65.

Thomassen, Jacques, and Hermann Schmitt (1997). 'Policy Representation', *European Journal of Political Research*, 32, 165–84.

Thomassen, Jacques, and Hermann Schmitt (1999). 'Issue Congruence', in Hermann Schmitt and Jacques Thomassen (eds.), *Political Representation and Legitimacy in the European Union*. Oxford: Oxford University Press, 186–208.

Tillman, Erik R. (2004). 'The European Union at the Ballot Box? European Integration and Voting Behavior in the New Member States', *Comparative Political Studies*, 37:5, 590–610.

Van der Eijk, Cees, and Mark N. Franklin (1991). 'European Community Politics and Electoral Representation: Evidence from the 1989 European Election Study', *European Journal of Political Research*, 19:1, 105–27.

Van der Eijk, Cees, and Mark N. Franklin (2004). 'Potential for Contestation on European Matters at National Elections in Europe', in Gary Marks and Marco Steenbergen (eds.), *European Integration and Political Conflict*. Cambridge: Cambridge University Press, 32–50.

Van der Eijk, Cees, and Eliyahu V. Sapir (2010). 'A User-driven and Flexible Procedure for Data Linking', *IASSIST Quarterly*, 2, 19–25.

Wagner, Markus (2012). 'When do Parties Emphasize Extreme Positions? How Strategic Incentives for Policy Differentiation Influence Issue Importance', *Journal of Political Research*, 51, 64–88.

Wessels, Bernhard (1999). 'System Characteristics Matter: Empirical Evidence from Ten Representation Studies', in Warren E. Miller, Roy Pierce, Jacques Thomassen, Richard Herrera, Sören Holmberg, Peter Esaiasson, and Bernhard Wessels, *Policy Representation in Western Democracies*. Oxford: Oxford University Press, 137–61.

Wessels, Bernhard, and Hermann Schmitt (2008). 'Meaningful Choices, Political Supply, and Institutional Effectiveness', *Electoral Studies*, 27:1, 19–30.

Strategic Incentives, Issue Proximity and Party Support in Europe

LORENZO DE SIO and MARK N. FRANKLIN

The Issue Yield model predicts that parties will choose specific issues to emphasise, based on the joint assessment of electoral risks (how divisive is an issue within the party support base) and electoral opportunities (how widely supported is the same issue outside the party). According to this model, issues with high yield are those that combine a high affinity with the existing party base, together with a high potential to reach new voters. In previous work, the model showed a remarkable ability to explain aggregate issue importance as reported by party supporters, as well as issue emphasis in party manifestos. This paper tests the implications at the individual level by comparing a conventional model where issue salience is determined from manifesto data with a revised model where issue salience is determined by issue yield. The empirical findings show that issue yield is a more effective criterion than manifesto emphasis for identifying the issues most closely associated with party support in the minds of voters.

Any assessment of the extent to which parties represent those who vote for them requires us to discover on what grounds people support the parties that they vote for. If those grounds do not include (directly or indirectly) a choice based on a preference for policies that parties promise to try and implement, then representation in policy terms is not taking place.

Determining whether policy representation takes place requires us to know which are the issues that parties promise to try and implement; but determining which issues these are is difficult. We might look at party manifestos, at media reports of stump speeches, at reports of positions taken in debate and at policies enacted when the parties concerned have the power to enact their policies, but still we would miss things. In this paper we examine the potential of starting from something we definitely can measure – the benefit to parties of stressing certain issues – and present evidence suggesting that parties do indeed stress, by some means or other, the issues from which they stand to benefit the most.

Determining which issues these are is complicated by the fact that there is disagreement in the literature over whether parties campaign on (and people choose between them on) the basis of position or valence. Position issues are those upon which parties (and voters) take positions that are for or against (some proposition), more or less (regulation), higher or lower (government expenditure, redistribution, etc.). Valence issues are those upon which most people are agreed (peace, security, economic growth) but, regarding which, different parties may be better or less well-positioned to credibly undertake to bring about the commonly desired objective. Certain parties may be so advantaged in these terms regarding certain issues that they could be said to 'own' those issues.

In previous work (De Sio 2010; De Sio and Weber 2011), one of the present authors has argued that many issues can be seen as combining valence and position aspects because even a position issue can approximate the character of a valence issue if the proportion of those supporting the issue is overwhelmingly large, so that it becomes something very close to a commonly desired objective. Moreover, the quasi-valence character of such issues can provide different opportunities to different parties. Certain issues can be safely exploited by some parties (whose supporters are largely in agreement about the issue) but not by others (whose supporters are more evenly split). In that work it was argued that parties take advantage of this variability between issues in order to focus on issues that promise them a high 'issue yield' – little chance of costing them the support of those who already vote for them together with a high potential to reach (and perhaps convert) other voters.

Findings demonstrate that the issue yield approach performs well in explaining aggregate issue importance as reported by party supporters (De Sio 2010), as well as issue emphasis in party manifestos (De Sio and Weber 2011). This paper addresses the implications of the model for individual-level voting behaviour. Our argument is that, if the configuration of strategic incentives encapsulated in the Issue Yield model does indeed influence party strategies, this will show up in the behaviour of voters – the final objective of party strategising – in terms of stronger support for parties that are close to them on issues that promise those parties high yield. We are agnostic as to the exact mechanism by which voters become aware of the strategic importance of certain issues for certain parties. It might be that parties focus in their campaigning on issues that promise high yield and voters respond to these campaign activities. Alternatively, parties may simply enjoy a long-standing reputation for their concern with these issues. Other mechanisms could be envisaged, but it is not our purpose to spell these out. We merely focus on establishing that voters behave as though some such mechanism exists.

In the pages that follow we will first summarise the Issue Yield model and describe our strategy for determining whether this model better explains party support than other approaches do. We then move on to introduce the data we employ and to describe the analysis we undertake in order to conduct our test. After reporting our findings the paper concludes.

The Issue Yield Model

At the very core of democratic representation is the fact that political debate during election campaigns is structured around a multiplicity of issues. Most such issues can be hypothesised to jointly contribute to the construction (or reactivation) of party preference – and ultimately to the determination of party choice, as election day approaches.

The literature has already confronted various problems connected to this multiplicity of issues. The dynamics of issue emergence have been framed in terms of their lifecycle and *evolution* (Carmines and Stimson 1986, 1989, 1993); attention has been drawn to the *priming* effects that allow issues that are salient in a specific campaign to play a special role in subsequent vote choice (Iyengar and Kinder 1987); finally, what is probably the most developed framework for the analysis of voting behaviour and party competition, Downsian theory, has been extended in order to accommodate the presence of multiple issue-bases of party competition.[1]

Attention has also been drawn – although without the development of a systematic framework – to the analysis of the risks and opportunities that different issues present to political parties. In this regard, pioneering work by William Riker (1982, 1986, 1996) developed the concept of *heresthetics*: the idea that a core resource in political competition is, rather than a change in position on the main dimension of conflict, the *selection of a favourable dimension of conflict*. In Riker's (1986: 1) words, 'For a person who expects to lose on some decision, the fundamental heresthetical device is to divide the majority with a new alternative, one the person prefers to the alternative previously expected to win'. The Issue Yield model builds on this idea to develop a systematic framework for comparative analysis by focusing on the systematic analysis of the electoral risks and opportunities that each issue presents to each party.

Underlying the Issue Yield model lies a generalised view of political issues that subsumes in a single concept two categories of issues that are usually seen as qualitatively distinct: traditional Downsian *positional* issues on the one hand, and *valence issues* on the other. While the former are characterised by the presence of a distribution of preferences over different policy alternatives (in other words, by the presence of disagreement about policy goals), the latter lack a distribution of preferences: they are characterised by complete agreement over particular objectives (usually in domains such as economic prosperity, national security, etc.). With valence issues, voters will evaluate different parties not on their proposed policy, but on the credibility they can claim for achieving what is perceived by everyone as a common goal (Stokes 1963, 1992).

A heresthetical unification of these two apparently incompatible issue types can be developed on the basis of a suggestion made by Stokes (1963: 373) himself: 'the question whether a given problem poses a position- or valence-issue is a matter to be settled *empirically* and not on *a priori* logical grounds'. In other words, *any* issue can be a valence issue, provided that there is a very large degree of agreement among citizens over a policy goal to pursue. A simple operationalisation of Stokes' suggestion can be achieved – using survey data – by measuring the percentage of respondents that lie on the 'agree' side of response items dedicated to specific policy issues. Comparative empirical analyses among the 27 EU member countries show that Stokes' suggestion is empirically confirmed: issues that are very controversial in some countries show a very high level of agreement in others, giving them a character very close to that of valence issues. As an example, a statement such as 'Income and wealth should be redistributed towards ordinary people' has 75 per cent support in France and Italy, 92 per cent in Slovenia, but only 49 per cent in Denmark, where it is a clearly divisive issue (De Sio 2010; De Sio and Weber 2011). This leads to the conclusion that, when adopting an indicator such as the *overall level of support* for one side of a policy issue, positional and valence issues can be considered as lying in different positions on the same continuum, with ideal type valence issues displaying close to 100 per cent agreement and 0 per cent disagreement (or the opposite), and ideal type position issues displaying close to 50 per cent agreement and 50 per cent disagreement.[2]

But the most useful application of this idea is to highlight the presence of an intermediate category of issues for which support lies in between these two extremes (for simplicity, those that register support from about 75 per cent and up). Though still positional,[3] such issues share some properties with valence issues: the policy at hand becomes something close to a *shared* goal (if not by 100 per cent of voters, then at least by a vast majority). For such issues we expect some of the dynamics of valence competition to come into play: parties will not necessarily take opposed views on such issues. Some may rather try to claim more credibility in being able to achieve the (almost) commonly desired outcome. Differences between parties in this regard are indeed quite likely. Since part of the electorate still disagrees on the policy concerned, the likelihood is that the distribution of preferences will be different for different parties. For some parties, all (or almost all) supporters will agree on the policy; for others, supporters might be more evenly split. This has clear implications in terms of party strategy. Parties for which the issue is internally divisive will hardly be able to claim credibility on the issue in valence terms; as a result, they will most likely refrain from emphasising the issue in a campaign. By contrast, parties whose supporters agree on the policy will be better positioned to safely campaign on the issue without the risk of losing existing support. For such parties the issue will clearly represent an attractive opportunity, given that it is supported by many who are not current adherents to that party: as such, it will represent a 'bridge' issue (De Sio and Weber 2011), allowing the parties to reach new supporters beyond their core support base.[4]

The Issue Yield model builds on these insights[5] to develop specific indicators for the configuration of risks and opportunities that each issue offers to each party. It does so based on two core indicators: the *overall level of support* that characterises each issue,[6] and the level of *differential support* (over or under) for the issue among adherents to a party.[7] These two core indicators can be combined into a party- and issue-specific index of *issue yield*, L, that expresses the combination of risks and opportunities that each issue presents to each party.[8] L can have a maximum value of 1 when all supporters of a party also support the issue. In this case, the issue will provide only opportunities for the party, with no risks of losing existing supporters. A value of 0 will instead correspond to a situation where the issue is supported by the same proportion of respondents as of party adherents (though obviously not the same ones): in this case it provides no opportunity for attracting additional support; and stressing it will probably cost as many existing party adherents as it stands to gain new supporters. Negative values correspond to issues for which support in the electorate as a whole is even *lower* than the level of support enjoyed by the party. Here, a stress on the issue will probably cost more party adherents than it will gain new ones.[9]

Empirical tests employing cross-national datasets show that issue yield is able to account in a general model for a large part of cross-national variation. Moreover, the nonlinear combination of risk and opportunity indicators that makes up the issue yield index performs significantly better than the indicators alone, providing empirical support for the theoretical hypothesis incorporated in the issue yield formula. These findings tell us that, in substantive terms, the Issue Yield model effectively captures an important part of the mechanisms that drive issue salience. Parties give a stronger emphasis in their manifestos to issues with a higher yield; and voters for such parties perceive those issues as more salient than others.

What is now of interest is to determine whether issue yield can explain the grounds on which voters choose specific parties.

We do not, however, expect yield-weighted issues to play an equal role for all parties. Past research (De Sio and Weber 2011) has shown that small parties are more greatly influenced by issue yield when deciding which issues to stress, and it would thus make sense for voters to respond more strongly to differences in issue yield when the party they are evaluating is a small one. Again the exact mechanism involved is not central; but we speculate that large parties generally benefit from widespread familiarity with their policies. Because of this familiarity, stress on specific issues in a particular manifesto (or campaign) will be less central to winning support. So large parties have less to lose from a poor choice of issues to stress and less to gain from a good choice. Small parties, by contrast, will have issue positions that are almost inevitably less widely known. At the same time, support for such parties almost by definition is based on fewer issues. So it matters more to small parties that they make good choices over what issues to stress. They have both more to gain and more to lose from this choice than large parties do.

Issue Yield and Individual Voting Behaviour

If parties are seen by voters to stand for issues that promise those parties high yield, this should be evident in voters' behaviour. At the margin, voters whose primary concerns are with issues that distinguish a particular party should be drawn more to that party than to parties that are seen to stand for other issues. Indeed, although not our purpose in this paper, such a focus on individual behaviour might even permit scholars to distinguish between issues stressed in party manifestos and issues stressed in campaigns, a point of contention for those who criticise the use of party manifesto data as a means of determining the issues that parties campaign on (for example, Benoit *et al.* 2009; Ray 1999). In this way we take a step forward from previous tests involving party manifesto data. In that research (De Sio and Weber 2011) it was found that parties do stress in their manifestos issues that promise high yield. Here we are concerned with whether voters also take account of issue yield in their party evaluations. Our expectations can be summarised into one main research hypothesis:

> *H: In assessing the importance that different issues have in driving support towards specific parties, predictions based on the Issue Yield model should outperform those based on party manifesto emphasis and both of these should outperform a model in which all issues have equal emphasis.*

This hypothesis is consistent with the expectation that only some of the issues stressed in a party manifesto are the focus of party campaign activities, since manifestos evidently serve additional purposes than simply attracting voters at election time. But it also expresses the expectation that considerations leading voters to assign different weights to issues are not completely idiosyncratic, but can be at least partially deduced from the general theoretical framework of issue yield. In other words, we expect the Issue Yield model to provide theoretical leverage in predicting which issues drive which voters towards which parties, and a test that pits the stress given to issues in party manifestos against the stress that would be given to issues with high yield should discover voters being attracted to parties on the basis of issues with high yield even more than on the basis of issues stressed in those parties' manifestos (which we already know reflect issue yield to some extent).

Finally, when considering the implications of the Issue Yield model for voting behaviour, we need to mention its relationship with existing rival spatial models of voting. Here, the important distinction is between *proximity* and *directional* theories, whose rivalry is prominent in the literature. We are fully agnostic regarding this debate, in that the Issue Yield model is positioned one step back in the causal chain. We expect issue yield to influence *which parties* stress *which issues*, and then – as a consequence – which issues will play a stronger role in driving voters towards specific parties. But our hypothesis will only concern the *relative weight* of different issues, not the specific dynamics (based on proximity or direction) that would best describe the relationship between party position, voter position and party support. It is true that the test we apply in assessing the weight of different issues could come out differently if we chose one or the other spatial model; but – as we explain in the next section – we will employ what is effectively a 'lowest common denominator' between the two theories, not requiring us to bind our empirical findings to the choice of a specific spatial theory.

Research Strategy

Being focused on the interaction between party strategy and voting behaviour, our research question inevitably calls for a composite dataset, comprising at least three distinct pieces of information. The first is a snapshot of issue support and party–issue alignments as shown in voters' attitudes: this first element is what is needed to build issue yield information, thus synthesising the risks and opportunities that issues present to parties; it typically requires voter-level survey data. A second piece of information relates to parties, in terms of both the party positions on the various issues (in order to compute party–voter proximity as a predictor of party preference) and the emphasis given in the party manifesto to each specific issue. Such information is typically acquired through manifesto data or expert surveys. Finally, these two elements can be used as predictors of the weights that voters implicitly employ in building party preferences: information about these latter (in terms of party support) must also be collected from voter-level survey data.

Our research design inevitably calls for the analysis of the largest possible number of parties, for at least two reasons. The first is, understandably, to increase the number of party*issue relationships that are the main object of interest; the second – not less important – is that the very general and abstract nature of issue yield calls for an empirical test of maximum generality, involving many different party systems, in order to demonstrate that the issue yield mechanism is able to travel across different contexts. Finally, we would ideally like to compare multiple elections under 'controlled conditions' to the largest extent possible, in trying to minimise the impact of contingent national factors.

For these reasons, we employ data from two of the comparative datasets collected by the PIREDEU study (http://www.piredeu.eu) of the 2009

European Parliament (EP) elections. EP elections may not appear the most appropriate context in which to study the dynamics of party competition in national party systems; however, EP elections are organised on a strictly national basis, and are contested by national parties. This presents a combination of country differences and cross-national context uniformity that can be seen as providing appropriate laboratory-like 'windows' into national political processes (see, for example, van der Brug *et al.* 2008; van der Eijk and Franklin 1996). Moreover, the PIREDEU project includes information about both voters and party manifestos, and its voter component (van Egmond *et al.* 2011) is a representative mass survey consisting of 27 virtually identical national samples, allowing for excellent comparability of issues across countries.[10] The same applies to the party manifesto component of the study (Braun *et al.* 2010), although the differences between the issue response items included in the voter study and the issue areas included in the manifesto study has required a 'conceptual matching' stage, whose choices are presented in Appendix Table A1.[11]

Using this dataset, we chose to operationalise our research question in terms of rival models of party support, employing as dependent variable a measure of propensity-to-vote (PTV). Following a proved measurement and analysis strategy (van der Eijk and Franklin 1996; van der Eijk and van der Brug 2007) respondents are asked to report separately for each party the likelihood that they will ever vote for that party. The dataset is then reshaped into a 'stacked' format by converting the PTVs reported for each party by each respondent into different values of the same 'generic' PTV variable for duplicate observations of the same respondent across different parties. This reshaping changes the unit of analysis in each country from the number of individual respondents (N) to $N*P$ respondent–parties (van der Eijk *et al.* 2006). Of course, for the analysis to produce meaningful results, predictors need to be tailored to the respondent–party unit of analysis.[12] In this study, our main focus is on the key issue-based predictor at the respondent–party level: the affinity between the respondent and the party on each of the issues included in the analysis.[13] This affinity was computed in three different versions, aiming at expressing the rival models whose comparison is at the core of our research hypothesis.[14]

The first version of the respondent–party issue affinity measure involves comparisons between individual issue positions and party positions as revealed in party manifestos. The position of the party on the issue is determined on a three-point scale,[15] based on the relative occurrence (and prevalence) of negative and positive mentions of the terms pertaining to the issue in the party manifesto.[16] Secondly, the position of the voter on the issue is determined on the same three-point scale, based on their response to a five-point survey item.[17] A party–respondent affinity score is then computed by multiplying the two scores together, leading to an overall affinity score of +1 when the party and the respondent lie on the same side, −1 when they lie on opposite sides, and 0 when either or both are neutral.[18] This measure assumes that all issues have the same degree of salience across voters and parties.

The second version additionally takes account of party manifesto emphasis, and is computed by taking the 'raw' affinity score calculated as described above and weighting it by the emphasis devoted to the issue in the party-specific manifesto:[19] it expresses a manifesto emphasis model, where respondents that report a high propensity to vote for a party are expected to do so because they have a high affinity with the party on issues that receive most emphasis by the party in its manifesto.

The third version is also a weighted score, but this one is instead constructed by computing each affinity score based on the issue yield of the issue for the party,[20] and then weighting it by the issue yield[21] so that issues whose affinity produces a higher propensity to vote for a party are those that have a higher yield for the party, regardless of the emphasis they received in the manifesto. Finally, because the three measures have different maxima and minima, all were converted to standard scores prior to analysis.

As should be clear from the operationalisation outlined above, the basic procedure for deriving the affinity measures (prior to weighting) essentially acts as a lowest common denominator between the proximity and directional approach to the relationship between voter and party positions. From a proximity point of view, the computed affinities are clearly equivalent to a party–voter proximity, albeit measured on an oversimplified three-point scale; from a directional point of view, the same affinities are equivalent to interactions between party and voter positions, when both are measured against a neutral position. In this regard, we then deem this operationalisation appropriate for expressing our agnostic views concerning the proximity-directional alternative (see Pardos-Prado and Dinas 2010 for corroborative reasoning).

Given the construction of each of these sets of predictors, our research strategy becomes straightforward. We estimated rival three-level random-intercept[22] models of propensity-to-vote for different parties (with PTV responses given by each respondent as the units of analysis). Our expectation is that, with a set of controls common to all models, yield-weighted issue affinities should predict PTVs more accurately than manifesto-emphasis-weighted affinities and both should perform better than the baseline unweighted affinities.

Findings

We proceeded to model estimation by including in all models a base set of control variables consisting of socio-demographics,[23] political awareness,[24] partisanship (whether a party was one that a respondent felt close to), and general competence.[25] Each of these groups of variables is represented by a single measure (dummy variable or y-hat).[26] The results of the estimation are presented in Table 1, which includes *b* coefficients (with standard errors), as well as goodness- of-fit statistics. The table reports coefficients for the socio-demographics (y-hats), political awareness (y-hats) and other control variables first, followed by coefficients for issue affinities.

Interpretation of affinity measures requires an understanding of the stacked nature of the data and the y-hat generation procedure. In a stacked dataset the dependent variable is no longer the propensity to vote for a particular party, but rather the propensity to vote for a party in general; and affinity measures are similarly divorced from reference to specific parties. For y-hats in particular, the *b* coefficient for a specific predictor (e.g. political awareness) does not express the effect of any particular indicator of political awareness, but rather the importance of political awareness in general (in this, y-hats are rather like factor scores, but tuned to provide the best available linear prediction of the dependent variable). So *b* coefficients for y-hat measures are always positive (in the absence of collinearity with other predictors they would all equal 1.0), and (in regard to multicollinearity) behave rather like beta coefficients (effects of standardised variables). But, in Table 1, y-hat affinities are used only for control variables, in contrast to the party–respondent issue affinities already described, whose values are the theoretically called-for product of respondent and party scores. Finally, information about goodness-of-fit is reported, by means of AIC and BIC coefficients, as well as of *R*-squared values.[27]

Model A is provided as a baseline, showing to what extent specific issue affinities predict party support. Model B tunes these affinities in terms of manifesto emphasis. It tries to eliminate correspondences that play no role in party preference formation by focusing on issues that the parties themselves focus on. Finally, model C tunes the affinities in terms of issue yield. As such, the three models provide alternative interpretations of the manner in which issues impact on the preference-formation process.[28]

We derive a substantive interpretation of the empirical results by comparing the *b* coefficients for unweighted issues and issues weighted by manifesto salience (Models A and B) with *b* coefficients for the same issues weighted by issue yield (Model C). What these comparisons tell us is that effects of yield-weighted issues are generally stronger than effects of unweighted or salience-weighted issues – so much so as to be generally greater by more than the 95 per cent confidence interval of the yield-weighted coefficients (see Figure 1).[29] While four yield-weighted issues have less effect than their corresponding salience-weighted counterparts, two of these effects are not significantly less (their spikes overlap) and the other two correspond to effects of yield-weighted issue affinities that are not significantly different from zero.[30] Moreover, all significant effects for yield-weighted issues in Model C are in the expected (positive) direction, in contrast to the unweighted and salience-weighted coefficients, which (for Q65) were seen to be significantly negative in Models A and B. Our interpretation of these findings is: (1) that voters assign different weights to an issue depending on

TABLE 1

ESTIMATED EFFECTS OF RIVAL THREE-LEVEL, RANDOM INTERCEPT MODELS OF PTVS, BASED ON DIFFERENT VERSIONS OF PARTY–RESPONDENT ISSUE AFFINITIES

	Model A Unweighted		Model B Salience-weighted		Model C Yield-weighted	
	b	s.e.	b	s.e.	b	s.e.
Control variables:						
Demographics (y-hats)	0.696	(0.008)***	0.704	(0.008)***	0.695	(0.009)***
Political awareness (y-hats)	0.528	(0.022)***	0.525	(0.025)***	0.515	(0.026)***
This is party R feels close to (Dummy)	2.738	(0.059)***	2.754	(0.063)***	2.701	(0.065)***
This is party best for MIP (Dummy)	4.347	(0.029)***	4.366	(0.031)***	4.271	(0.033)***
Party-respondent issue affinities:						
Q56. Immigrants should adapt	0.027	(0.009)**	0.131	(0.009)***	−0.001	(0.012)
Q57. Private enterprise best solution	0.124	(0.008)***	0.147	(0.009)***	0.211	(0.011)***
Q58. Prohibit gay marriages	0.145	(0.009)***	0.084	(0.009)***	0.208	(0.012)***
Q59. State should own public services	0.099	(0.008)***	0.062	(0.009)***	0.163	(0.012)***
Q60. Women should decide on abortion	0.153	(0.009)***	0.016	(0.010)	0.152	(0.011)***
Q61. Economy should be free of politics	0.095	(0.009)***	0.096	(0.010)***	0.058	(0.011)***
Q62. Harsher prison sentences	0.127	(0.010)***	0.099	(0.011)***	0.024	(0.013)
Q63. Redistribute income	0.095	(0.009)***	0.221	(0.010)***	0.199	(0.012)***
Q64. Schools should teach authority	0.060	(0.010)***	0.023	(0.011)*	0.124	(0.013)***
Q65. EU treaties require referendum	−0.041	(0.009)***	−0.060	(0.010)***	0.053	(0.012)***
Q66. Women should cut work for family	0.026	(0.008)**	0.018	(0.009)	0.070	(0.012)***
Q67. Immigration should be reduced	0.093	(0.008)***	0.106	(0.009)***	0.173	(0.013)***
Constant	3.028	(0.140)***	3.034	(0.140)***	3.037	(0.142)***
Random effects:						
Standard deviation of respondent intercepts	0.722		0.841		0.917	
Standard deviation of country intercepts	0.601		0.737		0.735	
Observations:						
Level 1 (response)	150,482		150,482		150,482	
Level 2 (individual)	27,069		27,069		27,069	
Level 3 (country)	27		27		27	
R^2	0.354		0.361		0.378	
AIC	703535		630357		566348	
BIC	703742		630552		566435	

Note: Significant at *0.05, **0.01, ***0.001 levels.

FIGURE 1
CONFIDENCE INTERVALS AROUND EFFECTS OF EACH SALIENCE-WEIGHTED (LEFT SPIKE) AND YIELD-WEIGHTED (RIGHT SPIKE) ISSUE AFFINITY, IDENTIFIED BY QUESTION NUMBER (SEE TABLE 1)

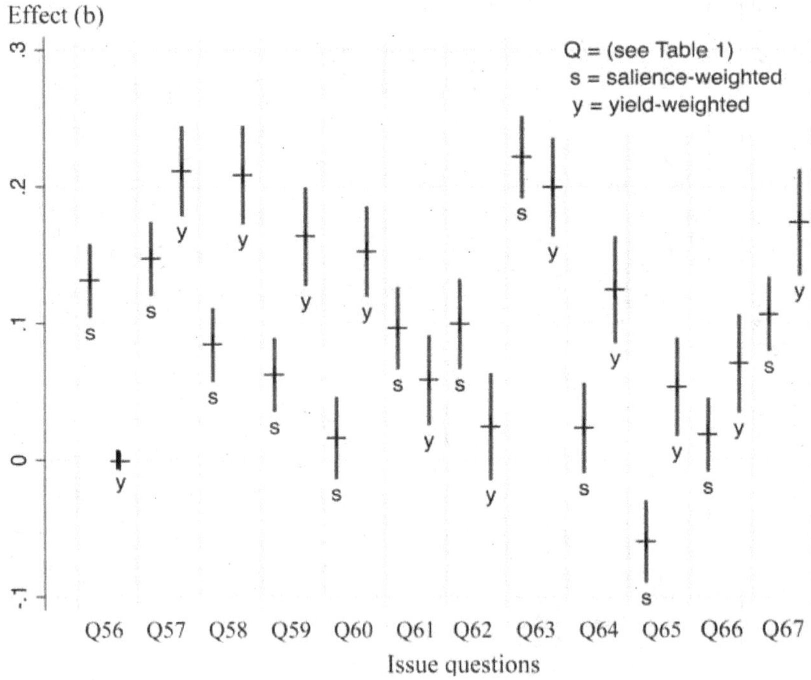

the party they are assessing (as Models B and C perform better than Model A); (2) that issue emphasis seen in party manifestos does not necessarily correspond to the weights that different issues have in the minds of voters – whether because of different emphasis adopted by parties in election campaigns than in manifesto content (Benoit *et al.* 2009; Ray 1999), or for other reasons;[31] such weights appear more accurately captured by the Issue Yield model, as seen in the better performance of Model C over Model B.[32]

It is based on this criterion that we judge the Issue Yield model to perform better than the other models. As reported in Model C, when issue affinities are weighted by issue yield they raise the predictive power of the overall model (*R*-squared increases by 0.017 (a 5 per cent increase in Model B's R^2), but the extent to which specific issues become more potent is even more marked, as already noted. In substantive terms, this confirms our hypothesis: issue yield effectively captures an important part of the configuration of issues that citizens take into account when assessing each party; and it does so better than does manifesto emphasis. In other words, the Issue Yield model apparently captures to a significant extent the overall issue identity of parties, as perceived by voters.

However, this does not mean that all issues are affected equally by the selection mechanism suggested by the Issue Yield model. Some issues are inevitably more important than others in motivating the judgements that voters assign to parties. This is clearly shown by differences between the issue coefficients in the last column of the table. But too much should not be made of the differences we see there. The two issues that fail to reach statistical significance in terms of the effects of issue-weighted yield ('Immigrants must adapt' and 'Harsher prison sentences') may well be issues whose yield is irrelevant to their importance – issues that get very little stress in any case.[33] But differences among the other issues listed in Table 1 could also be due to idiosyncratic distributional characteristics that affect their relative importance in random ways. Our next analysis will lend some support to this idea.

In this next step (see Table 2), we simplify the measure of issue yield so as to be able to introduce party size and the interaction of this variable with yield-weighted issues without creating a model with so many parameters as to raise to near certainty the likelihood that some of them will be falsely deemed significant (or falsely deemed non-significant). The method by which we simplify the model is the same method that we already employed to reduce the number of demographic variables. We are not interested in this research in the specific effects of individual demographic variables, only in controlling for the effects of demographic variables in general. So we generated a single measure of all demographics by using them as predictors of the dependent variable in an analysis with no other controls, and then used the values of the dependent variable predicted by these independent variables as a new variable that stands in for all of the individual demographic variables taken together, as seen in Table 1. In Table 2 we employ the same procedure to simplify the measure of yield-based issue affinities, by using all of them to predict a single y-hat variable that is then used to stand in for the full set of issue affinities. This stand-in variable (generic yield-weighted issue affinity) can then be interacted with party size without this requiring 12 separate interaction terms. Because party size is an explicit variable in this table, all models have a cross-nested hierarchical structure, with a party level as well as an individual level falling between the country and response levels.[34]

The first model in Table 2 (Model D) shows what happens when we replace separate measures of yield-weighted issues with a single measure. As can be seen, the effect of yield-weighted issues, viewed as a single variable, is on a par with the effects of demographic variables or of political awareness. This model produces a small increase in R^2 (0.017) over what we saw in the yield-weighted issue model (Model C) in Table 1, but this is the consequence of introducing a party level and its associated random intercepts into the model. The transformation has evidently cost us the ability to distinguish the effects of specific issues, but this might be

TABLE 2

ESTIMATED EFFECTS ON PROPENSITY TO VOTE FOR A PARTY DUE TO YIELD-WEIGHTED ISSUE AFFINITIES, ALONG WITH PARTY SIZE AND INTERACTIONS WITH PARTY SIZE

	Model D		Model E		Model F	
	b	**s.e.**	**b**	**s.e.**	**b**	**s.e.**
Control variables:						
Demographics (y-hats)	0.549	(0.009)***	0.568	(0.009)***	0.567	(0.009)***
Political awareness (y-hats)	0.460	(0.025)***	0.466	(0.026)***	0.466	(0.026)***
Party *R* feels close to (Dummy)	2.597	(0.064)***	2.330	(0.064)***	2.333	(0.064)***
Party best for MIP (Dummy)	4.096	(0.032)***	3.649	(0.033)***	3.666	(0.033)***
Party size and issue affinities:						
Generic yield-weighted (y-hat)	0.649	(0.008)***	0.661	(0.008)***	0.215	(0.059)***
Smaller party (smallest = 1)			−4.754	(0.091)***	−4.343	(0.091)***
Generic yield * smaller party					0.540	(0.071)***
Constant	2.638	(0.317)***	6.413	(0.346)***	6.402	(0.346)***
Random effects:						
SD of respondent intercepts	0.848		0.861		0.861	
Standard deviation of party intercepts	1.218		0.629		0.784	
Standard deviation of country intercepts	0.729		0.784		0.067	
Observations:						
Level 1 (response)	150,482		150,482		150,482	
Level 2a (individual)	27,069		27,069		27,069	
Level 2b (party)	2–11		2–11		2–11	
Level 3 (country)	27		27		27	
R^2	0.389		0.410		0.410	
AIC	563949		528557		528504	
BIC	564096		528662		528619	

Note: Significant at *0.05, **0.01, ***0.001 levels.

an advantage if idiosyncratic distributional differences have been rendered irrelevant by viewing issue yield in generic terms (as suggested earlier).

More importantly, this simplification of the model permits us to take account of party size – a variable that we theorised would impact on the influence of issue yield. Model E introduces party size on its own, and Model F adds interactions with yield-weighted issues. As can be seen, party size becomes the most powerful effect in the model, adding 0.021 to variance explained, or 5 per cent of Model D's R^2, when Model E is compared with Model D. The interaction of party size with issue yield is seen in Model E to add nothing further to R^2. However, the introduction of this interaction changes the issue yield constitutive term in the equation, which drops by more than two-thirds, from 0.661 in Model E to 0.215 in Model F.[35] The bulk of the work in terms of effects of issue yield is clearly being done by its interaction with party size (party size has been reversed, with small parties scoring more than large parties, so as to produce a positive interaction if our expectations are confirmed).

Since the interpretation of interaction terms is not straightforward, Figure 2 plots the effect of yield-based issue affinities for the largest and smallest parties found in our dataset. It can be seen that the slope for large parties, while palpable, is much less than the slope for small parties, as

FIGURE 2
EFFECTS OF YIELD-WEIGHTED ISSUE AFFINITIES ON PROPENSITY TO VOTE, SMALL PARTIES (LOWER LINES) AND LARGE PARTIES (UPPER LINES) COMPARED

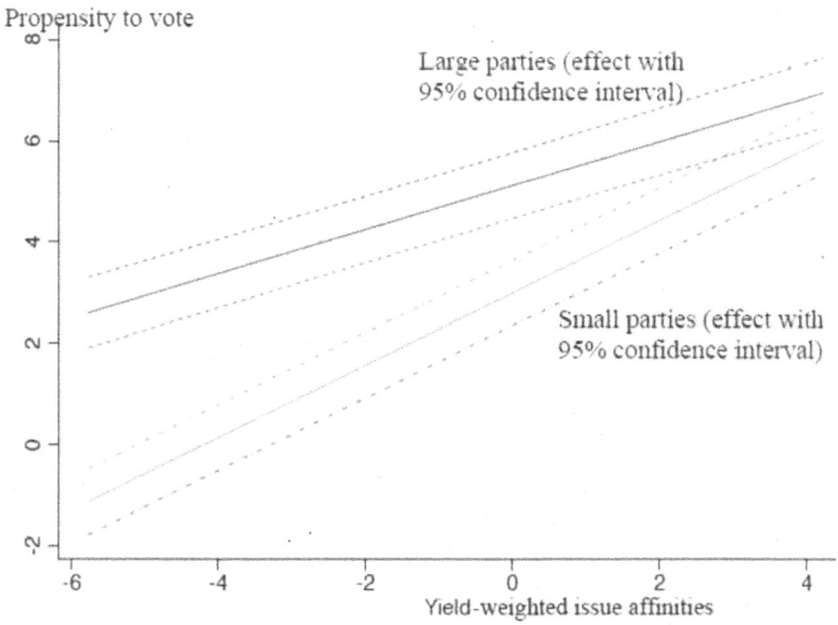

hypothesised. What we see is that a large party can maintain moderate levels of support (measured by propensity to vote) even among voters who have no (or indeed negative) issue affinity for the party, while a small party's support is quite low among voters with no issue affinity for it (and vanishes among voters whose issue affinity for it is negative).

Discussion

The question whether parties campaign on exactly the issues stressed in their manifestos has been raised several times in the literature on electoral politics and party choice (e.g. Ray 1999; Benoit *et al.* 2009). This question falls under a larger question, not previously posed as such but implicit in the theorising of Anthony Downs (1957), whether parties attempt to gain votes on the basis of strategic emphasis on issues that stand to benefit them the most. In this article we have contributed to answering this larger question by studying the final outcome of any and all attempts to gain votes on the basis of issue emphasis – the outcome in terms of voting behaviour.

We have establishing that voters make their choices on a basis that suggests an emphasis in their minds on those particular issues that indeed serve the strategic interests of the parties they vote for. How this emphasis was acquired is beyond the remit of this article, but somehow parties have succeeded in communicating to voters that they stand for policies that serve to increase their support, given the distribution of risks and opportunities represented by different issues in the minds of voters. In line with past findings, we observe that differing emphasis is given by voters to different issues (different issues have different salience in the minds of voters). Going beyond past findings, we also observe that differences in issue salience across voters and parties is such as to improve the electoral performance of parties over what would be observed if all issues had equal salience in voters' minds. Not surprisingly, and in line with past theorising, manifesto emphasis provides a good guide to the salience that parties appear to accord to different issues, but what this article has established is that the empirically observed differences in emphasis for different issues by different voters benefits parties even more than would have been the case if voters simply adopted the emphasis seen in manifestos.

This should not surprise us. Manifestos serve many purposes beyond telling voters what are the issues of most strategic importance to parties, and do not provide voters with their primary source of information about where parties stand. And indeed, according to our findings, voters acquire a somewhat different weight for issue affinities than the one that would be based purely on frequency of positive and negative mentions in party manifestos. The weights used by voters appear closer to those that would have been gained from campaigns in which parties stressed those issues that promise to maximise their potential gains from conversion while minimising their potential losses.[36]

We deem it most likely that our findings arise from conscious strategic decision-making by party leaders, who update their earlier strategic decisions reflected in manifesto content in the light of the somewhat different strategic context that they inevitably encounter during an actual electoral campaign; but other interpretations are possible. In particular, we may be seeing no more than that parties have long-term associations with particular issues in the minds of voters, though we doubt this could be the only mechanism at work. Only further research can settle this.

Nevertheless, parties that do not take conscious account of issue yield (or make equivalent judgements regarding which issues to stress during election campaigns) evidently should do so. The effects of issue yield are considerable. By picking an issue that promises high yield, a small party can effectively close the gap in the effects of issues that normally separate small from large parties – a gap that averages about three points on the 11-point propensity to vote scale, as shown in Figure 2. Large parties also gain from stressing issues with high yield, but not as much (as befits parties whose supporters have many other reasons to vote for them).

These findings emphasise the fact that elections involve strategic thinking. To be successful, it helps a lot for a party to be aware of the profile its supporters have in terms of support for different issues. Issues where supporters are divided are high-risk issues that parties need to avoid (as many apparently do). Issues where supporters are largely united are issues that present instead no risks, and could offer the possibility of gains if these issues find support outside the party.

That the strategy of issue emphasis is more vital for small parties comes as no surprise, but to the best of our knowledge this is the first study that has been able to document what appears to be successful strategic campaigning at work. More research is evidently needed to verify that parties do indeed stress the issues that the issue yield model predicts that they will stress – going beyond the already documented finding that the weights given to different issues in party manifestos themselves appear to take issue yield into account (De Sio and Weber 2011). But it would make sense for parties to direct their campaigns in this way.

Be that as it may, our findings also have implications for the process of political representation, suggesting the presence of mechanisms (presumably centred on efforts of political parties to realise strategic goals) that enable voters to progressively sort themselves into the support bases of parties that have the same profiles of issue concerns as they have themselves.

Acknowledgements

Mark Franklin is grateful for the support of the College of Arts and Social Sciences, Australian National University, which provided him with ideal working conditions during September 2011.

Notes

1. Albeit with mixed results, given that the cornerstone of Downsian theory is precisely that only the synthesising of political conflict into a single dimension (Black 1958; Downs 1957) can avoid the inherent disequilibria and decision cycles produced by issue multi-dimensionality (Arrow 1951; Riker 1982). As a result, most of the literature has concentrated on determining the conditions upon which the median voter theorem can be extended to multiple dimensions – conditions that are in general very restrictive (Ansolabehere and Snyder 2000; Davis and Hinich 1966; McKelvey 1986; Plott 1967).
2. This example should clarify the decoupling between the potential for a trade-off and the empirical presence of a difference of opinion regarding policy alternatives. Even in a country where 100 per cent of voters agreed on income redistribution, a potential trade-off would still exist on the issue: but, so long as the trade-off does not show up in public discourse, we would expect competition to take place on that issue in valence rather than in positional terms.
3. The 25 per cent disagreeing on the policy confirms the presence of a proper distribution of preferences.
4. We do not suppose that party leaders necessarily spend their time poring over polling figures trying to determine the issues on which their supporters are agreed. Politicians have other ways of gauging public opinion. Astute party leaders presumably have well-honed abilities to evaluate the potential of certain issues without necessarily requiring survey data. It is we who need survey data to understand the strategies that they eventually adopt.
5. These insights are not entirely new, as they are present – though part of a slightly different theoretical framework – in both the saliency theory (Budge and Farlie 1983) and the issue ownership (Petrocik 1996) approaches.
6. Defined as the share of respondents lying on the 'agree' side of the corresponding response item.
7. Compared to the default expectation that agreement and disagreement within each party is the same as in the whole electorate.
8. If we define p as the share of respondents that support a party, i as the share of respondents that support an issue, and f as the share of respondents that jointly support both, the formula for issue yield is $L = \frac{p(p-1)}{f+p(p-(1+i))}$ (see De Sio 2010; De Sio and Weber 2011).
9. Of course, it might be possible to convert opponents of the issue, both within and beyond a party, but this will produce a different proportion of supporters within and beyond the party and give rise to a different value of L.
10. The main quantities for computing issue yield indicators (party support, issue support, joint party–issue support) were derived from vote intention in national elections ('And if there was a general election tomorrow, which party would you vote for?') and from standard, five-point Likert response scales (strongly agree, agree, neither agree nor disagree, disagree, strongly disagree) on 12 issues presented in Appendix Table A1. These latter scales were dichotomised to calculate the measure of issue yield. Neutral values were coded 0.5, resulting in a conservative estimate of bridge issues because (dis)agreement is shrunk toward the midpoint.
11. The possibility for parties to exploit either the positive or the negative side of an issue has been taken into account in the analysis by separately computing issue yield for each side of each issue, then assuming that each party would exploit the side with the higher yield.
12. Otherwise, all predictors (being respondent-level) would have the same value across all the within-respondent observations: thus PTV differences across party-level observations for the same respondent could not be explained.
13. Control variables were included at the party–respondent level based on socio-demographics at the respondent level, and on respondents' party evaluations (which party did they feel closest to and which party did they think would perform best in terms of the most important problem facing their country). The specific procedure for doing so is based on multivariate regressions (run separately for each party) of a party's PTV on the

specific predictors: predicted values (y-hats) are then centred on their means and saved as scores for use in the later analysis as party–respondent-specific predictors (van der Eijk and Franklin 1996; van der Eijk *et al.* 2006).

14. A fourth version was computed as a robustness check (see below, note 32), but its detailed results are not reported.
15. With scores −1, 0, +1 corresponding to disagreement, neutral position, agreement.
16. In case of lack of any mention, the 'neutral' code is assigned.
17. Simplifying the five-point into a three-point scale is needed to render the voter and party scales comparable.
18. We also give a score of 0 when both are neutral, thus expressing the fact that this is a weaker form of agreement than when both are on the same side.
19. Actually, the difference between the emphases given to the two sides of the issue. For comparison, a model is provided in which issues are not weighted by manifesto emphasis.
20. Analogously to the manifesto emphasis score, this is based on the difference between issue yields for the positive or negative side of the issue.
21. As in the manifesto version, by the difference in yield between the positive and negative side of the issue.
22. With responses nested within respondents who are nested within countries. Random intercepts are specified at the country and respondent level. Since the model contains no party-level variables, we do not specify a party level in this model (see Table 2 for models that include a party level).
23. Education, union membership, marital status, employment status, social class (worker), family income, religion, and religiosity (church attendance).
24. Political interest and campaign interest.
25. Whether a party was considered best able to deal with the most important problem facing the country (the identity of the problem is not specified here).
26. Though one benefit of a stacked dataset is that it can include party-specific variables, we include no such variables in this model. We do have an expectation, detailed earlier, that party size and its interactions with yield-weighted issues will play a role in explaining party support. Specifically we expect support for small parties to be affected more strongly than support for large parties. However, in this initial test we have 12 measures of issue yield, and interactions between each of these and party size would produce more variables at the party level than we can handle in a multi-level model. Once we have established the ubiquity of the relationship we theorise, we can simplify the model so as to be able to include party size.
27. Obtained by squaring the correlation between observed values and values predicted by the model.
28. In this table we control for 'Party best for most important problem', which arguably already incorporates some effects of issue yield. We do this to provide the most conservative available test of those effects. Appendix Table A2 shows Models B and C without the Most Important Problem variable. Those models explain considerably less variance but show even greater gains for the Issue Yield model in comparison with a model employing salience-weighted affinities.
29. In Figure 1 we compare models B and C because this is the more critical comparison: models B and C have fewer significant differences than Models A and C. It is noteworthy that, with two exceptions, for issues where model C performs significantly better than Model B it also performs significantly better than Model A (it performs significantly better than Model A on an additional issue as well); but the two exceptions cancel out. For Q60, Model C performs significantly better than Model B but not than Model A, whereas for Q63 it is the other way around.
30. Effects for yield-weighted issue affinities do not indicate the importance of the issue. An issue with low yield, whose low yield is correctly anticipated, will get as high a coefficient as a correctly placed high yield issue. But this expectation breaks down for issues that promise no yield at all. An effect of zero for a yield-weighted issue implies that the issue

concerned is not a relevant basis for distinguishing between parties. That being the case, the yield-based effect will be zero, which would quite often be less than an issue effect calculated on a different basis.

31. Identification of the actual mechanism responsible for the superior performance of the Issue Yield model must wait on future research.
32. As a robustness check we created a fourth set of issue affinities for the 12 issues by generating y-hat predictors for each issue, in just the same way as for demographics and political interest. A y-hat affinity is, as already explained, 'tuned' to the dependent variable and can be regarded as the best affinity measure that can be gleaned without the benefit of any theoretical basis for linking voter preferences to parties. The overall predictive power of a model employing y-hat issue affinities is given by an R^2 of 0.367: more than the R^2 for Models A or B, but less than the R^2 for Model C. So yield-weighted issue affinities apparently work better even than a measure that posits a basis for these affinities derived purely from data-fitting (with y-hats, a correspondence such as the negative effect of Q65 in Models A and B, that makes no substantive sense, counts as 'correct' prediction).
33. See note 30.
34. Estimation was performed using *R*'s lme4 package. The quantities of interest for Figure 2 were simulated using Clarify (Imai *et al.* 2007; King *et al.* 2000). Because it is difficult (perhaps logically impossible) to simulate quantities of interest from a hierarchical model that contains random coefficients, we did not include random coefficients in any of the models in Table 2. However, a separate analysis (not shown but available on request) indicates that the standard error of the interaction term is only 0.005. So the effect of 0.5 shown for the interaction of party*size in Model E varies by no more than 0.01 (with 95 per cent probability) across countries. The effect of yield-weighted size itself varies rather more across countries, but by no more than 0.15 with 95 per cent probability. These variations are consistent with the standard errors for the same effects seen in Model E, suggesting no need to explicitly model these country-level variations. Moreover, the AIC is hardly reduced and BIC actually increases when random slopes are introduced into the analysis, supporting our choice of models to present in Table 2.
35. Because y-hat affinities are tuned to the dependent variable, in the absence of collinearity with other independent variables their effect would be 1.0. However, their indicated effect depends on the extent to which their uncontrolled effect is shared with other variables – the precise point of concern in this analysis. Model D tells us that about a third of the effect of party size is shared with other variables, probably mainly the Most Important Problem variable (because one-third is the extent to which 0.65 is less than 1.0). Model E shows no change in this situation, but Model F sees the bulk of the remaining effect of issue yield transferred to its interaction with party size. Substantively identical findings are obtained if, instead of *b* coefficients, we calculate standardised beta coefficients in these models, as explained earlier. But this would make it computationally challenging for us to plot the interaction of interest.
36. Indeed, voters adopt an emphasis on different issues that accords better with party needs than we would see if we adopted the blindly empiricist procedure of weighting each issue according to its observed covariation with party support (see note 32). The subtleties of the Issue Yield model do better in this respect than data-fitting.

References

Ansolabehere, S., and J.M. Snyder (2000). 'Valence Politics and Equilibrium in Spatial Election Models', *Public Choice*, 103:3, 327–36.

Arrow, Kenneth Joseph (1951). *Social Choice and Individual Values*. New York: Wiley.

Benoit, K., M. Laver, and S. Mikhaylov (2009). 'Treating Words as Data with Error: Uncertainty in Text Statements of Policy Positions', *American Journal of Political Science*, 53:2, 495–513.

Black, Duncan. 1958. *The Theory of Committees and Elections*. Cambridge: Cambridge University Press.

Braun, Daniela, Slava Mikhaylov, and Hermann Schmitt (2010). *European Parliament Election Study 2009, Manifesto Study*. GESIS Data Archive, Cologne. ZA5057 Data file Version 1.0.0, available at http://dx.doi.org/10.4232/1.10204, doi:10.4232/1.10204.

van der Brug, Wouter, and Cees van der Eijk (2007). *European Elections and Domestic Politics: Lessons from the Past and Scenarios for the Future*. Notre Dame, IN: University of Notre Dame Press.

van der Brug, Wouter Mark N. Franklin, and Gabor Toka (2008). 'One Electorate or Many? Differences in Party Preference Formation between New and Established European Democracies', *Electoral Studies*, 27:4, 589–600.

van der Eijk, Cees, and Mark N. Franklin (1996). *Choosing Europe? The European Electorate and National Politics in the Face of Union*. Ann Arbor, MI: University of Michigan Press.

van der Eijk, Cees, Wouter van der Brug, Martin Kroh, and Mark Franklin (2006). 'Rethinking the Dependent Variable in Voting Behavior: On the Measurement and Analysis of Electoral Utilities', *Electoral Studies*, 25:3, 424–47.

Budge, I., and D.J. Farlie (1983). *Explaining and Predicting Elections: Issue Effects and Party Stratégies in Twenty-three Democracies*. London: Allen & Unwin.

Carmines, Edward G., and James A. Stimson (1986). 'On the Structure and Sequence of Issue Evolution', *The American Political Science Review*, 80:3, 901–20.

Carmines, Edward G., and James A. Stimson (1989). *Issue Evolution: Race and the Transformation of American Politics*. Princeton, NJ: Princeton University Press.

Carmines, Edward G., and James A. Stimson (1993). 'On the Evolution of Political Issues', in William H. Riker (ed.), *Agenda Formation*. Ann Arbor: University of Michigan Press, 151–68.

Davis, O.A., and M. Hinich (1966). 'A Mathematical Model of Policy Formation in a Democratic Society', in J.L. Bernd (ed.), *Mathematical Applications in Political Science*. Dallas: Southern Methodist University Press, 175–205.

De Sio, Lorenzo (2010). 'Beyond "Position" and "Valence". A Unified Framework for the Analysis of Political Issues', working paper, European University Institute, available at http://cadmus.eui.eu/handle/1814/14814 (accessed 21 March 2011).

De Sio, Lorenzo, and Till Weber (2011). 'Issue Yield: A General Model of Issue Saliency Based on Party Competition Strategies, with an Application to the 2009 EP Elections'. ECPR Joint Sessions Workshops, St. Gallen.

Downs, Anthony (1957). *An Economic Theory of Democracy*. New York: Harper.

Egmond, Marcel van, Wouter van der Brug, Sara Hobolt, Mark Franklin, and Eliyahu V. Sapir (2011). *European Parliament Election Study 2009, Voter Study*. GESIS Datenarchiv, Köln. ZA5055 Datenfile Version 1.0.0, available at http://dx.doi.org/10.4232/1.10202, doi:10.4232/1.10202.

Imai, Kosuke, Gary King, and Olivia Lau (2011). Zelig: Everyone's Statistical Software, available at http://gking.harvard.edu/zelig/ (accessed 27 August 2012).

King, Gary, Michael Tomz, and Jason Wittenberg (2000). 'Making the Most of Statistical Analyses: Improving Interpretation and Presentation', *American Journal of Political Science*, 44:2, 347–61.

Iyengar, S., and D.R. Kinder (1987). *News that Matters*. Chicago: University of Chicago Press.

McKelvey, R.D. (1986). 'Covering, Dominance, and Institution-free Properties of Social Choice', *American Journal of Political Science*, 30:2, 283–314.

Pardos-Prado, Sergi, and Elias Dinas (2010). 'Systemic Polarisation and Spatial Voting', *European Journal of Political Research*, 49, 75–88.

Petrocik, J.R. (1996). 'Issue Ownership in Presidential Elections, with a 1980 Case Study', *American Journal of Political Science*, 40:3, 825–50.

Plott, C.R. (1967). 'A Notion of Equilibrium and its Possibility under Majority Rule', *American Economic Review*, 57, 787–806.

Ray, L., 1999. Measuring party positions on European integration: results from an expert survey. *The European Journal of Political Research*, 36:2, 283–306.

Riker, W.H. (1982). *Liberalism Against Populism.* San Francisco: Freeman.

Riker, W.H. (1986). *The Art of Political Manipulation.* New Haven: Yale University Press.

Riker, W.H. (1996). *The Strategy of Rhetoric: Campaigning for the American Constitution.* New Haven: Yale University Press.

Stokes, Donald E. (1963). 'Spatial Models of Party Competition', *American Political Science Review*, 57, 368–77.

Stokes, Donald E. (1992). 'Valence Politics', in Dennis Kavanagh (ed.), *Electoral Politics.* Oxford: Clarendon Press, 141–62.

APPENDIX

TABLE A1
ISSUE RESPONSE ITEMS IN THE VOTER SURVEY, AND THEIR MATCHING WITH MANIFESTO DATA

Voter survey	**Manifesto data**
Q56. Immigrants should be required to adapt to the customs of <country>	080100 Multiculturalism (r)
Q57. Private enterprise is the best way to solve <country>'s economic problems	050101 Free Enterprise
Q58. Same-sex marriages should be prohibited by law	090403 Homosexuals (r)
Q59. Major public services and industries ought to be in state ownership	050204 Publicly-Owned Industry; 050401 Nationalization
Q60. Women should be free to decide on matters of abortion	090502 Women
Q61. Politics should abstain from intervening in the economy	050201 Controlled Economy (r); 050600 Market Regulation (r)
Q62. People who break the law should be given much harsher sentences than they are these days.	080301 Law and Order
Q63. Income and wealth should be redistributed towards ordinary people	070300 Social Justice
Q64. Schools must teach children to obey authority	080200 Traditional Morality; 080301 Law and Order
Q65. EU treaty changes should be decided by referendum	020200 Democracy; 030102 Transfer of Power to the EC/EU (r)
Q66. A woman should be prepared to cut down on her paid work for the sake of her family.	080200 Traditional Morality; 090502 Women (r)
Q67. Immigration to <country> should be decreased significantly	080502 Immigration (r)

Note: (r) = reversed, i.e. the negative side of the manifesto item is matched to the 'agree' pole of the voter survey.

TABLE A2

ESTIMATED EFFECTS OF RIVAL THREE-LEVEL, RANDOM INTERCEPT MODELS OF PTVS, BASED ON DIFFERENT VERSIONS OF PARTY–RESPONDENT ISSUE AFFINITIES (OMITTING PARTY BEST FOR MOST IMPORTANT PROBLEM)

	Model B Salience-weighted affinities		Model C Yield-weighted affinities	
	b	s.e.	b	s.e.
Control variables:				
Demographics (y-hats)	0.857	(0.009)***	0.841	(0.009)***
Political awareness (y-hats)	0.720	(0.026)***	0.699	(0.027)***
This is party R feels close to (Dummy)	4.028	(0.067)***	3.948	(0.070)***
Party–respondent issue affinities:				
Q56. Immigrants should adapt	0.163	(0.010)***	0.040	(0.010)***
Q57. Private enterprise best solution	0.182	(0.009)***	0.267	(0.010)***
Q58. Prohibit gay marriages	0.049	(0.009)***	0.218	(0.012)***
Q59. State should own public services	0.064	(0.010)***	0.207	(0.012)***
Q60. Women should decide on abortion	0.029	(0.010)*	0.186	(0.011)***
Q61. Economy should be free of politics	0.113	(0.010)***	0.077	(0.012)***
Q62. Harsher prison sentences	0.104	(0.012)***	0.064	(0.013***
Q63. Redistribute income	0.245	(0.010)***	0.213	(0.012)***
Q64. Schools should teach authority	0.027	(0.011)*	0.169	(0.013)***
Q65. EU treaties should require referendum	−0.074	(0.010)***	0.057	(0.013)***
Q66. Women should cut work for family	0.022	(0.010)*	0.080	(0.013)***
Q67. Immigration should be reduced	0.124	(0.009)***	0.182	(0.013)***
Constant	3.407	(0.147)***	3.404	(0.353)***
Random effects:				
Standard deviation of respondent intercepts	0.677		0.776	
Standard deviation of country intercepts	0.765		0.775	
Observations: Level 1 (response)	150,482		150,482	
Level 2 (individual)	27,069		27,069	
Level 3 (country)	27		27	
R^2	0.223		0.254	
AIC	648102		601288	
BIC	648207		601482	

Note: Significant at *0.05, **0.01, ***0.001 levels.

The Causal Flow between Public Opinion and Policy: Government Responsiveness, Leadership, or Counter Movement?

ARMEN HAKHVERDIAN

This article examines the causal relationship between public opinion and policy. Does opinion affect policy or is it the other way around? Three hypotheses take centre stage. The responsiveness hypothesis postulates that changes in public opinion lead to subsequent changes in policy in the same direction. The leadership hypothesis reverses the causal arrow and states that a change in policy results in a subsequent change in opinion in the same direction. Finally, the counter hypothesis argues that policy change leads to a subsequent change in opinion in the opposite direction. These propositions are tested with time-series data from the United Kingdom from 1973 to 2006. Strong evidence is presented in support of policy responsiveness to public opinion. However, only conditional results were found for the other two hypotheses. Policy pushes public opinion in the same direction for popular incumbents (leadership), but in the opposite direction for unpopular incumbents (counter movement).

The relationship between public opinion and policy plays a key role in democratic government. Classic works on democratic representation define democracy in terms of a systematic opinion–policy link (Dahl 1971; May 1978; Pitkin 1967). According to these authors a polity cannot be called democratic unless a reliable public influence on government action exists. A vast literature has emerged that measures this opinion–policy nexus in all its facets.[1] One of the key issues to emerge from this literature revolves around the issue of causality. Does public opinion influence policy, or do governments shape public opinion? And if the latter holds, do governments align public preferences with their own preferences, or does the public move counter to government action?

Existing literature has found evidence in support of all these questions. The actions of elected political elites, however conceptualised and measured, depend on the wishes of the citizens which they represent (e.g. Achen 1978; Miller and Stokes 1963; Page and Shapiro 1983; Soroka and Wlezien 2010; Stimson *et al.* 1995). However, Paul Burstein (1998: 46) writes: 'Perhaps the most obvious objection to treating public opinion as an important determinant of policy change . . . is that public opinion is easily manipulated'. Even though 'leadership' is perhaps a more neutral term than 'manipulation', past scholarship has indeed shown that political elites manage to shape public opinion such that their actions cause a subsequent shift in mass opinion in the same direction (e.g. Gabel and Scheve 2007; Hill and Hurley 1999; McGraw *et al.* 1995; Ray 2003). Others, still, find the exact opposite of leadership – that shifts in policy in one direction lead to shift in public opinion in the other direction (e.g. Erikson *et al.* 2002; Wlezien 1995). These accounts show that the collective public possesses a type of rationality such that it adjusts its own demands for policy in relationship to the policies it receives.[2]

The abovementioned studies all have to overcome serious endogeneity concerns that surround the opinion–policy relationship. Some resort to experimental designs (McGraw *et al.* 1995), others to instrumental variables (Gabel and Scheve 2007), others still to time-series methods that allow for a precise temporal ordering of the main variables (Stimson *et al.* 1995). This study employs the latter method to examine the causal flow between public opinion and government action in the United Kingdom. It is important to remember that at its core the opinion–policy nexus is about power and influence. As Robert Dahl (1957: 204) wrote in his essay on power:

> A necessary condition for the power relation is that there exists a time lag, however small, from the action of the actor who is said to exert power to the responses of the respondent. This requirement merely accords with one's intuitive belief that [actor] *A* can hardly be said to have power over [actor] *a* unless *A*'s power attempts precede *a*'s responses.

We therefore follow Jacobs and Shapiro (1994: 14), who state that time-series approaches make it possible 'to investigate causal connections by comparing the temporal ordering of variables – whether a change in public opinion occurs after (leadership) or before (responsiveness)'.

This article presents empirical tests of the responsiveness, leadership, and counter hypotheses with new data drawn from the United Kingdom. In contrast to previous research which has mainly tested one of these conflicting hypotheses, the current study tests all three of these against the same data. Of course one can choose to examine policy and public opinion in separate issue domains such as defence, health care, immigration, and so on. Alternatively, one can move to a higher macro-level of political competition, namely, the left–right axis. However, even though scholars agree that post-war British politics has been conducted on an economic left–right axis (e.g. Budge 1999; Webb 2000), dense time-series of the left–right position of citizens and policy are virtually non-existent. This study employs a unique dataset of public preferences and government policy in the United Kingdom. For the policy series, we employ a measure developed by Hakhverdian (2009) who conducts computerised content analysis of legislative documents to derive the annual policy positions of most post-war British governments. For the opinion time-series we make use of a modified version of the classic left–right self-placement item from the Eurobarometer series. This enables us to examine the causal flow in the British political system on a policy dimension that is omnipresent in accounts of political competition, both in Britain and elsewhere.

The following section outlines the three main hypotheses concerning the opinion–policy relationship. Then the measurement of the key variables is explained and evidence for the validity of both variables is presented. The empirical section consists of two tests, one following Page and Shapiro's (1983) change-oriented design, the other using Granger causality tests. A final section argues for the conditional nature of the leadership and counter movement hypotheses.

The Relationship between Policy and Public Opinion

This section presents three different accounts of the causal direction between public opinion and government policy. The causal ordering of these two variables can be such that either opinion influences policy or, vice versa, policy influences opinion. A further distinction is possible for the latter relationship between those arguing for a positive effect of policy on opinion and those positing a negative relationship, yielding three theoretical expectations concerning opinion, policy, and their causal ordering:

1. *Responsiveness Hypothesis:* Public opinion change leads to a subsequent policy change in the same direction.
2. *Leadership Hypothesis:* Policy change leads to a subsequent opinion change in the same direction.
3. *Counter Movement Hypothesis:* Policy change leads to a subsequent opinion change in the opposite direction.

Government Responsiveness

The responsiveness of government policy to public preferences is one of the hallmarks of democratic governance (Dahl 1971; Pitkin 1967). A large and ever growing literature has been devoted to the empirical examination of that claim and found that public preferences indeed influence actions of governments and representatives. That is to say, as public preferences shift to one direction, policy outputs, however broadly defined, follow suit. The causal mechanisms behind this relationship are two-fold: the public influences policy by determining who governs and by altering the behaviour of those who actually govern (Hakhverdian 2010; Hobolt and Klemmensen 2008; Jennings and John 2009; Stimson *et al.* 1995; Wlezien 2004). In a seminal study, Stimson *et al.* (1995) label these two mechanisms 'electoral turnover' and 'rational anticipation'.

Electoral turnover as a representational mechanism has made its appearance in the scholarly literature under alternative monikers such as 'responsible party government' (Ranney 1954), 'partisan theory' (Hibbs 1977), 'promissory representation' (Mansbridge 2003), or 'mandate politics' (McDonald and Budge 2005). The basic idea is that the electorate votes a government into office that matches its own preferences, after which that government implements policy promises on the basis of which it was elected. In the British case, a left-of-centre electorate is expected to elect a Labour government, which, once elected, enforces left-of-centre policies, thus ensuring that public preferences indirectly influence government policy. If policy were to drift too far away from public opinion, the turnover of government at the next election would ensure that policy moves back to the preferred location of the electorate.

Electoral turnover is the conventional pathway to political representation in general. It constitutes the replacement mechanism that early classics in party government saw as central to representative democracy. Austin Ranney (1954: 12), for example, finds that 'only in the alternation in office of such [responsible and coherent] parties can the popular will be translated into government action'. Electoral turnover is based on the fundamental assumption that the behaviour of political actors is policy-oriented. However, as Anthony Downs (1957: 28) famously wrote: 'parties formulate policies in order to win elections rather than win elections in order to formulate policies'. This opens up a direct pathway of influence from public preferences to policy by introducing vote-seeking incentives to the mix. Governments will not stay put at their ideal policy location under the threat of electoral sanction. Rather, under the right circumstances, policy will shift to the position of the median voter and, as such, governments will anticipate electoral defeat. Rational anticipation can therefore be defined as the direct effect of public opinion on policy after partisan composition of the government has been controlled for (Stimson *et al.* 1995).

In sum, electoral turnover is the channel through which policy-oriented behaviour emerges, while rational anticipation is governed by vote-maximising motives. For vulnerable incumbents, vote-seeking might overshadow policy-seeking behaviour and vice versa for safe incumbents (Hakhverdian 2010; Hobolt and Klemmensen 2008). But both mechanisms of representation work together to ensure that changes in public opinion are followed by changes in government policy in the same direction.

Democratic Leadership

Previous research has demonstrated that policy shifts are, at least in part, based on public opinion shifts. Still, public opinion should by no means be treated as some sort of unmoved mover, completely exogenous to political context. Politicians can, and in fact do, influence public opinion (Gabel and Scheve 2007; Hill and Hurley 1999; Steenbergen *et al.* 2007). More specifically, political elites, be they parties, candidates, or governments, are often able to push public opinion closer to their own policy location. This manifestation of the opinion–policy nexus is often labelled leadership, persuasion, cueing, or even manipulation. While these labels are normatively distinct, the key point, to paraphrase John Geer (1996), is that democratic leadership occurs when a public's policy preferences align with that of the government.

Politicians certainly express their desire for opinion leadership. Theodore Roosevelt once famously proclaimed: 'I simply made up my mind what they [the people] ought to think, and then did my best to get them to think it' (quoted in Warren 1964: 23). In her second term as Prime Minister, Margaret Thatcher said: 'I came to office with one deliberate intent: to change Britain from a dependent to a self-reliant society – from a give-it-to-me, to a do-it-yourself nation. A get-up-and-go, instead of a sit-back-and-wait-for-it Britain.'[3] As Leader of the Opposition she even claimed that her job was 'to stop Britain going red'.[4]

The actual success of the politics of persuasion depends on a number of factors (see Druckmann and Lupia 2000 for an overview). When it comes to the side of the recipient, moderates have been shown to be the most prone to changing their beliefs (Kinder 1998; Zaller 1992). We might therefore expect a shift in government action to push the mean voter along. On a more contextual level, Hill and Hurley (1999) argue that elites are likely to influence masses on main lines of cleavage. The economic left–right axis certainly qualifies as this is perhaps *the* overarching line of conflict in British politics. Finally, source-effects also come into play, as the ability for persuasion rises with the trustworthiness and expertise of the source (Page *et al.* 1987).

Next to theories of persuasion, the leadership hypothesis can also be traced to theories of 'preference-shaping' (Dunleavy 1991; Dunleavy and Ward 1981). Patrick Dunleavy and Hugh Ward take issue with the treatment of preferences as exogenous in Downsian models of voting and argue it to be in conflict with the basic tenets of rational choice theory.[5] They write:

> The assumption that voters' preferences are invariant in response to party competition is not consistent with the assumption that the party winning the previous election takes states power. For within a framework of rational party decision making it would in some

> circumstances be rational for the party in power to seek to maximise its electoral chances by using state power to alter the distribution of preferences in the electorate in its favour. (Dunleavy and Ward 1981: 365–6)

Dunleavy and Ward outline a host of possible strategies that parties could employ to shape preferences *to their advantage*, both in and out of office. In fact, not doing so would be irrational, or so their argument goes. All in all, based on these strands of scholarship, a shift in public opinion ought to be preceded by a congruent shift in government action.

Counter Movement

Finally, public opinion may run counter to government policy (Erikson *et al.* 2002; Soroka and Wlezien 2010; Stevenson 2001; Wlezien 1995). When a government overshoots its target in terms of policy, the electorate provides feedback in the form of a correction back to the mainstream. A textbook example of this counter reaction is the strong post-Vietnam shift of the American public against military and other involvement abroad (Page and Shapiro 1992). Perhaps the boldest statement of feedback of this nature is Christopher Wlezien's (1995) notion of 'thermostatic' public opinion. According to Wlezien, public preferences will shift negatively in response to actual policy outputs. In terms of spending, the public adjusts its preferences for more spending downward (upward) at time *t* when appropriations have increased (decreased) at time *t*–1. Much like a thermostat, which sends a signal when the actual temperature differs from the favoured temperature until the heat is sufficiently adjusted, the public signals to policy makers about policy. Erikson *et al.* (2002) adopt Wlezien's framework in their examination of American public mood and find considerable evidence of negative feedback between opinion and policy activity. Kellstedt (2000) finds similar results in the United States for racial policy preferences and federal spending on key agencies in civil rights enforcement. Stevenson (2001) shows that higher social spending causes a shift to the right in public mood.[6] A counter movement of this nature is certainly expected to be present in the British political system since the first-past-the-post electoral system routinely produces governments to the left or to the right of the mean voter (Klingemann *et al.* 2006; Powell 2000). In the left–right terminology of the present article, the public is expected to adjust its preferences leftwards if it feels government policy has shifted too much to the right.

Counter movement of public opinion to policy is normatively appealing in the sense that it puts stock in public rationality. For negative feedback to occur, the public has to have valid and reliable information on government action. In the case of Wlezien's original model, the public has to possess knowledge on whether appropriations in defence and domestic domains have gone up or down. The mass media assumedly plays a large mediating role in conveying this message, and with spending data one can perhaps picture people adjusting their preferences for 'more' or 'less' spending based on media information they receive. All the public needs is to be given an indication of the broad direction of appropriations, not the exact amounts. But the public thermostat is not just expected to work with government action in terms of spending. Franklin and Wlezien (1997) apply the model to European integration, an area that has notoriously lacked voter and media attention, at least at the time of their writing. It appears that even the European public as a whole adjusts its preferences for more or less integration based on the volume of legislation emanating from Brussels. The policy measure that Franklin and Wlezien use is a simple annual count of the number of lines devoted to Regulations and Directives in the *Official Journal* of the European Community. With a media largely apathetic to European legislation, it is certainly impressive that the public annually updates its preference for more integration downward as the volume of European legislation increases.

Similar challenges present themselves when capturing policy and opinion on the left–right scale using legislative documents. The policy variable employed here is based on content analysis of the yearly Budget Statement. Still, the delivery of the Budget Statement is one of the best covered political events in the United Kingdom, so if voters would respond to any legislative action, this would be it. The media could certainly convey whether the government has, for example, decided to intervene in the economy, to raise or lower taxes, to increase or decrease the minimum wage, and so on. In precise terms, the British public would be expected to locate itself further to the left (right), as the government policy derived from the Budget Statement changes to the right (left).

Data and Measurement

The next two sections deal with the measurement of the key variables, policy and public opinion. Most existing time-series of these variables either have two few time-points or capture issue emphasis rather than position. Therefore, for the purpose of the present study, we combine a new measure of policy with a well-known indicator of public opinion. For policy, we rely on a computerised content analysis of government documents. For opinion, we employ the left–right self-placement item from the Eurobarometer.

Government Policy

Valid and reliable policy estimates of parties, governments, and voters are indispensable for testing theories of political competition, coalition formation, policy responsiveness, and cleavage politics, to name but a few. For the present study, we require a left–right measure for the observed policy behaviour of British government. When it comes to the longitudinal analysis of left-right positions of governments, the Comparative Manifesto Project (CMP) was long seen as the only game in town (Klingemann *et al.* 2006). Still, since the CMP coding scheme is based on party election manifestos, the post-war period only provides a maximum of 15 time-points for Britain.

As a result, more and more scholars have shifted their attention from election programmes to legislative speeches. In the British case, some have analysed the annual Queen's Speech, which contains the government's policy intentions for the coming year (Hobolt and Klemmensen 2008; Jennings and John 2009). The time-series variables employed there represent the relative importance of separate policy domains, such as social services, health care, defence, and so on. These studies contain annual observations for a period of at least 30 years, but, unlike the CMP data, most emphasis approaches cannot be transformed into left–right position scores, because their coding schemes are not designed with positional purposes in mind.

The challenge, then, is to construct a long time-series of the left–right policy position of government speeches with enough degrees of freedom to comfortably pursue regression techniques. The policy document of focus will be the Budget Speech, which is annually delivered by the Chancellor of the Exchequor to the House of Commons to outline policy in terms of spending and revenues, as well as monetary and fiscal matters. While election manifestos clearly constitute promises that a party makes vis-à-vis the electorate, the Budget Speech is more concerned with actual policy outputs. It contains information on the government's general role in shaping economic policy so it offers potential to distinguish between speeches in terms of their left–right policy content.[7]

Instead of applying pre-existing coding schemes specifically designed for party manifestos to code speeches, the dependent variable is constructed using a content analysis technique known as Wordscores (Laver *et al.* 2003; see also Hakhverdian 2009). Figure 1 depicts the movement of British government policy on the left–right scale from 1956 to 2006, measured in this fashion. Of course, as is the case with any newly constructed indicator, there are legitimate validity concerns. However, this particular policy variable has been shown to validly depict the left–right tendency of government policy in post-war Britain. First, the Wordscores measure compares well to expert survey data. Second, government policy is characterised by a general trend towards the right from the early 1970s onwards, which is consistent with studies on the restructuring of the welfare state. Third, a visual inspection of Figure 1 quickly reveals that, in the time-frame under investigation, every major policy shift to the right coincides with a change from Labour to Tory rule and vice versa. Fourth, the placement of individual administrations conforms to historical accounts of post-war British politics. In addition to these four sources of validation outlined in Hakhverdian (2009), the policy variable correlates well with

FIGURE 1
BRITISH GOVERNMENT POLICY ON THE LEFT–RIGHT SCALE

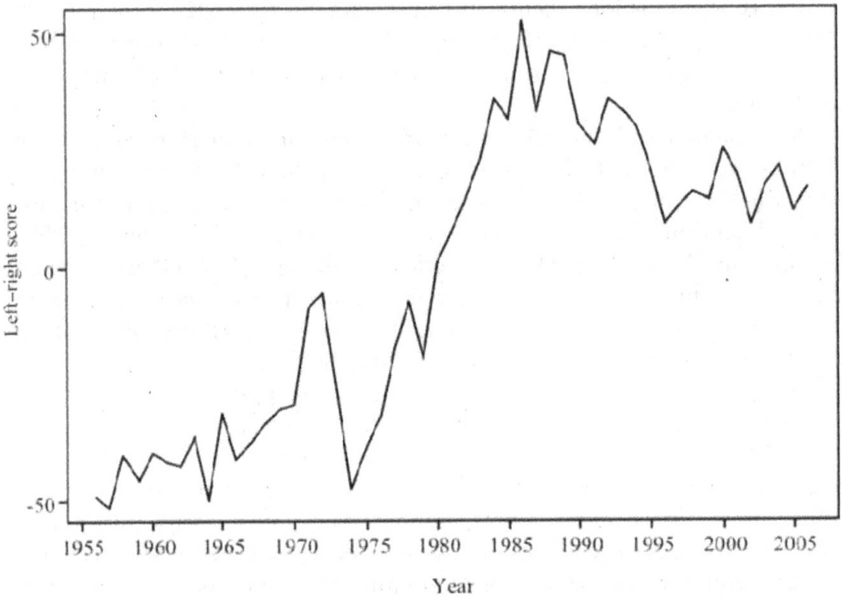

actual spending outputs. Using the annual spending data compiled by Soroka and Wlezien (2010) on education, health care, pensions, defence, and transportation, we find correlations of around –0.70 for the first three domains, 0.43 for the defence domain, and –0.22 for the transportation domain (not statistically significant). That is to say, right-wing values on government policy go together with lower social spending and higher defence spending, precisely as one would expect. This indicates to a considerable extent that the Budget Speech captures policy output for the parliamentary year ahead. All in all, Wordscores is thus able to replicate the CMP left–right time-series with the essential advantage of providing more points of observation.

Public Preferences

In order to carry out statistical tests of causality between opinion and policy, a long time-series of voter left–right preferences is just as important as a long time-series of government policy. As ever, though, theoretical ambitions are constrained by data availability. Geoffrey Evans and his colleagues (1996) argue that mass preferences are best captured by batteries of survey items (also see Ansolabehere *et al.* 2008). Since the political axis of interest is the economic left–right dimension, one would require survey data on matters pertaining to redistribution, the scope of government action, equality, and the like, and then combine these into some sort of left–right index. The reality of survey research, however, prohibits this strategy in time-series settings because of insufficient time-points. Fortunately, the Eurobarometer offers a solution since it asks of its respondents, over a period of 30 years, to place themselves on the left–right scale. These self-assigned ideological scores have been shown time and time again to reflect actual economic policy preferences (Huber 1989; Pattie and Johnston 2001). When the left–right preferences of all respondents in a given year are aggregated, a single mean score will emerge as an indicator of the preferences of the British electorate. The annual mean left–right self-placement score of the British population as a whole was calculated for all Eurobarometer surveys from 1973 onwards. It is important to note that missing data could potentially lead to severe biases in aggregate left–right self-placement. Since the lower educated and manual classes are more likely to refrain from answering, listwise deletion of incomplete data could bias the mean score to the right. Single imputation was therefore used to 'fill in the blanks' using as many independent variables as were available for the entire time frame. While there is a data-point in 1973, the Eurobarometer skipped the self-placement item in 1974 and 1975, but returned the item from 1976 onwards. The mean scores for these two missing years have been imputed from the individual level as well. Finally, it is important to note that the Eurobarometer item runs from 1 on the left to 10 on the right.

The movement of the mean voter on the left–right scale is displayed in Figure 2. The mid-1970s, which eventually culminated in the election of Margaret Thatcher in 1979, have been famously dubbed 'The Great Moving Right Show' (Hall 1979). Indeed, from 1973 to 1979 average voter ideology made a considerable shift to the right of about 0.44.[8] However, during the mid-1980s and 1990s, public opinion took a turn towards the political centre, and still further to the left. With the Tories in power for 18 years, public opinion shifted a massive 0.73 points to the left from 1979 to 1997.[9] Towards the end of Labour's third consecutive term, Philip Stephens, political commentator for the *Financial Times*, wrote that 'the zeitgeist has changed. Middle Britain has tired of bloated government. The pendulum has swung back to champions of a smaller state' (Stephens 2007). Figure 2 supports Stephens' statement. From 1997 to 2006, there has been a rightward movement in aggregate preference of 0.22 points.

Results

Now that both key variables have been captured on the left–right scale, we move along to the actual analysis of the causal flow in the British political system. The first section uses two separate, yet related, methods to examine the direction of causality between policy and public opinion. More specially, these methods consist of the 'change-oriented design' as used by Page and Shapiro (1983) and the more conventional Granger causality tests. Both are

FIGURE 2
LEFT–RIGHT SELF-PLACEMENT OF THE MEAN VOTER

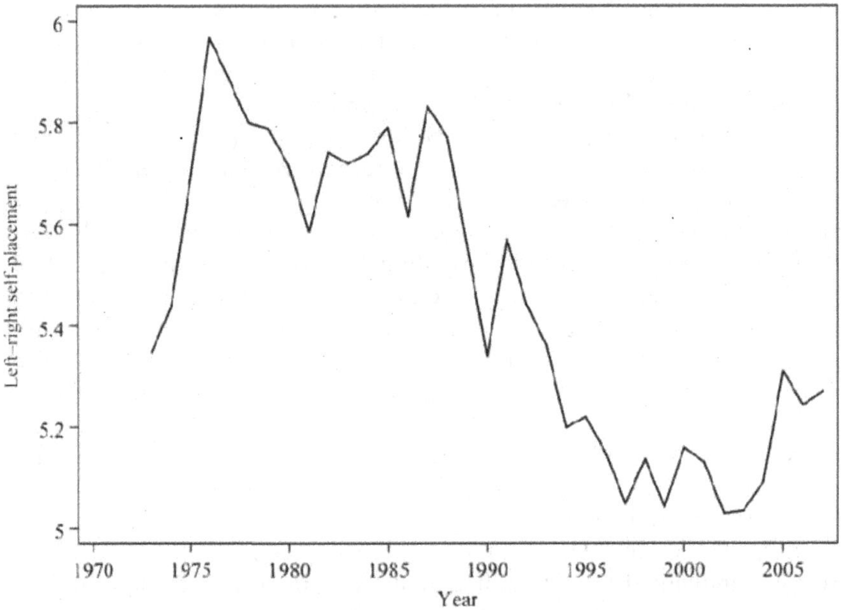

fundamentally based on the idea of analysing which temporal ordering of the variables fits the data the best. The second section focuses in more detail on the effects of policy on opinion and introduces a conditional result that resolves the apparent contradictory claims of the counter movement and leadership hypotheses.

Direction of Causality

A 'change-oriented' design. Before scholars had started to construct time-series of policy and opinion, or even had sufficient data to undertake such endeavours, Benjamin Page and Robert Shapiro (1983) devised a strategy with which they were still able to model these variables temporally. Their 'change-oriented' design attempts to 'ascertain whether policy moves in the same direction as policy – that is, *congruently* – or in the opposite direction, or not at all' (Page and Shapiro 1983: 176, emphasis original). Using survey marginals from a host of polling organisations, Page and Shapiro isolate those political items that showed a change of more than 6 percentage points from one time-point to another, the margin of errors of these samples tending to be ± 3 per cent. The resulting instances of change are then linked to comparable measures of government policy at various time-lags. Page and Shapiro go on to show that in two-thirds of all cases in which opinion changed in either direction, policy followed in the same direction a year after.

It is obviously beyond our scope to gather data on hundreds of survey marginals and policy outputs, but it is well within our reach to replicate a change-oriented design with the available opinion–policy time-series. In line with Page and Shapiro (1983), the responsiveness hypothesis requires that a change in policy to the left (right) ought to be preceded by a change in opinion to the left (right). More specifically, policy change and prior opinion change are expected to be positively related to one another. For the leadership and counter movement hypotheses we reverse the causal ordering such that a change in opinion is preceded by a change in policy. The leadership hypothesis posits a positive relationship between the two, while for a corroboration of the counter movement hypothesis the relationship would have to be negative.

Figure 3 shows that policy change and prior opinion change are largely congruent. Pearson's $r = 0.49$ and is significant at the 99 per cent confidence level, which means that the null hypothesis of no congruence can be confidently rejected. Erikson *et al.* (2002) use a similar bivariate design to measure the strength of responsiveness in the United States. While the focus above was on the annual Budget Statement, Erikson and his colleagues consider biennial legislative sessions (22 in total from 1953 to 1996) and presidencies (11 in the same time-frame). For Congress, they state that 'the most conservative legislative sessions, 1954 and 1982, followed the most conservative *Mood* periods and, similarly, the liberal 1960s lawmaking followed a period of high public liberalism' (Erikson *et al.* 2002: 340, emphasis original). For presidencies, they reach a similar conclusion: 'Net policy during a four-year presidential term is nearly perfectly predicted from knowing the public's *Policy Mood* during the prior four-year period' (Erikson *et al.* 2002: 342, emphasis in original). All in all, congruent with the findings of the Macro Policy team, Figure 3 provides evidence in support of the responsiveness hypothesis.

One might object that the explained variance of 25 per cent is unimpressive. Still, one has to bear in mind that the use of differenced variables greatly deflates R^2 statistics.[10] More importantly, while a positive relationship is found when pooling all governments together, one finds important heterogeneity below the surface. Existing research has shown that the relationship between policy and opinion is conditional upon an incumbent's electoral vulnerability (Hakhverdian 2010; Hobolt and Klemmensen 2008). In this study, vulnerability is conceived as simply the difference between the popularity of the government compared to the popularity of the main opposition party with positive values indicating an electoral buffer for the incumbent.[11] The sample is then split into two groups at the median value for incumbent vulnerability (3.8 per cent). The original correlation of 0.49 as depicted in Figure 3 holds when including all governments regardless of their electoral buffer. However, for vulnerable incumbents this correlation increases to a sizeable 0.67 ($p < 0.01$), but it drops to 0.26 ($p = 0.36$) for safe incumbents. The responsiveness of policy to

FIGURE 3
THE RELATIONSHIP BETWEEN POLICY CHANGE AND PRIOR OPINION CHANGE

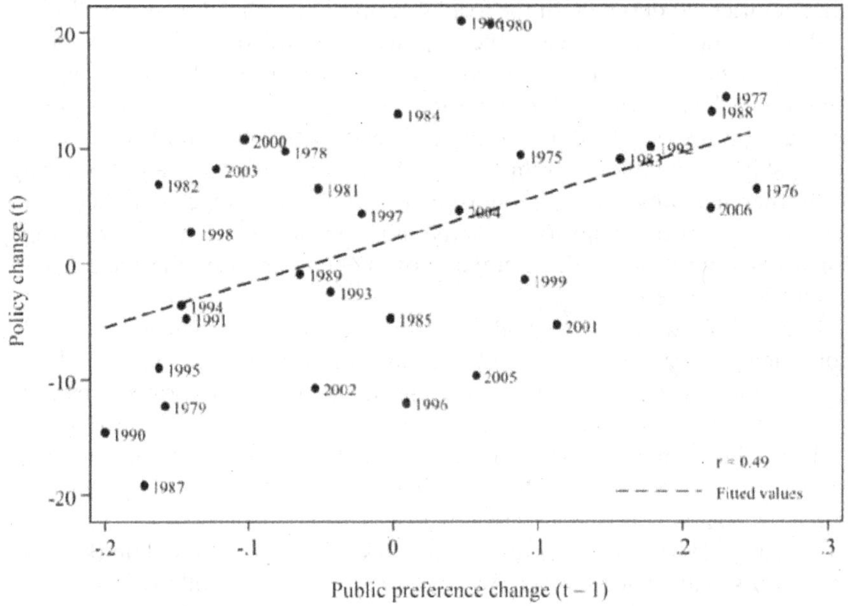

public opinion therefore hinges on electoral context. A serious threat to the re-election chances of the government ensures a strong relationship between policy and public opinion.

The responsiveness hypothesis receives empirical support, but what about the leadership and counter movement hypotheses? In order to test for the effects of policy change on subsequent opinion change, we swap the axes and time-lags of Figure 3. Figure 4 depicts the relationship between opinion change and prior policy change. It is apparent from the graph that this particular sequencing has a very poor fit with the data. Pearson's $r = -0.077$, but is nowhere near conventional levels of statistical significance. Opinion change certainly occurs, but whatever its sources, prior policy change does not seem to be one of them. Using these aggregate left–right data, policy change does not push opinion in the same or the opposite direction. All in all, both the leadership and counter movement hypotheses seem to collapse in the face of these findings. Based on Figures 3 and 4, we reach a similar conclusion to Page and Shapiro (1983: 188): 'Almost certainly the opposite process of opinion affecting policy is the more prevalent one.'

Granger causality. Another, more commonly used, test for causal ordering is the Granger causality test (Granger 1969). For the bivariate case, x 'Granger causes' y if past values of x contain information that helps predict

FIGURE 4
THE RELATIONSHIP BETWEEN OPINION CHANGE AND PRIOR POLICY CHANGE

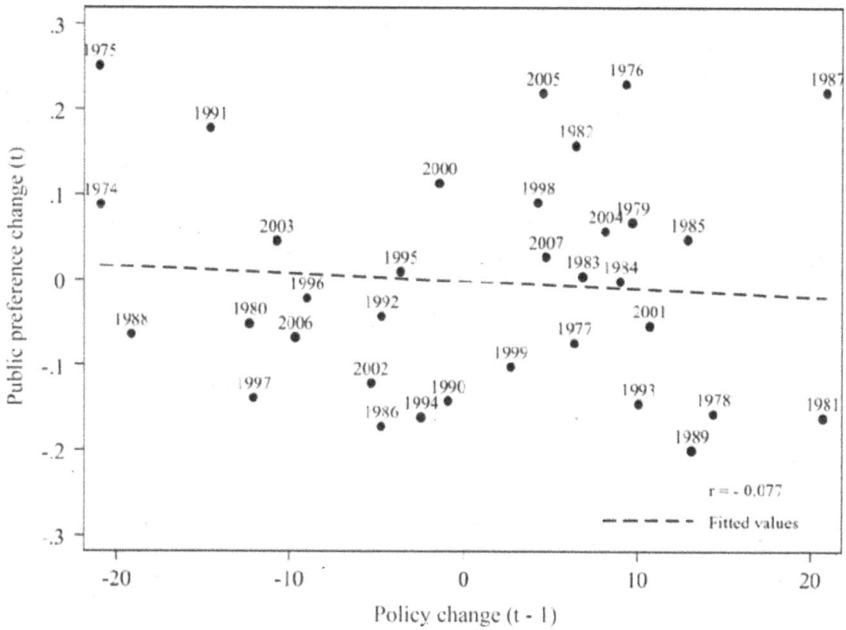

y above and beyond the information contained in past values of *y* alone. This notion of causality lies at the very heart of the dynamic representation approach that was introduced by Stimson *et al.* (1995) and also forms the backbone of most regression models of policy responsiveness. If public preferences have an effect on policy, after past values of policy have been controlled for, then public preferences 'Granger cause' policy. Swapping the independent and dependent variables allows one to assess which design fits the data best, which then reveals the likely direction of the causal flow.

The Granger causality test first involves estimating vector auto-regression (VAR) models with policy and preferences as the endogenous variables at various time-lags. These variables are required to be stationary, so the policy measure was de-trended first. In VAR, each variable is regressed on its own lagged values and the lagged values of all other variables – in our case, just public opinion – in level form. Various model selection criteria were used to determine the appropriate number of lags for the ensuing VAR models. The Akaike Information Criterion (AIC), the Bayesian Information Criterion (BIC), and a likelihood ratio test all point towards a model specification with one lag. The null hypothesis of the actual causality test then states that *x* does *not* 'Granger cause' *y*.

The first row in Table 1 shows that the null hypothesis can be confidently rejected here, meaning that public opinion 'Granger causes'

TABLE 1
GRANGER CAUSALITY TESTS OF POLICY AND PUBLIC OPINION

Causal flow	χ^2	*p*-value
Preferences cause policy	11.68	0.001
Policy causes preferences	0.82	0.36
Lagrange-multiplier Test	3.40	0.49

Note: The χ^2 entries are derived from Wald tests.

government policy. In line with the earlier findings from Figure 3, the responsiveness hypothesis receives strong support. The second row reveals a failure to reject the null hypothesis in the opposite direction, indicating that policy does not 'Granger cause' public opinion. In other words, having additional knowledge of government policy does not help us in predicting movements in public opinion above and beyond what we could have predicted using public opinion alone. Again, in line with the abovementioned results, and in direct opposition to both the leadership and counter movement hypotheses, there is no evidence of a causal flow from government policy to opinion. In line with Stimson *et al.* (1995: 546), the conclusion from these Granger causality tests has to be that 'previous opinion predicts current policy, even controlling for previous policy, whereas previous policy fails . . . to have statistically discernible ability to predict current opinion'.

The Conditional Nature of Leadership and Counter Movement

Based on the tests conducted above, the causal flow between public opinion and government policy in the British political system points unambiguously towards public opinion affecting policy, but not the other way around. Public opinion change seems to be impervious to government action, invalidating explanations based on leadership theories as well as counter movement accounts of public opinion. If anything, these results are indicative of public ignorance or apathy regarding government policy.

However, a visual inspection of Figures 2 and 4 quickly reveals that a closer examination of the leadership and counter movement hypotheses is in order. As for Figure 2, there is no denying that in certain years public opinion has moved counter to government ideology. We see a clear move to the right under the Labour-led Callaghan government of the mid-to-late 1970s, a sharp turn to the left under John Major's Conservative government in the early 1990s and what appears to be the beginnings of a rightward shift in the later Blair years of the 2000s. Moreover, consistent with leadership principles, public opinion clearly moves to the right in the early 1980s under Margaret Thatcher's rule. While such a rough visual analysis is by no means conclusive, it does open up the possibility that leadership and counter movement dynamics both operate at the same time, yet for different types of governments. In other words, under certain conditions policy change results in subsequent public opinion change in the same direction, under other conditions in the opposite direction, but we end up with the null finding of Figure 4 when all years are pooled together. Just as responsiveness was shown to be conditional on electoral context, the same might hold for leadership and thermostat.

When would we expect policy shifts to lead to consequent changes in mass opinion? Put differently, under what conditions can the public be persuaded by elites to change its views? The literature on elite cueing in the European integration process offers some guidance. The existence of top-down influences from leaders to citizens appears to be conditional on a host of individual-level as well as contextual factors (Ray 2003; Steenbergen *et al.* 2007). For instance, leaders are only able to influence followers on issues that are perceived as salient by those same followers. More importantly for our purposes, Ray asserts that persuasion is more effective when the

FIGURE 5
THE CONDITIONAL NATURE OF LEADERSHIP AND COUNTER MOVEMENT

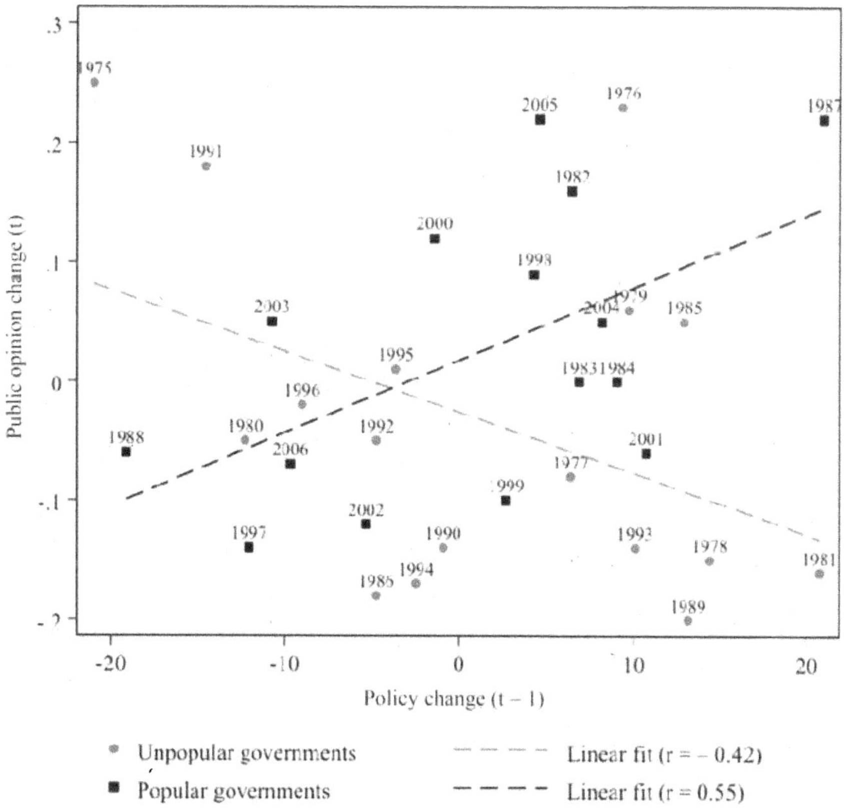

recipient displays positive affect for the source of communication. Simply put, the public is more likely to shift its position in the same direction as a result of a shift in government action when that government is popular. Also, both Ray (2003) and Steenbergen *et al.* (2007) show that elite cueing suffers from internal dissent among the party leadership. Given that dissent is less likely when the governing party is popular, we would expect leadership of public opinion to occur especially for popular governments. It should come as no surprise that most empirical accounts of leadership focus on popular leaders such as Ronald Reagan, Margaret Thatcher, or Tony Blair. On the other hand, unpopular governments should be more prone to the counter movement as predicted by the thermostat hypothesis.

To test for these conditional effects, Figure 4 is reproduced but, just as before, the sample of governments is divided into two equal groups based on their popularity vis-à-vis the opposition (the median value for this electoral buffer is 3.8 per cent). Figure 4 has already shown that for the combined sample no relationship emerges between opinion change and prior policy change. However, Figure 5 puts that finding into perspective. The positive relationship between opinion change and prior policy change only exists for popular governments, while the negative relationship only holds for unpopular governments. The correlation for the former equals $r = 0.55$ ($p = 0.036$), for the latter $r = -0.42$ ($p = 0.096$). Both the leadership and thermostat hypotheses therefore seem to receive conditional support from the data, much in line with the abovementioned visual inspection of the opinion time-series (Figure 2). These findings suggest that the contradictory claims of these two hypothesis may reflect the conditional nature of the policy–opinion linkage.

Conclusion

This article set out to examine the relationship between public opinion and government policy in the United Kingdom. Three hypotheses were derived from the literature on the opinion–policy link and tested with time-series data from 1973 to 2006. The responsiveness hypothesis received strong support, indicating that opinion change often leads to policy change in the same direction in the subsequent year. However, no evidence was found for reverse effects of policy on opinion when altering the temporal ordering of these variables. While this finding entails a poor fit of the leadership and counter movement hypothesis using these British left–right data, a closer inspection revealed that the non-relationship was the result of conditional effects. That is to say, popular governments proved able to change public opinion in the same direction as their prior policy shift, as the leadership hypothesis would predict. On the other hand, the public moved counter to government policy when this policy was enacted by unpopular governments. As such, these conditional findings are in line with previous research which found that elite cueing and persuasion depend on a number of recipient-, context-, and source-specific factors (e.g. Hill and Hurley 1999; Ray 2003; Zaller 1992).

These results indicate that much is to be gained by examining variance in the strength and causal direction of the opinion–policy nexus and subsequently provide explanations for that variance. Some sources of conditionality have been covered by others, chief among them institutional context (Hobolt and Klemmensen 2008; Soroka and Wlezien 2010, 2012). For example, Soroka and Wlezien (2010) rightly point out that public responsiveness to policy requires that the public possesses accurate information about government activity. Confusion about policy responsibility hampers the negative feedback that forms the core of their thermostatic model. As a consequence, public responsiveness to policy is notably weaker in federal than unitary states (Soroka and Wlezien 2012). The same logic should apply to leadership and counter movement effects. This study has shown that the electoral context plays a key role, both in strengthening government responsiveness to public opinion, and in providing a background against which either leadership or counter movement effects might operate, but it has done so in a very specific institutional setting, namely the Westminster system. Given that clarity of responsibility is well established in the United Kingdom with its system of one-party government (the current exception notwithstanding), the likelihood of the policy signal being confused is small compared to countries with coalition governments. Soroka and Wlezien's research would suggest that similar findings are unlikely to emerge in contexts where policy signals have multiple sources. Whether leadership and counter movement dynamics hold in these 'confused responsibility' settings is an important avenue for future research.

Acknowledgements

A previous version of this paper was presented at the 2011 Joint Sessions of the ECPR in St. Gallen, Switzerland. I would like to thank the participants of the workshop 'Issue Congruence and Policy Responsiveness in European Governance' and the convenors, Mark Franklin and Christine Arnold. I am also grateful to Sara Hobolt, Geoff Evans, Steve Fisher, Mark Franklin, Paul Warwick, and Chris Wlezien for comments on previous drafts. All remaining errors are my own.

Notes

1. For overviews, see Burstein (2003), Weakliem (2003), and Wlezien and Soroka (2007).
2. For the sake of completeness we note that the actual 'thermostatic model' consists simultaneously of two equations, one concerning the effects of opinion on public spending, the other concerning the effects of public spending on opinion (e.g. Soroka and Wlezien 2010). We present these as separate hypotheses here, since they entail different constellations of the policy–opinion nexus, but this does not mean that these hypotheses

are contradictory in nature. Quite the contrary, Soroka and Wlezien would argue that this keeps the representative system in equilibrium.

3. Speech to Small Business Bureau Conference, 8 February 1984, Frimley.
4. Quoted in *The Times*, 3 November 1977.
5. Anthony Downs is notoriously ambivalent on the matter of preference exogeneity. On the same page of *An Economic Theory of Democracy*, he states that 'at the beginning of our study we assumed that voters' tastes are fixed, which means that the voter distribution is given', but then admits that 'though parties will move ideologically to adjust to the distribution in some circumstances, they will also attempt to move voters towards their own locations' (Downs 1957: 140).
6. To be fair, these adoptions of the thermostatic model differ from the original in terms of the precise model specification. Erikson *et al.* (2002), Kellstedt (2000), Stevenson (2001) and the present paper include a measure of policy activity on the right-hand side of the equation. In Wlezien's thermostatic model relative public preferences depend on what the public gets *and* what the public wants. We therefore refer to this hypothesis as a 'counter movement hypothesis', since it does not provide an actual test of the thermostatic model as developed by Wlezien and his co-authors. However, in terms of the theoretical foundations of counter movement, all these accounts cover common ground.
7. On average the Budget Speech is almost 10 times as long as the Queen's Speech, which is likely to contribute to the reliability of position estimates (Laver *et al.* 2003).
8. The conservative turn in mass attitudes has also been documented by Sarlvik and Crewe (1983) and Heath *et al.* (1991).
9. The swing to the left is also described by Crewe and Searing (1988) and Heath *et al.* (1991).
10. DeBoef and Keele (2008) illustrate this point with simulated examples in which they compare an Autoregressive Distributed Lag (ADL) model with an Error Correction Model (ECM). The ADL and ECM are functional equivalents and fit the data equally well, yet the ADL uses a dependent variable in level form while the ECMs dependent variable is differenced. Accordingly, the ADL explains 94 per cent of the variance, while the ECM 'only' explains 45 per cent.
11. Popularity data are taken from Gallup (pre-1980) and Ipsos-MORI. These polls contain monthly data on party support so the annual mean is a more reliable measure than using one item from the Eurobarometer.

References

Achen, Christopher (1978). 'Measuring Representation', *American Journal of Political Science*, 22:3, 475–509.

Ansolabehere, Stephen, Jonathan Rodden, and James Snyder (2008). 'The Strength of Issues: Using Multiple Measures to Gauge Preference Stability, Ideological Constraint, and Issue Voting', *American Political Science Review*, 102:2, 215–32.

Budge, Ian (1999). 'New Patterns of Party Competition?', in Geoffrey Evans and Pippa Norris (eds.), *Critical Elections: British Parties and Voters in Long-term Perspective*. London: Sage, 1–21.

Burstein, Paul (1998). 'Bringing the Public Back in: Should Sociologists Consider the Impact of Public Opinion on Public Policy?', *Social Forces*, 77:1, 27–62.

Burstein, Paul (2003). 'The Impact of Public Opinion on Public Policy: A Review and an Agenda', *Political Research Quarterly*, 56:1, 29–40.

Crewe, Ivor, and Donald Searing (1988). 'Ideological Change in the British Conservative Party', *American Political Science Review*, 82:2, 362–84.

Dahl, Robert (1957). 'The Concept of Power', *Behavioural Science*, 2:3, 201–15.

Dahl, Robert (1971). *Polyarchy: Participation and Opposition*. New Haven, CT: Yale University Press.

De Boef, Suzanna, and Luke Keele (2008). 'Taking Time Seriously: Dynamic Regression', *American Journal of Political Science*, 52:1, 184–200.

Downs, Anthony (1957). *An Economic Theory of Democracy*. New York: Harper & Row.

Dunleavy, Patrick (1991). *Democracy, Bureaucracy and Public Choice*. London: Pearson Education.

Dunleavy, Patrick, and Hugh Ward (1981). 'Endogenous Voter Preferences and Parties with State Power: Some Internal Problems of Economic Theories of Party Competition', *British Journal of Political Science*, 11:3, 351–80.

Druckmann, James, and Arthur Lupia (2000). 'Preference Formation', *Annual Review of Political Science*, 3, 1–25.

Erikson, Robert, Michael Mackuen, and James Stimson (2002). *The Macro Polity*. Cambridge: Cambridge University Press.

Evans, Geoffrey, Anthony Heath, and Mansur Lalljee (1996). 'Measuring Left–Right and Libertarian-Authoritarian Values in the British Electorate', *British Journal of Sociology*, 47:1, 93–112.

Franklin, Mark, and Christopher Wlezien (1997). 'The Responsive Public: Issue Salience, Policy Change, and Preferences for European Unification', *Journal of Theoretical Politics*, 9:3, 347–63.

Gabel, Matthew, and Kenneth Scheve (2007). 'Estimating the Effect of Elite Communications on Public Opinion Using Instrumental Variables', *American Journal of Political Science*, 51:4, 1013–28.

Geer, John (1996). *From Tea Leaves to Opinion Polls: A Theory of Democratic Leadership*. New York: Columbia University Press.

Granger, Clive (1969). 'Investigating Causal Relations by Econometric Models and Cross Spectral Methods', *Econometrica*, 37:3, 424–38.

Hakhverdian, Armen (2009). 'Capturing Government Policy on the Left–Right Scale: Evidence from the United Kingdom, 1956–2006', *Political Studies*, 57:4, 720–45.

Hakhverdian, Armen (2010). 'Political Representation and Its Mechanisms: A Dynamic Left–Right Approach for the United Kingdom', *British Journal of Political Science*, 40:4, 835–56.

Hall, Stuart (1979). 'The Great Moving Right Show', *Marxism Today*, January, 14–20.

Heath, Anthony, Roger Jowell, John Curtice, Geoffrey Evans, Julia Field, and Sharon Witherspoon (1991). *Understanding Political Change*. Oxford: Pergamon.

Hibbs, Douglas (1977). 'Political Parties and Macroeconomic Policy', *American Political Science Review*, 71:4, 1467–87.

Hill, Kim and Patricia Hurley (1999). 'Dyadic Representation Reappraised', *American Journal of Political Science*, 43:1, 109–37.

Hobolt, Sara, and Robert Klemmensen (2008). 'Government Responsiveness and Political Competition in Comparative Perspective', *Comparative Political Studies*, 41:3, 309–37.

Huber, John (1989). 'Values and Partisanship in Left–Right Orientation: Measuring Ideology', *European Journal of Political Research*, 17:5, 599–621.

Jacobs, Lawrence, and Robert Shapiro (1994). 'Public Opinion, Institutions, and Policy Making: Studying Substantive Democracy', *PS: Political Science and Politics*, 27, 9–17.

Jennings, Will, and Peter John (2009). 'The Dynamics of Political Attention: Public Opinion and the Queen's Speech in the United Kingdom', *American Journal of Political Science*, 53:4, 838–54.

Kellstedt, Paul (2000). 'Media Framing and the Dynamics of Racial Policy Preferences', *American Journal of Political Science*, 44:2, 245–60.

Kinder, Donald (1998). 'Communication and Opinion', *Annual Review of Political Science*, 1, 167–97.

Klingemann, Hans-Dieter, Andrea Volkens, Judith Bara, Ian Budge, and Michael McDonald (2006). *Mapping Policy Preferences II: Estimates for Parties, Electors, and Governments in Eastern Europe, European Union and OECD 1990–2003*. Oxford: Oxford University Press.

Laver, Michael, Kenneth Benoit, and John Garry (2003). 'Extracting Policy Positions from Political Texts Using Words as Data', *American Political Science Review*, 97:2, 311–31.

Mansbridge, Jane (2003). 'Rethinking Representation', *American Political Science Review*, 97:4, 515–28.

May, John (1978). 'Defining Democracy: A Bid for Coherence and Consensus', *Political Studies*, 26:1, 1–14.

McDonald, Michael, and Ian Budge (2005). *Elections, Parties, Democracy: Conferring the Median Mandate*. Oxford: Oxford University Press.

McGraw, Kathleen, Samuel Best, and Richard Timpone (1995). 'What They Say or What They Do? The Impact of Elite Explanation and Policy Outcomes on Public Opinion', *Annual Journal of Political Science*, 39:1, 53–74.

Miller, Warren, and Donald Stokes (1963). 'Constituency Influence in Congress', *American Political Science Review*, 57:1, 45–56.

Page, Benjamin, and Robert Shapiro (1983). 'The Effects of Public Opinion on Policy', *American Political Science Review*, 77:1, 175–90.

Page, Benjamin, and Robert Shapiro (1992). *The Rational Public: Fifty Years of Trends in Americans' Policy Preferences*. Chicago: University of Chicago Press.

Page, Benjamin, Robert Shapiro, and Glenn Dempsey (1987). 'What Moves Public Opinion?', *American Political Science Review*, 81:1, 23–43.

Pattie, Charles, and Ronald Johnston (2001). 'Routes to Party Choice: Ideology, Economic Evaluations, and Voting at the 1997 British General Election', *European Journal of Political Research*, 39:3, 373–89.

Pitkin, Hanna (1967). *The Concept of Representation*. Berkeley: University of California Press.

Powell, Bingham (2000). *Elections as Instruments of Democracy: Majoritarian and Proportional Visions*. New Haven, CT: Yale University Press.

Ranney, Austin (1954). *The Doctrine of Responsible Party Government*. Urbana: University of Illinois Press.

Ray, Leonard (2003). 'When Parties Matter: The Conditional Influence of Party Positions on Voter Opinions about European Integration', *Journal of Politics*, 65:4, 978–94.

Sarlvik, Bo, and Ivor Crewe (1983). *Decade of Dealignment: The Conservative Victory and 1979 and Electoral Trends in the 1970s*. Cambridge: Cambridge University Press.

Soroka, Stuart, and Christopher Wlezien (2010). *Degrees of Democracy: Politics, Public Opinion, and Policy*. New York: Cambridge University Press.

Soroka, Stuart, and Christopher Wlezien (2012). 'Political Institutions and the Opinion–Policy Link', *West European Politics*, 35:6, 1407–1432.

Steenbergen, Marco, Ericka Edwards, and Catherine de Vries (2007). 'Who's Cueing Whom? Mass–Elite Linkages and the Future of European Integration', *European Union Politics*, 8:1, 13–35.

Stephens, Philip (2007). 'Middle Britain Wants Value for Money', *Financial Times*, 15 October.

Stevenson, Randolph (2001). 'The Economy and Public Mood: A Fundamental Dynamic of Democratic Politics?', *American Journal of Political Science*, 45:3, 620–33.

Stimson, James, Michael Mackuen, and Robert Erikson (1995). 'Dynamic Representation', *American Political Science Review*, 89:3, 543–65.

Warren, Sidney (1964). *The President as World Leader*. New York: McGraw-Hill.

Weakliem, David (2003). 'Public Opinion Research and Political Sociology', *Research in Political Sociology*, 12, 49–80.

Webb, Paul (2000). *The Modern British Party System*. London: Sage.

Wlezien, Christopher (1995). 'The Public as Thermostat: Dynamics of Preferences for Spending', *American Journal for Political Science*, 39:4, 981–1000.

Wlezien, Christopher (2004). 'Patterns of Representation: Dynamics of Public Preferences and Policy', *Journal of Politics*, 66:1, 1–24.

Wlezien, Christopher, and Soroka Stuart (2007). 'The Relationship between Public Opinion and Policy', in Russell Dalton and Hans-Dieter Klingemann (eds.), *Oxford Handbook of Political Behavior*. Oxford: Oxford University Press, 799–817.

Zaller, John (1992). *The Nature and Origins of Mass Opinion*. New York: Cambridge University Press.

Political Institutions and the Opinion–Policy Link

CHRISTOPHER WLEZIEN and STUART N. SOROKA

The link between public opinion and policy is of special importance in representative democracies. Policymakers' responsiveness to public opinion is critical. Public responsiveness to policy itself is as well. Only a small number of studies compare either policy or public responsiveness across political systems, however. Previous research has focused on a handful of countries – mostly the US, UK and Canada – that share similar cultures and electoral systems. It remains, then, for scholars to assess the opinion–policy connection across a broad range of contexts. This paper takes a first step in this direction, drawing on data from two sources: (1) public preferences for spending from the International Social Survey Program (ISSP) and (2) measures of government spending from OECD spending datasets. These data permit a panel analysis of 17 countries. The article tests theories about the effects of federalism, executive–legislative imbalance, and the proportionality of electoral systems. The results provide evidence of the robustness of the 'thermostatic' model of opinion and policy but also the importance of political institutions as moderators of the connections between them.

A growing body of literature addresses the relationships between public opinion and public policy. Much of the literature focuses on policy responsiveness to opinion. Research also considers public responsiveness to what policymakers do – an equally important condition for effective representation. Results suggest that representative democracy functions rather well, at least in certain countries. Governments regularly react to public opinion, not just via election results but dynamically over the election cycle (e.g. Erikson *et al.* 2002; Soroka and Wlezien 2010). And citizens adjust their preferences alongside policy. As policy goes up, preferences for policy change go down, and vice versa. The 'thermostatic' model of public opinion and policy (Wlezien 1995) works, at least in Canada, the United Kingdom and the United States.

There are however some caveats and limitations. Opinion and policy move together in salient policy domains, but this is not the case for non-salient domains.[1] The evident connections are likely strongest only at a highly aggregated level, e.g. welfare or health or education. The preferences of poorer citizens may be less well represented in the domain in which they have the greatest stake – welfare (see also Enns and Wlezien 2011; Soroka and Wlezien 2008). And the strength of the opinion–policy link, even in highly salient domains, can be constrained or enhanced by political institutions.

The argument that some institutions are more conducive to a link between opinion and policy has been made in work by comparative institutionalists (e.g. Lijphart 1999). It has also been investigated by those interested in the effects of electoral systems in particular (e.g. Powell 2000). This work does not focus on policy per se, however; nor does it examine dynamics – that is, relationships between opinion and policy over time. So while the vote–seat function is well understood, as are, for instance, the advantages of proportional representation and/or federal institutions in managing ethnolinguistic diversity, the impact of these institutions on the ways in which opinion and policy interact is still rather mysterious.

Recent research has begun to address this issue. We build on that work here: specifically, research that develops an argument about the functioning of the thermostatic model under varying degrees of both vertical and horizontal divisions of power (Soroka and Wlezien 2004, 2005, 2010; Wlezien and Soroka 2007, 2011; also see Hobolt and Klemmensen 2008).[2] A desire for directly comparable measures of both opinion and policy over the long term meant that our previous work was constrained to three Anglo-American democracies – the US, the UK and Canada. Here, we relax our longitudinal requirements in an effort to gain cross-national and, especially, cross-institutional variance.

Our goal is to examine differences in opinion–policy connections across political-institutional environments. What makes the analysis possible is the availability of public preferences for spending data from the four Role of Government waves of the International Social Survey Program (ISSP). We combine these data with measures of government spending from OECD spending datasets. For the analysis, we focus on total government spending. As in our previous work, we analyse both policy representation (the reflection of public preferences for spending in actual spending change) and public responsiveness (the tendency for public preferences to adjust, thermostatically, to changes in spending). Doing so across a wider range of countries means that we can explicitly test existing theories about vertical decentralisation and the executive–legislative balance of power as well as the proportionality of electoral systems. The results provide evidence of the robustness of the thermostatic model, but also the importance of political institutions as mediators of the connection between public opinion and public policy.

The Thermostatic Model

The thermostatic model of public opinion and policy describes a system of two equations – one for public preferences and the other for policy (Soroka and Wlezien 2010; Wlezien 1995, 2004).

The Public Responsiveness Equation

The public's preference for 'more' or 'less' policy – its relative preference, R – represents the difference between the public's preferred level of policy (P^*) and policy (P) itself:

$$R_t = P_t^* - P_t. \tag{1}$$

Thus, R can change because either P^* or P changes; a change in P^* positively influences R and a change in P negatively influences R. The negative feedback of policy on opinion is the crux of the thermostatic model. It provides the basis for effective accountability and control.[3]

In practice, the theoretical equation cannot be directly estimated. Most importantly, we typically do not observe P^*. Survey organisations rarely ask people how much policy they want. Instead, these organisations usually ask about relative preferences – whether we are spending 'too little', whether spending should 'be increased' or whether we should 'do more'.[4] This, presumably, is how people think about most policies. (Imagine being asked about your own preferred level of health or education spending.) The public preference, however defined, is also necessarily relative. This is important, as we can measure the thermostatic signal the public sends to policymakers. Because we cannot directly measure P^*, and the fact that the metrics of R and P also differ, we must rewrite our equation 1 as follows:

$$R_t = a + \beta_1 P_t + \beta_2 W_t + e_t, \tag{2}$$

where a and e_t represent the intercept and the error term, respectively and W designates the instruments for the public's preferred level of policy (P^*). The most critical part of equation 2 is β_1. If the public responds thermostatically to policy, β_1 will be negative.

We already know that the thermostatic model works well in certain spending domains in the US (Wlezien 1995, 1996), the UK (Soroka and Wlezien 2005), and Canada (Soroka and Wlezien 2004).[5] (For a general assessment across the three countries, see Soroka and Wlezien 2010.) That is, the public adjusts its preferences in response to spending, other things being equal: when spending increases, relative preferences decrease; when spending decreases, relative preferences increase. The thermostat does not work in all policy domains, however (Soroka and Wlezien 2010). To begin with, the public salience of the policy domain matters – the public pays more attention to policymaking in domains it considers to be important. The effect of policy on preferences depends on the salience (S) of different policy domains j; formally, it equals β_1 times S_j. In some very low salience domains, there may be no public responsiveness to policy.

The Policy Representation Equation

Now if there is representation, policy change (ΔP_t) will be a function of relative preferences for policy (R_{t-1}), which reflect support for policy change. Other things also matter for policy, of course, including the partisan control of government (G_{t-1}). Note that both R and G are lagged so as to reflect preferences and party control when budgetary policy, the focus of our empirical analysis, is made.[6] For any particular domain, then, the equation is:

$$\Delta P_t = \rho + \gamma_1 R_{t-1} + \gamma_2 G_{t-1} + \mu_t, \tag{3}$$

where ρ and μ_t represent the intercept and the error term, respectively. This equation captures both indirect and direct representation. The former – representation through election results and subsequent government partisanship – is captured by γ_2, and the latter – adjustments to policy reflecting shifts in preferences – is captured by γ_1. Other variables can be added to the model, of course.[7]

The coefficient γ_1 is most critical for our purposes. It captures policy responsiveness, the kind of dynamic representation that we expect to differing degrees across policy domains. A positive coefficient need not mean that politicians literally respond to changing public preferences, of course, as it may be that they and the public both respond to something else, e.g. changes in the need for more spending. All we can say for sure is that γ_1 captures policy responsiveness in a statistical sense – the extent to which policy change is systematically related to public preferences, other things being equal. This is of (obvious) importance, as we want to know whether public policy follows public preferences.

As public responsiveness varies across domains, so may policy representation. Indeed, there is reason to expect the two relations to be symmetrical – in domains where the public responds to policy, policymakers are more likely to reflect public preferences. There are two reasons. First, public responsiveness is more likely in publicly salient domains, where policymakers have a stronger incentive to represent preferences. Second, where the public responds to policy, expressed preferences actually contain meaningful information. Thus, we expect that the coefficient of direct policy representation (γ_1) in equation 3 varies across domains j with the coefficient of public responsiveness (β_1) in equation 1. (For more details, see Soroka and Wlezien 2010).

Political Institutions and Opinion–Policy Dynamics

There also is reason to think that representation and feedback differ across countries. Indeed, as noted earlier, there is some evidence to suggest that they do, partly due to differences in political institutions. Recent research has examined the influence of government institutions. Electoral systems also may matter.

Government Institutions

We have suggested in previous work that the division of powers – both vertical and horizontal – structures the relationships between opinion and policy over time. First, the vertical division of powers, or decentralisation, makes it more difficult for the public to gauge and react to government policy change, and thus dampens public responsiveness. Second, the horizontal division of powers, as in 'Madisonian' presidential systems, makes governments more responsive to changes in public opinion. Let us briefly trace the reasoning.

The vertical division of powers. Thermostatic public responsiveness requires that people acquire accurate information about what policy-makers are doing. This clearly depends on the supply of information, as we have discussed. It also depends on the clarity of that information. More precisely, it depends on the extent to which responsibility for policies is clear, and this is in part a function of how government itself is organised. Federalism, the vertical division of powers, increases the number of different governments making policy and thus makes less clear what any particular level of 'government' is doing (see e.g. Downs 1999). Put differently, the government policy signal may be confused – i.e. there may be different signals from multiple sources. This can dampen public responsiveness.

Different federal arrangements may have different effects on public responsiveness, of course, and there are two ideal types worth considering briefly here. Where governments have complete control for different domains – what is in the American context referred to as dual federalism – there is no mistaking the source of policy in each policy area. Multiple governments may still produce complications, but we might expect a comparatively high level of responsiveness on the part of the public in politically important domains, regardless of which level of government is in charge. Even so, the existence of multiple governments may make for a more complicated information environment, and public responsiveness may suffer.

In most federal systems, governments actually share responsibilities in a number of policy areas. There may be direct involvement in a policy domain by multiple levels; there may also be transfers – 'conditional' or 'unconditional' – from one level of government to the other. In either case, the actions of governments are more difficult to discern. The point is not that federalism destroys the potential for representative democracy but that it presents challenges. The most fundamental challenge is the 'confusion' it creates.

We expect that a high level of federalism makes it harder for citizens to assign responsibility for policy, to know what any one level of government is doing. This makes it more difficult for citizens to express informed preferences about what different levels of government should do.[8]

The horizontal division of powers. The horizontal division of powers also may structure the relationship between opinion and policy over time. The concentration of powers in parliamentary systems – as opposed to presidential systems – affords voters more direct control over government on Election Day. This may aid indirect representation: To the extent election outcomes reflect public opinion, policy representation will follow quite naturally, at least to the extent we have responsible parties.

The same seemingly is not true about direct representation, however. Indeed, there is reason to suppose that parliamentary governments are less reliable in their attendance to public opinion in between elections. Scholars have long noted the dominance of cabinets over parliaments (see e.g. the classic statements by Bagehot 1867 and Jennings 1959; also see Cox 1987; Laver and Shepsle 1996; Tsebelis 2002). These scholars portray a world in which cabinet governments exercise substantial discretion, where the cabinet is the proposer – it puts legislation to the Commons – and the legislature ultimately has only a limited check on what the government does. Strom (2003) concludes that parliamentary government deals much better with 'adverse selection' than it does 'moral hazard'. Once established, the cabinet is difficult to control on a recurring basis.

This has fairly direct implications for government responsiveness. When there are differences between what the cabinet and parliament want, the latter cannot as effectively impose its own contrary will. The process of amendment and veto is compromised, at least by comparison with Madisonian presidential systems. In the latter the executive cannot effectively act without the legislature, at least with respect to statute. The legislature is the proposer – it puts statute to the executive – and, while the executive can veto legislation, the legislature can override it. Most changes in policy require agreement between the executive and legislature, or else a supermajority in the latter. This is likely to reduce disjunctures between public opinion and policy change, even when the executive attempts to represent changing public opinion. In effect, Madisonian systems allow for 'error correction' during the policymaking process. There already is some support for this supposition from the United States, where Congress has been shown to alter presidential proposals to better reflect changing public opinion (Wlezien 1996).

Although the separation of powers makes presidential systems more deliberate in their actions, it may also make them more reliably responsive to public opinion over time. Research comparing the US, UK and Canada bears out these expectations, as policy is more responsive to changing public opinion in the former (Soroka and Wlezien 2004, 2005, 2010; Wlezien, 2004). Hobolt and Klemmensen's (2008) different examination further shows that policy representation in Denmark is comparable to that in the UK and lower than in the US. The combined evidence is thus far supportive but clearly limited, as it concerns but four countries. It also does not consider differences in the executive–legislative balance of power within presidential and parliamentary systems. Presidents are advantaged in some presidential systems, after all, and here we would expect opinion to be a less significant predictor of policy change. Likewise, the executive has less discretion in some parliamentary systems, and there we would expect a more reliable connection between public preferences and policy change. These possibilities can be settled empirically.

Electoral Institutions

Electoral systems are the emphasis of most of the broader literature on representation. Most of this research focuses on differences between the majoritarian and proportional visions, using Powell's (2000) language, and how these differences matter. Lijphart (1984) provides the first direct statement on the matter. He distinguishes between 'consensual' democracies – characterised by, most notably, proportional representation, multiparty systems and coalition governments – and 'majoritarian' systems – characterised by simple plurality election rules, a two-party system and single-party government (exactly as Duverger (1951) would predict). Most importantly, Lijphart suggests that consensual democracies provide better descriptive representation and general policy congruence than do majoritarian systems.

Powell (2000) provides further empirical support, focusing specifically on the differences between majoritarian and proportional election rules and their implications for representation. Powell finds that proportional representation tends to produce greater congruence between the government and the public; specifically, that the general ideological disposition of government and the ideological bent of the electorate tend to match up better in proportional systems. According to Powell, this reflects the greater, direct participation of constituencies the vision affords (also see Miller *et al.* 1999).

Recent research challenges Powell's findings. Blais and Bodet (2006) argue that, while proportional systems do encourage coalition governments, thus pulling the government more to the centre, they also encourage a greater number and diversity of parties in the first place, which promotes representation of more extreme positions. Their analysis reveals little difference in the congruence between citizens and governments in proportional and majoritarian systems. Golder and Stramski (2010) show much the same.[9] Powell's (2011) own very recent analysis, which encompasses a broader period than his original work, also demonstrates little difference between electoral systems.[10]

Even accepting Powell's original (2000) results, they pertain to elections and their immediate consequences. What about in the periods between elections? Are coalition governments more responsive to ongoing changes in opinion? Although proportional systems may provide more indirect representation, it is not clear that they afford greater direct representation. In our previous work (Soroka and Wlezien 2004, 2005, 2010), we have argued that there is reason to think that governments in majoritarian systems are more responsive to opinion change.[11] First, it is presumably easier for a single party to respond to changes than a multi-party coalition, as coordination in the latter is more difficult and costly. This partly reflects the increased transaction costs but also the constraints posed by coalition agreements. Second, majoritarian governments may have more of an incentive to respond to opinion change. Since a shift in electoral sentiment has bigger consequences on Election Day in majoritarian systems, governments in these are likely to pay especially close attention to the ebb and flow of opinion.[12]

Thus, it may be that the two systems both work to serve representation, but in different ways, where proportional systems provide better indirect representation via elections and majoritarian systems better direct representation in between elections. In this paper, we are especially interested in the latter. Unfortunately, there is little empirical work on the subject. Only Hobolt and Klemmensen's (2005, 2008) research directly addresses the issue, and their findings are inconclusive. They show that government rhetoric in one proportional system (Denmark) is more responsive than in one majoritarian system (the UK) but not in another (the US). Perhaps most importantly, actual policy is more responsive in the US than the two other countries, as noted above. As for analysis of government institution effects, it is hard to tell what these results could tell us given the focus on only three countries.[13]

Data and Methodology

Here we test our three conjectures relating to political institutions. The measure of relative public preferences – the variable R in the equations above – is critical. For this, we rely on the International Social Survey Program 'Role of Government I–IV cumulative file', combining results from the four years in which the survey has included a battery of questions on government policies, namely, 1985, 1990, 1996 and 2006.[14] The surveys include questions about spending in a number of different policy domains. While we intend to address these in subsequent work, we focus here on a single measure of relative preferences (R) – namely, a question about government spending in general: 'Here are some things the government might do for the economy. Please show which actions you are in favour of and which you are against: Cuts in government spending (strongly in favour, in favour, neither in favour nor against, against, strong against).'[15]

We produce a net support for spending measure by taking the (weighted) average of responses, where responses are scored strongly in favour (−100), in favour (−50), neither in favour nor against (0), against (+50), strongly against (+100). The measure ranges in theory from −100, meaning that all respondents strongly favour spending cuts, to +100, meaning that all respondents oppose spending cuts. Of course, the actual results do not have quite this range; indeed, the net support measure tends to be negative, meaning that on average respondents are more likely to agree to cuts then to oppose them. This allows measures in 17 countries over the period. The data are listed by country and year in Appendix Table A1.

From the ISSP datasets we also draw a measure to tap the public's underlying preferred levels of policy (P^*) in the public responsiveness equations. The measure is based on the question,

> On the whole, do you think it should be or should not be the government's responsibility to: (1) Keep prices under control, (2) Provide health care for the sick, (3) Provide a decent standard of living for the old, (4) Provide a job for everyone who wants one, (5) Provide industry with the help it needs to grow, (6) Provide a decent standard of living for the unemployed, (7) Reduce income differences between the rich and poor, (8) Give financial help to university students from low-income families, (9) Provide decent housing for those who can't afford it, (10) Impose strict laws to make industry do less damage to the environment.

Each item is scored as follows: definitely should not be (0), probably should not be (34), probably should be (67), definitely should be (100); country-level scores take the (weighted) average of this measure, ranging in theory from 0, meaning no support for government action, to +100, meaning clear support for government action in all cases. Support for Government Action scores are listed by country and year in Appendix Table A2.

All opinion data are adjusted to account for the fact that the ISSP is not fielded at exactly the same time in all countries. For waves 1–3, one or two countries fielded the survey one year late; for wave 4, field dates range from 2005 to 2008. We make the appropriate adjustments, so that opinion data are used here in the year in which they were actually measured (and so that they are both driving and reacting to policy at the appropriate times).

To measure government spending, we rely mainly on OECDStat 'Table 11. Government expenditure by function'. The table lacks data for Australia, so we add those from the Australian Bureau of Statistics, '5204.0

Australian System of National Accounts, Table 35. Government Final Consumption Expenditure, by Level of government and purpose'. All data were initially recorded in national currency units (NCUs) at current prices. We convert them to constant NCUs using inflation (average consumer prices, 2000 = 100) available from the International Monetary Fund's (IMF) World Economic Outlook Database (2010; http://www.imf.org/external/data.htm).

Spending data present a particular difficulty in these time-series cross-sectional models, since NCUs differ considerably both in level and in variance.[16] For models of policy representation, we deal with the problem by using a percentage change measure of spending. For models of public responsiveness, where we need levels rather than changes in spending, we rely on spending as a proportion of GDP. GDP also is drawn from the IMF World Economic Outlook Database.

Measures of institutional variation are from a variety of sources. For the proportionality of the electoral system, we use the effective number of electoral parties (ENPP) for national elections from 1985 to 2000, drawn directly from Golder (2010).[17] To capture the executive–legislative balance, we use Lijphart's (1999) measure of executive dominance, which is available for 14 of the 17 countries. For federalism, we use Rodden's (2002, 2004) measure of own-source state–local revenue as a proportion of total government revenue. Although our theory is a general one, we employ a fiscal-specific measure because our empirical analyses focus on fiscal policy and preferences. The measure is based on revenues because they reflect the decentralisation of fiscal policymaking authority more clearly than spending.[18] Values for all institutional variables are listed by country in Appendix Table A3.

While the institutional variables are constant by country, the other variables used in the analysis vary across both space and time. Much of the variance still is cross-national. This is clear in Table 1, which summarises a space–time analysis of variance for each variable. Note that we include all the variables discussed above, as well as unemployment, which appears below in models of public responsiveness. The numbers in the table are the percentages of variance explained by year and country dummy variables.

TABLE 1
THE VARIABLES: AN ANALYSIS OF VARIANCE ACROSS SPACE AND OVER TIME

	Year	Country	*N*
Net preferences	12.33*	72.05*	46
Support for government action	0.01	76.74*	46
Unemployment	21.42*	59.83*	44
% government spending/GDP	1.80	77.28*	42
%Δ total government spending	50.88*	11.02	42

*$p < 0.05$. Cells contain the proportion of the total variance explained by year and country, based on ANOVAs including the two variables. Spending and unemployment results include cases for which preferences data are available only.

The results indicate that most of the variance we observe in the 'level' variables is cross-national, approximately 70 per cent on average. It does differ somewhat, however, being most pronounced for the spending measure and less so for unemployment. Importantly, our measure of relative preferences (though not our instrument for the public's preferred level of spending) also shows significant temporal variation. The differenced measure of spending does too – see the last row of Table 1. This allows us to assess dynamics, at least to some degree. We want to see whether the thermostatic model works in this broader set of countries and whether and how political institutions matter.

The Analysis of Public Responsiveness

Recall that we are interested in seeing whether the thermostatic model applies generally and whether and to what extent the public's response to spending is a function of the vertical division of powers. This can be assessed directly, by extending equation 2 from above across countries k as follows:

$$R_{kt} = a_k + \beta_1 P_{kt} + \beta_2 D_{kt} + \beta_3 D_{kt} * P_{kt} + \beta_4 W_{kt} + e_{kt}, \tag{4}$$

where D is the level of fiscal federalism. We are especially interested in the coefficients β_1 and β_3, which capture the direct and interactive effects of policy (P). If there is thermostatic responsiveness and federalism dampens it, β_1 would be less than 0 and β_3 would be greater than 0. This would tell us that policy feeds back negatively on preferences but that the tendency declines as the decentralisation of policymaking authority increases. That is, we would find that the public is more responsive in the UK and Ireland, on the one hand, than in Canada and the US, on the other.

Figure 1 displays the simple bivariate relationship between policy change and opinion change in the 15 countries for which we have data between 1996 and 2006. Here we can see a weak negative relationship between the two. In general, when spending goes up (down), preferences for more spending go down (up) – the Pearson's r is –0.35 ($p = 0.20$). To the extent there is thermostatic public responsiveness to policy over the decade, it is coarse and unreliable. To provide a more rigorous estimate over the four waves of the ISSP, we estimate pooled models of spending preferences for all 17 countries and four years – the distribution of the variable is shown in Appendix Table A1. Because some of our independent variables are a constant in each country, we estimate a random effects model using maximum likelihood.[19] Table 2 presents the results of different models.

The first column in the table summarises the results of estimating a basic model of spending preferences including just the spending measure. Consistent with what we saw in Figure 1, spending has a negative effect on preferences. The effect does meet minimal levels of statistical significance, though it is not highly reliable. It also accounts for little (6 per cent) of the

FIGURE 1
CHANGE IN GOVERNMENT SPENDING AND CHANGES IN NET PREFERENCES
(~1996–2006)

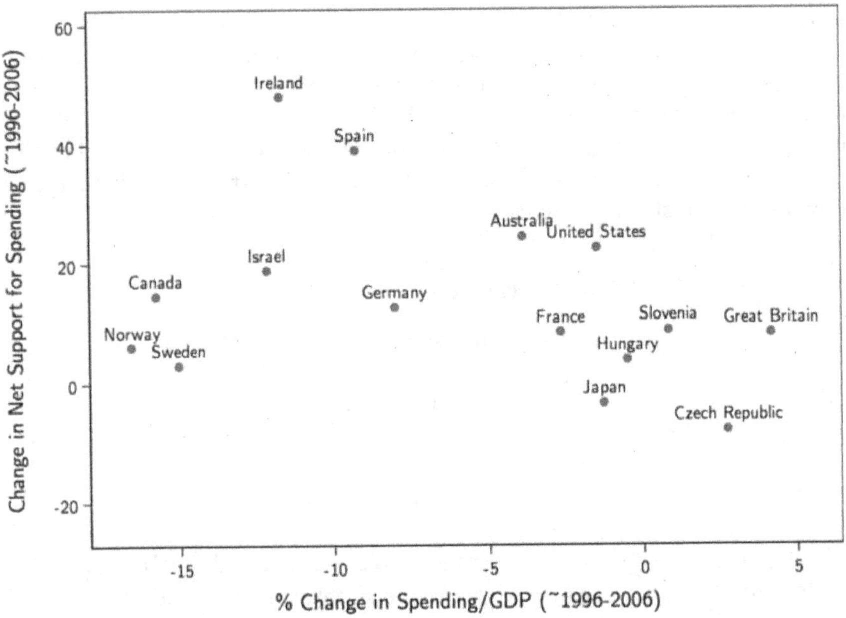

variance in preferences, even less across countries.[20] Of course, we have yet to incorporate our proxy variables for the public's preferred levels of spending. The main variable is the index of public attitudes toward the role of government (Support for Government Action) described above. Other variables may matter, and one likely suspect is the economy. Durr (1993) showed that support for policy is positively related to economic conditions: when the economy improves, people become more liberal; when things worsen, people become more conservative (see also Soroka and Wlezien 2010). To measure conditions, we rely on unemployment, which is available in all of our countries.[21] We expect it to be negatively related to spending preferences, that is, when unemployment worsens (improves), support for more spending decreases (increases).[22] Of course, it may be that the public responds counter-cyclically to economic conditions. To the extent this is true, preferences will be positively related to unemployment. The empirical analyses will reveal which, if either, is true.

The results of estimating a model including the two proxies for P^* are reported in the second column of Table 2. Here we see that both variables impact on preferences in expected ways. Support for Government Action positively influences support for spending while the level of unemployment negatively influences it, and both effects are statistically significant. When these variables are included, moreover, spending continues to have a

TABLE 2
PUBLIC RESPONSIVENESS, USING TOTAL GOVERNMENT SPENDING/GDP

	DV: Net preferences$_{kt}$		
% government spending/GDP$_{kt}$	−0.878*	−0.754**	−0.707**
	(0.450)	(0.379)	(0.258)
P Instruments*			
Support for government action$_{kt}$	–	0.552**	0.597**
		(0.225)	(0.202)
Unemployment$_{kt}$	–	−3.011**	−1.755
		(0.574)	(1.349)
Net preferences$_{kt-1}$	–	–	0.766**
			(0.117)
Constant	−7.506	−17.118	8.270
	(20.114)	(18.504)	(11.808)
sigma u	16.734**	18.184**	0.000
	(3.784)	(3.448)	(5.836)
sigma e	11.722**	7.229**	11.749**
	(1.859)	(1.133)	(1.570)
N	38	38	28
N (panels)	17	17	17
LR Chi2	4.022	23.936	33.809
rho	0.671	0.864	0.000

$*p < 0.10$; $**p < 0.05$. Cells contain MLE coefficients with standard errors in parentheses.

significant negative effect. Of course, the two variables only imperfectly tap differences in the public's preferred levels of spending across countries and time. Taking into account lagged preferences allows us to better capture the influence of other omitted variables. As can be seen in the third column of Table 2, doing so alters the coefficients in isolated ways. (It also substantially reduces the number of observations.) Specifically, the effect of unemployment is smaller and unreliable. The size and significance of the other coefficients are largely unchanged.

Now, we have explicit hypotheses about differences across countries. We expect that public responsiveness to policy change varies with the level of fiscal federalism. The greater (lesser) the decentralisation of policymaking authority, the lesser (greater) the responsiveness. This is easy to test following equation 4. Recall that our measure of federalism is the ratio of state and local revenue to total government revenue from Rodden (2002, 2004). To test the effects of federalism on public responsiveness, we include this measure as well as its interaction with spending in our model.[23] Table 3 summarises the results. The first column shows the model without lagged preferences. Here we see that the spending still has a negative direct impact on preferences, but it is much larger and more reliable. We also see that it has an interactive effect with federalism. This effect is positive. In other words, as federalism increases, the thermostatic influence of spending declines. This is exactly as we hypothesised. The effects do not change when lagged preferences are included in the model – see the second column of Table 3.

The influence of fiscal federalism on public responsiveness is in fact quite pronounced. This is clear in Table 4, which shows how public responsiveness varies across different levels of federalism – for this illustration, we show results for countries at the 25th, 50th and 75th percentiles. In highly unitary countries, estimated responsiveness is three times what we found (in Table 2) when not taking federalism into account. In modestly federalised countries, responsiveness is twice what we saw previously. Perhaps most notably, in highly federalised countries we expect no responsiveness whatsoever. The vertical division of powers really matters for thermostatic public responsiveness.[24]

TABLE 3
PUBLIC RESPONSIVENESS, MODERATED BY FEDERALISM

	DV: Net preferences$_{kt}$	
% government spending/GDP$_{kt}$	−3.169**	−2.298**
	(1.152)	(0.979)
Federalism$_k$	−3.920**	−2.357
	(1.840)	(1.485)
Spending$_{kt}$ * Federalism$_k$	0.094**	0.060*
	(0.040)	(0.033)
P Instruments*		
Support for government action$_{kt}$	0.635*	0.617**
	(0.385)	(0.308)
Unemployment$_{kt}$	−2.991**	−0.506
	(0.894)	(1.751)
Net preferences$_{kt-1}$	–	0.644**
		(0.141)
Constant	88.622	62.541
	(61.346)	(46.210)
sigma u	12.814**	0.000
	(3.813)	(6.139)
sigma e	11.976	11.517**
		(1.698)
N	31	23
N (panels)	13	13
LR Chi2	22.875	29.812
rho	0.534	0.000

$*p < 0.10$; $**p < 0.05$. Cells contain MLE coefficients with standard errors in parentheses. Federalism is a revenue-based measure (rescaled from 0 to 100) from Rodden (2004).

TABLE 4
IMPLIED FEEDBACK COEFFICIENTS, BY LEVEL OF FEDERALISM

	Implied feedback coefficient
Federalism	
Low	−2.327**
Medium	−1.952**
High	−0.173

$**p < 0.05$. Levels of federalism correspond to the 25th, 50th and 75th percentiles in the data, i.e. 9, 13 and 32. Based on results in column 1 of Table 4.

The Analysis of Policy Representation

We also are interested in assessing policy representation and whether and how it is regulated by political institutions. As we have noted, one hypothesis is that the horizontal division of powers increases representation. The other is that the proportionality of electoral systems weakens representation. Whether one or the other is true needs to be settled empirically. The form of our tests follows our assessment of the effects of federalism on public responsiveness. Specifically, we incorporate the additive and interactive effects of institutions into our representation equation (3). In the case of the proportionality hypothesis, we would estimate the following model:

$$\Delta P_{kt} = \rho_k + \gamma_1 R_{kt-1} + \gamma_2 E_{kt-1} + \gamma_3 E * R_{kt-1} + \gamma_4 G_{kt-1} + \mu_{kt}, \qquad (5)$$

where E taps the electoral system's proportionality. If there is representation and it varies negatively with proportionality, then γ_1 will be greater than 0 and γ_3 will be less than 0. This would tell us that preferences positively influence policy, but that the relationship declines as proportionality increases. That is, we would find that governments are more representative

FIGURE 2
LEVELS OF NET PREFERENCES (~1996) AND CHANGE IN GOVERNMENT SPENDING (~1996–2006)

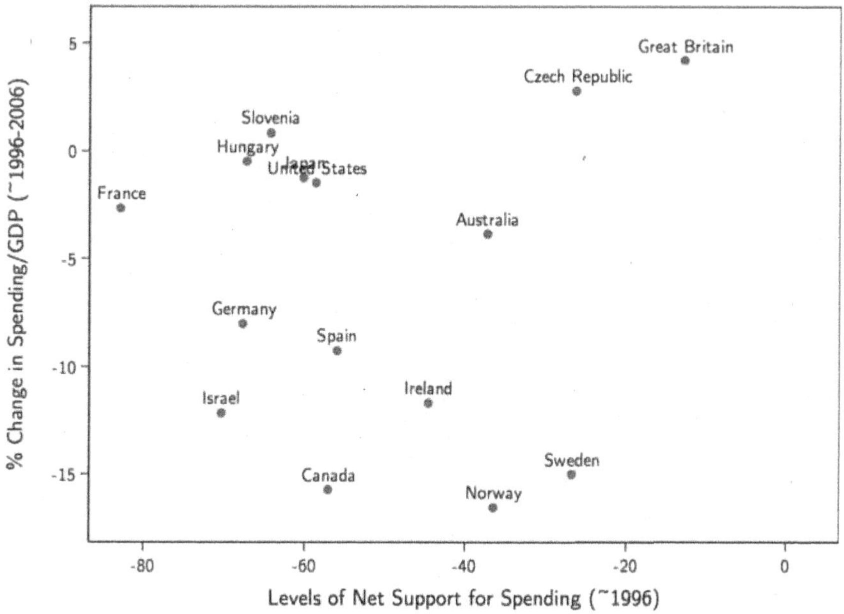

in the US and UK than in France. Of course, it may be that proportional systems are more responsive to opinion change, as some might infer from Powell (2000) and Lijphart (1999).[25] If so, then both γ_1 and γ_3 will be greater than 0 – the sum of γ_1 and $\gamma_3 * E$ will increase as E increases. We can settle the issue empirically.

To begin with, Figure 2 plots the bivariate relationship between public preferences in 1996 and the change in spending between 1996 and 2006. There is no clear pattern here – the Pearson's r is just 0.04 ($p = 0.87$). If there is representation of preferences, it is barely in evidence here. That said, the figure illustrates changes in spending over a 10-year period, while our estimation focuses on much more fine-grained (annual) effects. We turn to those estimations now.

Table 5 shows results from our basic model of policy representation.[26] The first column shows results from regressing the annual change in spending in year t on net preferences in year $t - 1$. Here there is evidence of policy representation – the coefficient (0.074) is positive and easily exceeds conventional levels of statistical significance. It is necessary to include other controls, of course. For this analysis, we do not include a measure of government partisanship of government (G) – thus, the models in Table 5 cannot capture whether representation really is direct or indirect, mediated by the partisan composition of government. The reason is that comparable measures of government partisanship are not available for all countries and time points encompassed by our analysis. For instance, the Armingeon *et al.* (2010) data set does not include Israel or figures for Australia and the United States before 1990. That said, preliminary tests using this measure show no impact of percentage of left seats in the cabinet – see Appendix

TABLE 5
POLICY REPRESENTATION

	DV: % Δ Total government spending$_{kt}$		
Net preferences$_{kt-1}$	0.074**	0.060**	0.043*
	(0.024)	(0.026)	(0.024)
% ΔGDP (deflated NCUs)$_{kt-1}$	–	0.291	0.506**
		(0.244)	(0.230)
% ΔDebt (deflated NCUs)$_{kt-1}$	–	–	−0.075
			(0.059)
Constant	5.278**	3.686**	2.404
	(1.220)	(1.742)	(1.565)
sigma u	1.725**	1.198	–
	(0.582)	(0.782)	
sigma e	2.195**	2.331**	2.624**
	(0.347)	(0.403)	(0.323)
N	36	35	33
N (panels)	16	16	16
LR Chi2	8.428	12.068	12.391
rho	0.382	0.209	0.000

*$p < 0.10$; **$p < 0.05$. Cells contain MLE coefficients with standard errors in parentheses.

Table A4. This may be because government partisanship does not matter, or, more likely, because the impact is difficult to capture across a wide range of countries with very different party systems, pooled together in a dataset with a very limited number of observations over time.[27] Because the government partisanship variable is insignificant, we opt to drop partisanship from the analysis, allowing us to retain more cases.

We do however add other important control variables. In the second and third columns of Table 5, we incorporate indicators of fiscal capacity – the percentage change in GDP, and the percentage change in debt, both measured in the previous year. Our expectation is that an expanding economy will tend to increase spending and that growing public debt will tend to decrease it.[28] The coefficients for the variables are in the expected direction here, though only GDP is significant in the final model. That debt is not significant says something about how little governments have been constrained by it over the years, and also may challenge interpretations of the impact of the current global fiscal crisis.

The institutional variables are added in Table 6. The first column includes executive–legislative balance, using Lijphart's (1999) measure of Executive

TABLE 6
POLICY REPRESENTATION, MODERATED BY PROPORTIONALITY AND PRESIDENTIALISM

	DV: % Δ Total government spending$_{kt}$		
Net preferences$_{kt-1}$	0.053	0.136*	0.504**
	(0.103)	(0.072)	(0.166)
Executive dominance$_{kt}$	−1.318*	–	−2.913**
	(0.740)		(0.869)
Prefs$_{kt}$ * Executive dominance$_{kt}$	−0.022	–	−0.043**
	(0.015)		(0.015)
ENPP$_{kt}$	–	−0.471	−5.248**
		(1.573)	(2.023)
Prefs$_{kt}$ * ENPP$_{kt}$	–	−0.005	−0.099**
		(0.034)	(0.043)
%ΔGDP(deflated NCUs)$_{kt-1}$	0.565**	0.515**	0.555**
	(0.251)	(0.234)	(0.210)
%ΔDebt(deflated NCUs)$_{kt-1}$	−0.078	−0.064	−0.044
	(0.058)	(0.058)	(0.052)
Constant	3.486	7.893**	28.747**
	(4.524)	(3.743)	(8.560)
sigma u	0.000	0.000	0.000
	(0.000)	(0.000)	(0.790)
sigma e	2.610**	2.292**	2.021**
	(0.321)	(0.306)	(0.270)
N	33	28	28
N (panels)	16	13	13
LR Chi2	12.728	17.265	24.332
rho	0.000	0.000	0.000

*$p < 0.10$; **$p < 0.05$. Cells contain MLE coefficients with standard errors in parentheses. ENPP is the effective number of parliamentary parties from Golder (2010), and Executive dominance is from Lijphart (1999).

Dominance. Recall that we estimate both its direct impact and its interactive effect with preferences, but that the latter is of special interest to us. In the table we can see that the preferences coefficient remains positive and significant and the interactive coefficient is negative, implying that representation decreases as executive power increases. The effect of executive balance on representation is not quite statistically significant ($p = 0.07$), so we stop short of crediting the relationship.

In the second column of the table, we see a similar set of results for proportionality, using Golder's ENPP measure. The coefficient is negative, suggesting that representation decreases with proportionality, though the effect is not significant.[29] Although proportional systems do not reliably dampen the representation of public preferences over time, it is fairly clear that they do not enhance the representation connection.

The third column of Table 6 shows the effects of incorporating both institutional variables in the same model.[30] Here we see much more definitive evidence, as the additive effect of preferences remains positive and significant and both the interactive coefficients are negative and significant ($p < 0.05$). The results imply that there is policy representation but that high levels of executive power and electoral system proportionality decrease it.[31] It is not clear from these results just how much institutions matter, however. To get some sense of this, we simulate the effects of the two variables. To do so, it is necessary to model the joint effects of the variables, as every system is a combination of the two.

Table 7 shows the implied representation coefficients at different institutional combinations. The results are for countries at the 25th, 50th and 75th percentiles of the data, using coefficients from model 3 in Table 6. From our estimates, representation clearly decreases sharply as the proportionality (ENPP) of the system increases. Indeed, going from low to high levels of proportionality, the effect of representation completely disappears regardless of the level of executive dominance. Executive dominance has a slightly less pronounced effect. Consider that countries with high levels of executive power still are expected to be significantly responsive to public preferences in low proportionality systems. This is not true as proportionality increases, however.

The estimates in Table 7 help us characterise dynamic representation in different types of systems. It is expected to be strongest in Madisonian presidential systems that use plurality elections, as in the US. By contrast, representation is expected to be weakest in systems where the executive is dominant and electoral systems are highly proportional. That said, none of the countries in our data set have both of these characteristics – i.e. the lower right-hand quadrant of the Table 7 is empty. A number do have highly proportional systems and weak executives, namely, Israel and Italy, and these are expected to be largely unresponsive to changing public preferences. By contrast, in countries with low proportionality and dominant executives, such as the United Kingdom, we still expect some

TABLE 7
IMPLIED REPRESENTATION COEFFICIENTS, BY EXECUTIVE DOMINANCE AND ENPP

	Executive dominance		
	Low	**Medium**	**High**
ENPP			
Low	0.142**	0.110**	0.045**
Medium	0.083**	0.050	−0.014
High	0.025	−0.008	−0.072

$^*p < 0.10$; $^{**}p < 0.05$. Levels of institutional variables correspond to the 25th, 50th and 75th percentiles in the data; for ENPP, 2.74, 3.34, 3.93; for Executive dominance, 2.09, 2.86, 4.36. Based on results in column 3 of Table 6.

policy representation. That is, both types of institutions influence representation but electoral systems appear to matter more.

Discussion and Conclusions

This is the first time that the thermostatic model has been tested across such a wide range of countries. That the model works, then, is an important finding all on its own. Publics can and do react to policy change, and governments can and do respond to changing public preferences.

The strength of both public responsiveness and policy representation is conditioned, however, by political institutions. We have previously provided evidence that federalism constrains public responsiveness and that executive–legislative balance enhances policy representation. Both effects are in evidence here as well. We thus see this work in part as a further testing and confirmation of hypotheses we have developed elsewhere. And we also examine hypotheses that have been posited in previous research but not subjected to empirical scrutiny, specifically about the effects of electoral systems on dynamic representation. Our results indicate that governments in proportional systems are less responsive to changing public opinion. Indeed, we see this work as the start of a larger research agenda focused on the ways in which a wide range of institutions can condition opinion–policy relationships.

There clearly is more to do. First, we need to extend our models from overall levels of spending to government activity in specific policy domains for which data are available in the ISSP. Second, we can consider additional institutional measures. Each of the institutions we explore here can be measured in different ways and, while we have already tested several versions of each, there are more to consider. There are other political institutions to consider as well, including party systems themselves. Finally, we can explore the effects of government institutions, which are far more complex than we have shown here. Take federalism; although the decentralisation of policymaking authority dampens the clarity of policy responsibility, at some point it may prove to be beneficial – that is, where the public only needs to monitor what the local (rather than national) governments are doing. Likewise, while executive dominance and proportionality may reduce the direct representation of public preferences, they may improve indirect representation through elections. The value of these systems ultimately seems to depend on the net effect of direct and indirect representation. These and the other issues discussed above remain subjects for future research.

In the meantime we have additional support for the thermostatic model and the conditioning effects of vertical and horizontal divisions of power and new evidence of the effects of electoral systems. These institutions impact on dynamic representation. The effect of executive power and proportionality is direct, as it makes governments less responsive to public preferences. The former – federalism – is indirect, through preferences. As federalism dampens thermostatic public responsiveness of the public to policy, it compromises representation as well. That is, because they are less informed by policy, the public preference inputs into the policymaking process are less meaningful to begin with. Political institutions evidently do matter and in different ways.

Acknowledgements

Previous versions were presented at the European Consortium for Political Research Joint Sessions of Workshops, St. Gallen, Switzerland, 12–17 April 2011, the Annual Meeting of the Elections, Public Opinion and Parties specialist group of the Political Studies Association, Exeter, UK, 9–11 September 2011, the Ash Center at the Kennedy School, Harvard University, 19 October 2011, Koc University, Istanbul, 26 January 2012, and the Annual Meeting of the Midwest Political Science Association, 12–15 April 2012. We are grateful to participants at each presentation, especially Christine Arnold, Susan Banducci, Shaun Bowler, Ali Carkuglo, Nicole Doerr, Mark Franklin, Archon Fung, Brigitte Geissel, Armen Hakhverdian, Will Jennings, Quinton Mayne, Francisca Rojas, Hollie Russon-Gilman, Belgin San Akca, Eser Sekercioglu, Paul Warwick and Kamil Yilmaz. We also are grateful to Kevin Arceneaux and Luke Keele for helpful advice with aspects of the statistical analysis.

Notes

1. Indeed, we have little sense for the connection between opinion and policy in very low salience domains, i.e. domains in which we do not even gather opinion data (Burstein 2003). A lack of a connection between opinion and policy in non-salient domains would be neither surprising nor a bad thing, since public preferences in these domains surely are less informed.

2. We have in addition developed an argument about the effects of electoral systems (Soroka and Wlezien 2010), which we summarise and test below.
3. Unlike the thermostat that governs the heating (and/or air conditioning) units in our homes, which sends a dichotomous signal, *R* is a continuous variable, and captures both direction and magnitude.
4. There some exceptions such as abortion or desegregation. Consider, e.g. the GSS question on 'whether or not you think it should be possible for a pregnant woman to obtain a legal abortion' under six different conditions. These instances are rare, however – very few policy domains lend themselves to questioning about specific levels of policy.
5. There is other evidence of thermostatic public responsiveness as well, including Franklin and Wlezien (1997), Erikson *et al.* (2002), and Jennings (2009).
6. Note that this dovetails with public responsiveness to spending. Public opinion in year t reacts (negatively) to policy for year t and policymakers adjust policy (positively) in year t + 1 based on current (year t) opinion. Now, if studying policy that, unlike budgetary policy, is not lagged, then policy change could represent year t public opinion, which in turn responds to lagged (year t – 1) policy. That is, the model can be adjusted to reflect the reality of the policy process.
7. Note that different economic variables, including unemployment, inflation and business expectations, were included in the model though to little effect.
8. For a more extended (and nuanced) discussion, see Wlezien and Soroka (2011).
9. They do, however, show that proportional systems produce more representative legislatures.
10. Powell finds that what mostly matters is the polarisation of the party system.
11. For related work considering dynamic representation in majoritarian (and non-majoritarian) systems, albeit using MIP responses or ideology rather than policy, see Hakhverdian (2010) and Hobolt and Klemmensen (2005, 2008).
12. This generalises Rogowski and Kayser's (2002) argument relating to the comparatively higher seats–votes elasticities in majoritarian systems.
13. Also note that Hobolt and Klemmensen do not actually assess responsiveness to public preferences for policy and focus instead on public mentions of the 'most important problem' facing the country.
14. The file is distributed by GESIS, ZA file #4747/4748.
15. Note that the question used here is about 'cuts' rather than 'spending' ('more', 'less', or 'about the same'), the latter of which is the focus of our own past work. The ISSP asks questions about spending 'more' or 'less' in various specific policy domains (e.g. health, defence), but the only question capturing overall spending preferences asks about 'cuts'. Results for the question used here nevertheless move alongside the average across all eight specific-domain 'spending' questions.
16. Converting to a constant currency, such as US dollars, presents other difficulties – namely, it means that trends in spending are affected by shifts in exchange rates over time.
17. We use ENPP instead of the effective number of electoral parties (ENEP) because of our conceptual focus on how electoral systems influences parliamentary control. Using ENEP makes little difference, however, as does using (logged) median district magnitude.
18. That is, state and local spending includes funds from the national government that are difficult to disentangle. Note also that there are other alternative measures of federal revenues, including in particular Vatter's (2009), but the one used here has the practical advantage of being available for more of the countries in our sample.
19. Employing generalised least squares (GLS) techniques makes no substantive difference.
20. This is not surprising given the difficulty of comparing responses to the items across countries, that is, they may not be registering the same things.
21. The measure is from the International Monetary Fund's (IMF) World Economic Outlook Database (2010). We have described this in the data section, above.
22. Our previous research on preferences for spending has included a linear time trend to account for increases in the underlying preferred levels of spending over time that would

reflect growing economic capacity over time. We do not include such a variable here because our measure of spending takes into account GDP. When included, trend is not a robust predictor and it makes little difference for the estimated effects of the other variables.

23. Note that Rodden's measure is not available for all 17 countries, so these estimations rely on 13 only. The excluded countries are: Czech Republic, Hungary, Japan and Slovenia.
24. There is reason to suppose that it does not matter as much as our analysis implies – i.e. that the results overstate the size of federalism's effect. Consider that they imply little public responsiveness in highly federalised countries, such as the US and Canada, where our previous research of time-serial dynamics has demonstrated a significant amount.
25. Recall that Powell and Lijphart focus on the congruence between the median voter and government position in the wake of elections, not the responsiveness of governments to shocks to preferences in between elections.
26. Note that this model relies on 16 countries – Poland is excluded from models of representation because the field date for the final ISSP survey was late, in 2008, and our spending data end in that year.
27. Consider findings in other work exploring the impact of partisanship with more data, e.g. Blais *et al.* (1996).
28. This would be in line with past work, including, e.g. Blais *et al.* (1996) and Soroka and Wlezien (2004).
29. The same is true when we use the median district magnitude. This again points towards the possibility that more proportional electoral systems decrease rather than increase dynamic representation, but the pattern also is too unreliable to credit.
30. Again, some countries are excluded due to missing data: in addition to Poland (see Note 26), Hungary, Japan and Slovenia.
31. The US is an extreme case on both dimensions, and so it is worth noting that the effects are larger and more reliable when it is excluded from the analysis.

References

Armingeon, Klaus, Romana Careja, Sarah Engler, Panajotis Potolidis, Marlène Gerber, and Philipp Leimgruber (2010). *Comparative Political Data Set III 1990–2008*. Berne: Institute of Political Science, University of Berne.

Bagehot, Walter (1867/1966). *The English Constitution*. Ithaca, NY: Cornell University Press.

Blais, Andre, and Marc Andre Bodet (2006). 'Does Proportional Representation Foster Closer Congruence Between Citizens and Policymakers?', *Comparative Political Studies*, 39, 1243–62.

Blais, Andre, and Donald Blake, and Stephene Dion (1996). 'Do Parties Make a Difference: A Reappraisal', *American Journal of Political Science*, 40, 514–20.

Burstein, Paul (2003). 'The Impact of Public Opinion on Public Policy: A Review and an Agenda', *Political Research Quarterly*, 56:1, 29–40.

Cox, Gary W. (1987). *The Efficient Secret: The Cabinet and the Development of Political Parties in Victorian England*. Cambridge: Cambridge University Press.

Downs, William M. (1999). 'Accountability Payoffs in Federal Systems? Competing Logics and Evidence from Europe's Newest Federation', *Publius: The Journal of Federalism*, 29:1, 87–110.

Durr, Robert (1993). 'What Moves Policy Sentiment?', *American Political Science Review*, 87, 158–70.

Duverger, Maurice (1951). *Les Partis Politiques*. Paris: Seuil. (English trans. *Political Parties: Their Organization and Activity in the Modern State*. New York: Wiley, 1954.).

Enns, Peter, and Christopher Wlezien, eds. (2011). *Who Gets Represented?* New York: Russell Sage Foundation.

Erikson, Robert S., Michael B. MacKuen, and James A. Stimson (2002). *The Macro Polity*. Cambridge: Cambridge University Press.

Franklin, Mark, and Christopher Wlezien (1997). 'The Responsive Public: Issue Salience, Policy Change, and Preferences for European Unification', *Journal of Theoretical Politics*, 9, 347–63.

Golder, Matt (2010). 'Democratic Electoral Systems around the World, 1946–2000', *Electoral Studies*, 24, 103–20.

Golder, Matthew, and Jacek Stramski (2010). 'Ideological Congruence and Electoral Institutions', *American Journal of Political Science*, 54, 90–106.

Hakhverdian, Armen (2010). 'Political Representation and its Mechanisms: A Dynamic Left–Right Approach for the United Kingdom, 1976–2006', *British Journal of Political Science*, 40, 835–56.

Hobolt, Sara Binzer, and Robert Klemmensen (2005). 'Responsive Government? Public Opinion and Policy Preferences in Britain and Denmark', *Political Studies*, 53, 379–402.

Hobolt, Sara Binzer, and Robert Klemmensen (2008). 'Government Responsiveness and Political Competition in Comparative Perspective', *Comparative Political Studies*, 41, 309–37.

Jennings, Sir Ivor (1959). *Cabinet Government, 3rd ed.* Cambridge: Cambridge University Press.

Jennings, Will (2009). 'The Public Thermostat, Political Responsiveness and Error-Correction: Border Control and Asylum in Britain, 1994–2007', *British Journal of Political Science*, 39, 847–70.

Laver, Michael, and Kenneth A. Shepsle (1996). *Making and Breaking Governments: Cabinets and Legislatures in Parliamentary Democracies*. Cambridge: Cambridge University Press.

Lijphart, Arend (1984). *Democracies: Pattern of Majoritarian and Consensus Government in Twenty-One Countries*. New Haven, CT: Yale University Press.

Lijphart, Arend (1999). *Government Forms and Performance in Thirty-Six Countries*. New Haven, CT: Yale University Press.

Miller, Warren E., Roy Pierce, Jacques Thomassen, Richard Herrera, Soren Holmberg, Peter Esaisson, and Bernhard Wessels (1999). *Policy Representation in Western Democracies*. Oxford: Oxford University Press.

Powell, G. Bingham (2000). *Elections as Instruments of Democracy: Majoritarian and Proportional Views*. New Haven, CT: Yale University Press.

Powell, G. Bingham (2011). 'Party Polarization and the Ideological Congruence of Governments', in Russell Dalton and Christopher Anderson, *Citizens, Context, and Choice*. Oxford: Oxford University Press, 197–213.

Rodden, Jonathan (2002). 'The Dilemma of Fiscal Federalism: Grants and Fiscal Performance around the World', *American Journal of Political Science*, 46, 670–87.

Rodden, Jonathan (2004). 'Comparative Federalism and Decentralization: On Meaning and Measurement', *Comparative Politics*, 36, 481–500.

Rogowski, Ronald, and Mark Kayser (2002). 'Majoritarian Electoral Systems and Consumer Power: Price-Level Evidence from the OECD Countries', *American Journal of Political Science*, 46:3, 526–39.

Soroka, Stuart N., and Christopher Wlezien (2004). 'Opinion Representation and Policy Feedback: Canada in Comparative Perspective', *Canadian Journal of Political Science*, 37:3, 531–60.

Soroka, Stuart N., and Christopher Wlezien (2005). 'Opinion–Policy Dynamics: Public Preferences and Public Expenditure in the United Kingdom', *British Journal of Political Science*, 35, 665–89.

Soroka, Stuart N., and Christopher Wlezien (2008). 'On the Limits to Inequality in Representation', *PS: Political Science and Politics*, 41, 319–27.

Soroka, Stuart N., and Christopher Wlezien (2010). *Degrees of Democracy*. New York: Cambridge University Press.

Strom, Kaare (2003). 'Parliamentary Democracy and Delegation', in Kaare Strom, Wolfgang Muller, and Torbjorn Bergman (eds.), Delegation and Accountability in Parliamentary Democracies. Oxford: Oxford University Press, 55–106.

Tsebelis, George (2002). *Veto Players: How Political Institutions Work*. Princeton, NJ: Princeton University Press.

Vatter, Adrian (2009). 'Lijphart Expanded: Three Dimension of Democracy in Advanced OECD Countries', *European Political Science Review*, 1, 125–54.

Wlezien, Christopher (1995). 'The Public as Thermostat: Dynamics of Preferences for Spending', *American Journal of Political Science*, 39, 981–1000.

Wlezien, Christopher (1996). 'Dynamics of Representation: The Case of U.S. Spending on Defense', *British Journal of Political Science*, 26, 81–103.

Wlezien, Christopher (2004). 'Patterns of Representation: Dynamics of Public Preferences and Policy', *Journal of Politics*, 66, 1–24.

Wlezien, Christopher, and Stuart Soroka (2007). 'The Relationship between Public Opinion and Public Policy', in Russell Dalton and Hans-Dieter Klingemann (eds.), *Oxford Handbook of Political Behavior*. Oxford: Oxford University Press, 799–817.

Wlezien, Christopher, and Stuart Soroka (2011). 'Federalism and Public Responsiveness to Policy', *Publius: The Journal of Federalism*, 41, 31–52.

APPENDIX

TABLE A1
NET PREFERENCES FOR TOTAL GOVERNMENT SPENDING

	1985	1990	1996	2006
Australia	−48.0	−45.3	−37.3	−12.8
Canada			−56.9	−42.4
Czech Republic			−26.1	−34.1
France			−82.8	−74.4
Germany	−53.0	−51.8	−67.5	−54.9
Great Britain	−1.5	−7.9	−12.8	−4.5
Hungary		−63.3	−67.2	−63.4
Ireland			−44.6	3.4
Israel		−73.0	−70.3	−51.5
Italy	−44.9	−42.2	−43.5	
Japan			−60.2	−63.7
Norway		−40.8	−36.4	−30.2
Poland			−43.8	−68.6
Slovenia			−64.2	−55.5
Spain			−56.0	−17.0
Sweden			−26.6	−23.6
United States	−55.7	−53.6	−58.5	−36.1

Question wording: Here are some things the government might do for the economy. Please show which actions you are in favour of and which you are against: Cuts in government spending ('strongly in favour of' to 'strongly against'). Coded so that positive values reflect support for increases in spending (that is, opposition to cuts).

TABLE A2
SUPPORT FOR GOVERNMENT ACTION

	1985	1990	1996	2006
Australia	37.1	26.8	32.8	41.7
Canada			31.2	39.2
Czech Republic			45.9	33.9
France			54.0	50.1
Germany	39.8	41.0	42.7	39.3
Great Britain	62.0	55.4	52.2	41.5
Hungary		55.6	51.8	56.2
Ireland		64.4	61.0	61.5
Israel		53.6	57.7	59.1
Italy	66.0	59.2	57.9	
Japan			39.0	28.2
Norway		54.0	54.7	54.6
Poland			58.2	61.2
Slovenia			67.9	63.7
Spain			74.3	67.1
Sweden			50.4	42.6
United States	16.4	23.6	22.5	36.1

Question wording: On the whole, do you think it should be or should not be the government's responsibility to: Keep prices under control, Provide health care for the sick, Provide a decent standard of living for the old, Provide industry with the help it needs to grow, Provide a decent standard of living for the unemployed, Reduce income differences between the rich and poor, Give financial help to university students from low-income families, Provide decent housing for those who can't afford it, Impose strict laws to make industry do less damage to the environment ('definitely should be' to 'definitely should not be'). Coded by taking the average across all questions, where positive values reflect support for increasing levels of government responsibility.

TABLE A3
INSTITUTIONAL VARIABLES

	ENPP (Golder)	Executive Dominance (Lijphart)	Federalism (Rodden)
Australia	2.42	4.02	33
Canada	2.55	4.17	47
Czech Republic	3.93		
Germany	3.31	5.52	13
Spain	2.75	4.36	17
France	3.34	5.52	12
Great Britain	2.19	5.52	8
Hungary	3.59		
Ireland	3.08	2.49	8
Israel	5.77	1.40	9
Italy	5.87	1.10	5
Japan	3.01	2.98	
Norway	3.93	2.56	22
Poland	5.90	2.09	9
Sweden	3.81	2.73	32
Slovenia	5.56		
United States	1.96	1.00	39

TABLE A4
POLICY REPRESENTATION, WITH PARTISANSHIP

	DV: % Δ Total government spending$_{kt}$		
Net preferences$_{kt-1}$	0.076**	0.053**	0.046*
	(0.025)	(0.024)	(0.025)
% Left seats in cabinet	−0.003	−0.011	−0.010
	(0.012)	(0.012)	(0.012)
% Δ GDP (deflated NCUs)$_{kt-1}$	–	0.417*	0.510**
		(0.226)	(0.236)
% Δ Debt (deflated NCUs)$_{kt-1}$	–	–	−0.067
			(0.059)
Constant	5.325**	3.405**	2.819*
	(1.324)	(1.557)	(1.610)
sigma u	1.730**	–	–
	(.610)		
sigma e	2.216**	2.669**	2.616**
	(0.377)	(0.334)	(0.327)
N	32	32	32
N (panels)	15	15	15
LR Chi2	8.162	11.431	12.707
rho	0.379	0.000	0.000

*$p < 0.10$; **$p < 0.05$. Cells contain MLE coefficients with standard errors in parentheses.

Index